Preaching through
Exodus

Applying the Book of Exodus to Today

By Pastor Paul Wallace

© December 2018
by Paul Wallace
Sedona, Arizona
All rights reserved
Printed in the United States of America

ISBN # 978-1-949249-04-0

Unless otherwise stated all Scripture citation is from the HOLY BIBLE, the "English Standard Version"®. (ESV®)Copyright © 2001 by Crossway, a publishing ministry of Good News Publishers. All rights reserved. ESV Text Edition: 2007

Scripture citations marked (NIV) are from the NEW INTERNATIONAL VERSION®. Copyright ©1973, 1978, 1984, by International Bible Society. Used by permission of Zondervan Publishing House. All Rights Reserved. The "NIV" and "New International Version" trademarks are registered in the United States Patent and Trademark Office by International Bible Society. Use of either trademark requires the permission of International Bible Society.

Contents

Societal Engineering Exodus 1 5
God in the Trials Exodus 2:1-10 10
My Way! Exodus 2:11-15 16
God's Preparatory Academy Exodus 2:16-25 21
God Encounter Exodus 3:1-10 25
The Name Exodus 3:11-22 30
Why You Can! Exodus 4:1-17 35
My Deliverer is Coming Exodus 4:18-31 40
God, Why? Exodus 5:1-23 45
I Am the Lord Exodus 6 50
Supreme God Exodus 7 55
A Hard Heart Exodus 8-9:7 60
The God Hardened Heart Exodus 9:8 –10:29 65
Final Plague Exodus 11; 12:29-32 70
Passover Exodus 12 75
Remember Exodus 13 80
Obedient Waves Exodus 14 85
Redeemer Healer Exodus 15 91
God's Provision Exodus 16 96
Testing God Exodus 17:1-7 102
It's a War! Exodus 17:8-16 107
Saved x 2 Exodus 18 112
Prepare To Meet God! Exodus 19 118
Ten Words (part 1) Exodus 20:1-12 123
Ten Words part 2 Exodus 20:13-21 129
Book of the Covenant Exodus 21-23:9 134
Draw Near Exodus 24 140

From the Inside Out Exodus 25-27	145
Jesus in the Tabernacle Exodus 25-27	150
Priestly Robes Exodus 28	155
Consecration Exodus 29	160
Rebels Without A Cause Exodus 32	165
Divine Presence Exodus 33:1-16	171
Glory Revealed Exodus 33:17-34:35	175
Stirred Hearts Exodus 35:20 - 36:7	180
Heaven Came Down Exodus 40	186

Societal Engineering Exodus 1

How did the family of Israel (Jacob) get into this mess? That story is in the book of Genesis. If you weren't with us through the study of Genesis, I encourage you to go to the web site above and read a sermon for a devotional each morning or evening. It will only take you about 20 minutes a day and you'll get caught up with how they ended up here. Briefly, man rebelled against God in the Garden of Eden. Because of his sin, the earth was cursed. Critics of faith in God often point to the suffering in the world. It is a complex issue, but the basis of suffering is man's rebellion against God. We brought it on ourselves. When the catastrophes of this fallen world strike, we turn to God or turn against God, but it forces us out of neutrality to a decision.

The descendants of the first couple quickly multiplied and became increasingly evil. God picked Noah and family to preserve the race and destroyed those living in slavery to sin. Again the human race quickly multiplied and turned their back on God, building the tower of Babel to try to stick together and probably as a part of astrological worship. God confounded their languages and people began to spread out over the earth according to their language groups.

God called Abram out of Ur of the Chaldees and made a covenant with him. Abram's name was changed to Abraham and he bore the son God had promised him when he was 100 years old. The son of promise was Isaac. Isaac had two sons, Jacob and Esau. Jacob bought the birthright from his brother and stole his father's blessing through deception. He had four wives that produced the 12 sons of Jacob whose name was changed to Israel. Next to the youngest son was Joseph who was the favorite. In jealousy over his favored status, his brothers sold him to traders that were on the way to Egypt. The last portion of Genesis is all about how God directed Joseph to interpret the Pharaoh's dream and save the world from starvation. Our passage begins by describing the family of Israel that went into Egypt to avoid starvation. They were given the best of the land, Goshen.

Archeological remains of Israelite construction in Goshen remain to this day. According to the chronology of the Apostle Paul (Acts 13:19-20) and Jephthah in Judges 11:26, the exodus occurred during the reign of Amenhotep II (1453 – 1425 B.C.).

The Hebrew title for Exodus is *elleh semot*, which means "These are the names..." The phrase, "These are the names of the sons of Israel who went..." is identical with the first six words of Genesis 46:8. This is to help the readers see the continuity with the Book of Genesis. The text actually begins with the word "and", which also helps us see it as a story already in progress. Though there is a 400-year gap, it is quickly covered in the first fourteen verses.

The family of Israel had landed in the best of Egypt. The Nile Delta provided the perfect pasture for their flocks. The promise of God to Abraham had come to pass for they had multiplied into a great nation.

(Genesis 46:3) It looked like the best possible place for the family to live, but before Joseph's death, he had made his family promise to take his bones back to the land God had promised to Abraham. (Genesis 50:24) Ironic, isn't it, that the posterity of the brothers who sold their brother into slavery ended up as slaves in Egypt. What looks like a paradise can end up being a prison camp.

It is quite possible that Joseph was in power during the reign of a Hyksos Pharaoh, a foreign people who were eventually driven out of Egypt. That may have added to the fear factor and ease at which Pharaoh convinced the country to abuse the Hebrews for Israel and the Hyksos were both Semitic peoples.

To say the Pharaoh didn't know of Joseph was another way to say he did not honor any agreements made with him by the foreign power that was ruling at the time. 10 "Come, let us deal shrewdly with them, lest they multiply, and, if war breaks out, they join our enemies and fight against us and escape from the land." The Pharaoh's solution was to keep them worn out with work and limit the male population. The idea behind the labor was not only to physically break them but probably also to separate the men from their wives making it less likely they would reproduce as well as starving them by keeping them away from their flocks and fields.

It is amazing how we see ourselves as better than others and can actually use people like one would use a tool. Sometimes the basis for that is fear, as in the case with the Egyptians. Most of the time it is simply greed. History is replete with examples of one group enslaving another. Most nations of antiquity, including Rome in the days of Jesus, saw conquered people as a physical asset to perform acts of labor. Americans used blacks to make cotton production profitable. They reasoned that one of the sons of Noah was black because his name, Ham, could be interpreted that way. Ham was cursed because of his sexual sin. That became their justification for using blacks as slave labor.

Japanese used Koreans before World War 2 as cheap expendable labor. Hitler decided to use the Jewish people as a scapegoat for all the nations problems. He used the increasingly popular theory of evolution to say that the Germans were the superior race and the Jews were less evolved. In the process of trying to exterminate them, they robbed the wealth of the business savvy Jews. We could go on and on. It is the often used tactic of ethnic fear to justify violating their rights. The balance between being reasonable in keeping a nation secure and unreasonable in violating the rights of people as human beings is often a very fine line. Pharaoh was about to step way over the line and used ethnic fear and loathing to justify it.

In our society we take the life of the unborn to save us from the expense and trouble having a child would bring at that point in our life. The justification is that the child will grow up in poverty. We are one of the wealthiest nations on earth. Our poor live like wealthy of in the third world. The other excuse is it is the mother's body to do with as she chooses, but who will speak up for the body of the baby?

The problem stems from man's sinful nature. If man accepted the Genesis account that tells us man is made in the image of God, every life would be sacred from the Haitian in the slum to the baby in the womb. Do your realize that the death blow to slavery came when the pope declared that slaves could partake in communion? It wasn't long after that declaration that Europe could no longer tolerate slavery. If a person was your brother or sister in Christ, or has the potential to become one, how can you enslave them? How can you say you own them? Jesus bought them and they are His! (1Corinthians 7:23) We are all His servants.

Pharaoh saw the family of Israel as a commodity, building tools, to do his bidding. Since their birth rate was probably higher than that of the Egyptians, there was the fear that they would join with enemies of Egypt or rise up and overtake Egypt. The end of verse 10, "leave- the country" has been shown to possibly be an idiom for rising up and taking over the country. (See use in Genesis 2:6 and Hosea 1:11) If there were too many Israelites, Pharaoh reasoned that he should get rid of some.

It should remind us of the Christians of the early church. The more they were persecuted the more they evangelized. When missionaries in China were booted out by the Communists, they feared the little progress they had made would be exterminated. A few decades later we learned the opposite was true. The Chinese church is now 100 million strong and not propped up by Western support but completely indigenous and sending out missionaries. When Christianity thrives in spite of the conditions, those in governmental power become fearful. It is happening around the world even today. What secular societies don't realize is that Christians are instructed by Scripture to be good citizens and to honor the government. (Romans 13:1) We should be the best of citizens. Of course, in a democratic republic, we might not vote to throw the babies in the Nile and that is seen as a threat to the agenda of some as well.

12 But the more they were oppressed, the more they multiplied and the more they spread abroad. And the Egyptians were in dread of the people of Israel.
This again reminds us that the promises to multiply the seed of Abraham had come to pass in spite of Pharaoh. (Genesis 26:3-4) God keeps his promises but the conditions may not always be what we imagined.

In verse 10 Pharaoh says, "lest they multiply" "*pen-yeribe*", and in this verse God says *"ken-yeribe"* the more they shall multiply". All through the story it's as if Pharaoh is set in opposition to God. God wants them to go to the Promised Land. Pharaoh doesn't want them to leave. God wants to be honored through them. Pharaoh wants to be honored through them. Pharaoh wants to reduce their number. God has promised to multiply their number. God wants them to serve Him. Pharaoh wants their service. Pharaoh is really a type of antichrist in the story. He has set himself in opposition to God and His people. We are never told the name of this Pharaoh because he represents all powers that set themselves against God. The story is about the greatness of God in spite of every power set against Him. It is a chapter in the age-old battle between God and Satan.

Verse 14 gives us five different expressions of how difficult life had become. "Lives bitter," "hard labor," "all kinds of work," "hard labor," and "used them ruthlessly" follow after "worked them ruthlessly" at the end of verse 13 to hammer home the point that the situation was intolerable.— New American Commentary

One of the interesting literary features of Exodus is that significant words often come in groups of seven. One example of this occurred back in verse 7, which used seven different words to describe the miraculous multiplication of the Israelites. Another example occurs here in verses 13 and 14, which use seven words (some of which are repeated) for Israel's slavery. Umberto Cassuto claims that each word is like another blow from a slave driver's whip. – (from Preaching the Word – Exodus: Saved for God's Glory.)

Pharaoh's next strategy at limiting the Israelites was infanticide. *17 But the midwives feared God and did not do as the king of Egypt commanded them, but let the male children live.* He ordered the midwives to kill any male child that was born. I suppose he thought they could just smother the baby before it took its first breath and say it was stillborn.

The fear of God can keep us from evil and its consequences. Though the Ten Commandments had not been given, they knew that life was sacred. (Genesis 9:6) How many miraculous births had the midwives witnessed? How many mothers had they comforted when their baby did not survive? They refused to obey the Pharaoh. The heroic resistance of the midwives earned a place for their names in Scripture, Shiphrah and Puah. Compare that with the fact that the elders' names and the Pharaoh's is never mentioned. (3:16, 18) These two women, who were probably the older overseers of a number of midwives, are the heroines of the first chapter. Their civil disobedience could have cost them their life, but they chose to obey God rather than man. (Acts 5:29)

When we give God the respect that is due Him and live in accord with His will, blessings follow. *20 So God dealt well with the midwives. And the people multiplied and grew very strong. 21 And because the midwives feared God, he gave them families.* It sounds as if they were childless and up in years. While Pharaoh tried to stop the growth of Israel, even these matrons were blessed with children because of their fearless obedience to God.

Did God reward the midwives for lying? Did they lie? There is much debate over this passage. The word for "vigorous" may also be translated "involved". It could very well be that Hebrew women were more involved in the birth process and therefore it would have been impossible to strangle or suffocate the baby without them knowing it. They said they gave birth even before they arrived. It could have been that the midwives intentionally delayed their arrival so as not to be able to carry out the Pharaoh's decree. So, while they may not have exactly been telling the whole story, they may have not been lying either. Whatever the case, they had more fear of God than they did of an irate Pharaoh. (Ecclesiastes 12:13)

The mixed conditions in the story show the mixed conditions of life. The blessings to Abraham of making him the father of many had come to pass, but the many are oppressed. Ultimately the oppression will result in the liberation of Israel. They probably would have stayed in comfortable Egypt had Pharaoh not oppressed them. God often has to use difficulty to get us to finally do what we were meant to do. Even with all they endured, they were still tempted to go back. (Numbers 14:3-4) And what suffering have you endured that turned your heart from this world and fixed it upon God? It's not so easy to look at conditions in life and label them as the favor or displeasure of God. His ways are certainly different from man's ways. (Isaiah 55:8) Some of our greatest blessings come from our deepest trials.

The midwives' faithfulness to God made Pharaoh come out in the open with his social engineering plan. If the job can't get done in secret, if there is enough power in the hands of the one that leads, he will just come out and openly declare his intentions. It's a familiar pattern of human nature. You can bet there was a lot of explanation and justification given for this decree. 22 Then Pharaoh commanded all his people, "Every son that is born to the Hebrews you shall cast into the Nile, but you shall let every daughter live."

Now all Egyptians were to participate in Pharaoh's ethnic cleansing program. The Nile was considered to be one of the great gods of Egypt. While it brought the much-needed water, it also carried away the waste. If the baby disappeared in the waters of the Nile it was thought to be the Nile's judgment and thus take the guilt from the one that threw the baby into its waters. The Nile was viewed as both the giver and taker of life. The Egyptians may have even considered it an act of worship of the Nile. What the Egyptians have sown they would soon be reaping when they chase Israel through the Red Sea.

Some scholars believe that Moses wrote the Book of Exodus near the end of his life to the younger generation that would enter the Promised Land. Many were Egyptians and slaves from other nations that had been in Egypt and left with the Israelites during the Exodus. (Exodus 12:37-38) Even the Israelites had to learn again of the God of their fathers and the covenant they had with Him. This retelling of the national history gave them all a sense of purpose and identity. It helped them to become a family.

That is what Scripture does for us today. We are very much like the mixed rabble in the desert. Hopefully, by the grace of God, we are more like the younger generation that is willing to enter the Promised Land, a people who believe God. Though we too are from various backgrounds, we have been adopted into the family of God. We have a national history, for we have been grafted into the tree of Israel. Now their past is ours as well. The promises to them are promises to us as well. (Galatians 3:29) I'm not saying we have replaced them. I'm saying we have joined the people of faith. We were in bondage to sin, and Satan is a hard taskmaster. But we too were led out of bondage. The stories are repeated again and again. Nations fear us, then persecute us (1Peter 2:21), and God brings deliverance and finally the ultimate Deliverer.

Though I believe this is an accurate historical account, I also believe it foreshadows a spiritual reality. We will see how Egypt is symbolic of the world system that is under the control of the evil one. We will see how the history of the Israelites is our history as well and that God calls us out of the world system to wander in the wilderness until we are ready to reach the Promised Land. We'll see the tests and trials along the way, the stretching of our faith, while suffering turns our hearts from this world to our Promised Land. We'll see our failings in some, and desire to be like Shiphrah and Puah. But most of all we'll see a God that no one can stop. A God who knows the end from the beginning (Isaiah 46:10), and who always keeps His promises, and foils the enemy of our soul time and time again. He even takes a stuttering failure and raises him up to become a picture of the great Deliverer, our Redeemer and Savior, Jesus.

Questions
1 Can you summarize the book of Genesis?
2 How does Moses connect the stories?
3 How many years take place between the two stories?
4 Why was it easy to incite persecution of the Hebrews?
5 What was Pharaoh's fear/excuse?
6 What was his first plan?
7 How does the Bible give value to every life?
8 Why does persecution strengthen rather than diminish?
9 How was Pharaoh an antichrist?
10 What was his next tactic?
11 Why do we have the midwives names?
12 What is their example to Israel and us?
13 How are we like the first that read Exodus?

God in the Trials Exodus 2:1-10

Last week we recalled how the descendants of Abraham ended up in Egypt and the national social engineering program of Pharaoh. Fear motivated the Pharaoh and the Egyptians to enslave the Hebrews as a work force in an effort to limit their population growth. God had promised he would multiply them like the stars in the heavens. (Genesis 15:5) When man goes against the promises of God, guess who wins? The more they were oppressed the more they multiplied. The brave midwives took a stand and refused to follow Pharaoh's instructions at the risk of their own lives. God not only spared their lives but also blessed them with families. Then Pharaoh tried a crude form of population control; throw all male babies in the Nile.

We don't know how long this horror had gone on before Moses was born. We do know it must have traumatized and demoralized the Hebrew people. This is again one of those times when man would cry out, "How could God let this happen?" The subject is much bigger than we have time to deal with this morning, but let me give you a summary.

Man and some angels have been given free will. Why would God do such a thing knowing it would bring a curse on the earth, untold suffering, the loss of lives in Haiti as earthquakes are surely part of the curse connected with the sin of Adam and Eve's rebellion? How could God allow these babies to be thrown to crocodiles, and the resultant pain in the mothers' hearts? Sin by its very nature brings destructive consequences that ripple out in waves of damage.

The alternative is that we all be automatons, no choices allowed. We could have been made to obey. But where there is forced obedience, love cannot exist. If there is to be a love relationship, there must be the freedom to choose. Good cannot be appreciated as it should without an understanding of the destructiveness of evil.

God is always present with His hand stretched out to us, inviting us to turn from darkness to light, to reject bitterness and choose love, to comfort us in the pain that is the consequence of the evil choices of man. (Hebrews 4:15-16) Often it is in the pain and suffering that we turn to God for His help and comfort. God is more concerned about our eternal good than our temporal happiness.

Pharaoh is just one man in a long line of rebels against God, Cain, Lamech, Nimrod, Jezebel, Hamen, Antiochus Epiphanies, Stalin, Hitler, Mao, to name just a few. Some only took the lives of a few but were noted for the hardness of heart in doing so. Some took the lives of millions. They are pawns in Satan's army of the unbelieving. Don't you think Satan loves it when we question God for the pain and suffering he, Satan, instigates? What better propaganda in this war of good and evil than to blame the other side for your crimes. You'll notice that this is a common tactic, accusing others of what the accuser is guilty. Those intolerant of righteousness and truth will call believers intolerant.

So while Pharaoh convinced his nation to participate in the genocide of the Hebrew people, a few brave souls like Shiphrah and Puah lived by faith. We find later that the names of the parents of Moses are Amram and Jochabed. (Exodus 6:20) At this point, the focus is just on the baby so we are not yet told their names. The book of Hebrews tells us they were people who lived by faith. (Acts 7:20) What happened to people who tried to hide their baby boys? Surely there were some that did, and there must have been a punishment severe enough to deter others from trying to do so. Hebrews 11:23 (ESV) Tells us, *23 By faith Moses, when he was born, was hidden for three months by his parents, because they saw that the child was beautiful, and they were not afraid of the king's edict.*

Imagine Jochabed trying to keep her newborn quiet and hidden. That little baby must have kept the angels very busy. Imagine the tension each time they heard the baby cry out, and trying to anticipate the baby's needs before it cried. But by the time he was 3 months old, the little boy's lungs were just too strong, and discovery was inevitable.

Exodus 2:3 (ESV) *3 When she could hide him no longer, she took for him a basket made of bulrushes and daubed it with bitumen and pitch. She put the child in it and placed it among the reeds by the riverbank.* She obeyed the Pharaoh. The baby was thrown in the river, technically. It was a last ditch effort to put the child in the hands of the true God. Like Shiphrah and Puah before her, she decided she could not obey a decree that violated her conscience. Remember, the Law had not yet been given, but the stories of murder that were passed down from the time of Cain and through Noah and his sons were told around the Hebrew cooking fires. They knew life was a precious gift of God. The very wonder of birth assured them that to take that life was a horrible crime against God who gave it. (Genesis 9:6)

Now, the baby's sister waited and watched to see what would happen. Jochabed would not have had her watch if she did not have faith that God would intervene. What mother would have her daughter watch if she suspected the worse? As Providence would have it, the daughter of Pharaoh passed by on her way to bathe. She heard the cries and sent a servant out to get the basket and bring it to her. Exodus 2:6 (ESV*) 6 When she opened it, she saw the child, and behold, the baby was crying. She took pity on him and said, "This is one of the Hebrews' children."* What woman's heart is not touched by the cry of a baby? The daughter of Pharaoh was no different. I wonder if she deplored what was happening to the Hebrew babies, or if it was just the sight of the baby and the sound of his crying that caused her to open her heart?

Sometimes the pain of others is easier to ignore as long as we don't have to face it up close. The situation in Haiti hurts us all. News agencies realize this and they are already limiting the reporting as it isn't good for ratings. But if you were there, if you stood among the hungry, if you talk to a family about the loss of loved ones, you become overwhelmed and have to act. You would do what you could until the pain in your heart becomes so great that you have to separate yourself. I've heard that many who leave Haiti after a time want to return and do more. The cry of that baby grabbed the heart of the daughter of Pharaoh and would not let go.

Opportunity was knocking. Exodus 2:7 (ESV*) 7 Then his sister said to Pharaoh's daughter, "Shall I go and call you a nurse from the Hebrew women to nurse the child for you?"* There were numerous Hebrew women who would love to have a replacement for the baby they lost, but God had the baby nursed by his own mother, and even paid her to do so. (Ephesians 3:20) Just as the midwives were rewarded for their defiance of the evil edict, so Jochabed was rewarded for her resistance to an ungodly decree. (Acts 5:29)

Many of our nations spiritual leaders came together to write the Manhattan Declaration. It draws a moral line in the sand and declares we will not move away from the godly issues of life and morality. You can go on-line and see if you agree and are willing to sign it. It marks you as one of those conservatives that will not obey laws that require you to violate your conscience. It declares the signers will not devalue life or the sanctity of marriage even if a law is passed that tells us that we must. It is a non-violent resistance of the steady erosion of Biblical principles in our culture by the passing of ungodly laws. It is doing what our heroes in this story did, by defying the culture and laws that defy God.

Pharaoh has done everything he can to stop the proliferation of the Hebrews, but God keeps His promises. (Genesis 12:2) Now, trying to keep them from leaving and going to the land God has promised them, he is destroying the baby boys. But the irony is that the one that would lead them back to the Promised Land is saved by that Pharaoh's very own daughter.

Think how bleak it must have looked for the Hebrews, worked literally to death, baby boys thrown into the Nile, mothers that sunk into depression and probably even suicidal. It couldn't have been bleaker. I doubt that any of us have been in a worse situation. Certainly we all face our dark hours, but compared to this, you must admit our dark hours would pale in comparison. But look what God is doing. In the midst of all the suffering in this the earliest of Jewish pogroms, God has plucked out a savior, drawn him out of the slaughter, and set him in the safest place in the land, in the house of Pharaoh. It reminds us of a verse in the last chapter of Genesis. *20 You intended to harm me, but God intended it for good to accomplish what is now being done, the saving of many lives.* Genesis 50:20 (NIV)

I don't know if the Hebrews thought anything of it. They may have even been upset that the one surviving boy was adopted and being taught the ways of the Egyptians. It is usually impossible for us to know what God is up to. We look at our situations and come up with dire conclusions, ones that are usually completely wrong, because it is hard to even imagine the plan that God has set in action. (Isaiah 55:8) What is God doing in our country, in our church, or in your life? Well, the Holy Spirit might reveal it to you, but more often than not I find I even misinterpret that.

There is one thing you can count on, however. God is always true to His character. (Malachi 3:6) In spite of the ruin that sin wreaks, God is at work in hearts and lives, raising up the very answer to our desperate situations, drawing us out of impossible situations and setting His plan in motion. (Jeremiah 32:17) Do you believe it? Really? Are you applying that truth?

We have a book that tells a similar story over and over and over again. In the midst of worldwide judgment there is Noah. During the fall of the nation there is a Jeremiah. In the hopeless captivity there is a Nehemiah and an Ezra. Under the oppression of Rome, and even under a much greater oppression, our enslavement of sin, there is Jesus. But what about today? Is our situation hopeless? As long as there is God, and people with faith, then there is hope. Jesus already won the victory! Think of how the Jews had just suffered the worse persecution in their history when they were miraculously granted the restoration of their nation, 1900 years after they had lost their land. (Deuteronomy 30:4) Think of how the iron curtain seemed like an impossibility and nuclear war the inevitable outcome of the arms race, and overnight the situation was transformed. The Gospel poured like a flood past what was once the iron curtain and into all of Russia. Nothing is too hard for God! (Jeremiah 32:27) Today we think that there is no solution to Iran or radical Islam. God will have His way. (Ezekiel 12:25)

This does not mean it will be easy, but that God has a plan that is set in motion and all the forces of hell, all their evil men and angels cannot stop

God. (Psalm 2:4) The cry of a baby changed the future of a nation! Think about that. God can use anything to turn the course of mankind and reveal His glory. (1Corinthians 1:27)

Exodus 2:10 (ESV) *10 When the child grew up, she brought him to Pharaoh's daughter, and he became her son. She named him Moses, "Because," she said, "I drew him out of the water."* It is the Hebrew verb, "to draw out", but for what purpose. Moses is a picture of all God's children who are drawn out of the world system to be God's servants. The very idea of holiness is to be set apart or drawn out for God's use. It is the call of God upon every life. *"Come out from among them and be separate, says the Lord, and I will be a Father to you, and you will be my people."* 2Corinthians 6:17

The Princess knew some Hebrew to give him the name Mashah, thinking it meant to draw out, but her Hebrew wasn't that good. Mashah is better translated "one who draws out of". She unknowingly named him for the destiny he would live out. Just as he was drawn out of the water, so he would be the "one who draws out of" Egypt and through the Red Sea the people of God. God is in the details.

Mose is Egyptian for "born of". We see it in the names Thutmose or Rameses, which means Thuth or Ra has given birth to him. The name has a double etymology (Hebrew/Egyptian) adding to the historical credence.

Moses was nursed in the Hebrew camp probably at least to the age of 3, and you can be sure that Jochabed told Moses of his true identity and the plight of his people. She surely told him the old stories, creation, the flood, the tower of Babel, the stories of the Patriarchs, and finally of the great Prince Joseph who once ruled the empire of Egypt. Pharaoh was afraid of the Hebrew men, but the biggest danger to his empire was a mother relaying the word of God to a baby.

After being weaned, he *"was educated in all the wisdom of the Egyptians"* (Acts 7:22). This was the finest training the world then had to offer—a first-class secular education. We know that from the time of Thutmose III (middle of the fifteenth century B.C.) it was customary for foreign-born princes to be reared and educated in the Egyptian court. The "children of the nursery," they were called; and as a child of the nursery, Moses was trained in linguistics, mathematics, astronomy, architecture, music, medicine, law, and the fine art of diplomacy. In other words, he was being trained for Pharaoh's overthrow right under Pharaoh's nose! - Preaching the Word – Exodus He was a boy caught between two cultures, but he was also a boy in the hands of Almighty God. (Proverbs 21:1)

What does this short passage speak to us today? Your situation may be unique and God may be addressing a situation in your life that no one else is aware of, telling you to trust Him. He is at work. (Hebrews 4:13) The situation may look desperate, but God has a plan. He is working even now to take what the enemy of our soul meant for evil and turning it to something that will grow us. That is why the Scriptures tell us to, *2 Count it all joy, my brothers, when you meet trials of various kinds, 3 for you know that the testing of your faith produces steadfastness. 4 And let steadfastness have its full effect, that you may be perfect and complete, lacking in nothing.* James 1:2-4 (ESV) And again, *... we rejoice in our sufferings, knowing that suffering produces endurance, 4 and endurance produces character, and character produces hope, 5 and hope does not put us to shame, because God's love has been poured into our hearts through the Holy Spirit who has been given to us.* Romans 5:3-5 (ESV)

How could God allow suffering? Do you have a better idea? Careful with your answer. Maybe a better question is, "Why does man choose evil with its inevitably painful consequences?" Or how about this question, "Why does God so patiently put up with us and allow us to go on?" The answer is that He is not willing that any should perish. (2Peter 3:9)

Whatever your situation, or however you see the world today, know that God is at work in ways we can't comprehend. We should grieve at the consequences of sin. God does. But we should also have hope, for every story of history has some kind of good that comes out of the darkness, some surprise that develops to change lives and turn people to faith in God. He is at work in all the darkness man has brought on himself. (Romans 8:28) You can trust Him. Have hope. Even now God is moving in some way we do not imagine, in the route a princess takes to her bath, in floating basket, in the cry of a baby, in the watching sister, in the Bible stories a mother tells her child. God will have His glorious way in the earth. (Romans 11:33) No wonder the prophet would call God's incarnation Immanuel. In this great story of the Hebrew people, He was Immanuel. Through the whole story He is Immanuel. Since man was formed He has been and ever will be God with us.

Our Savior was also born in poverty and under a death penalty. Herod first tried to kill Jesus secretly, asking the Magi to return and reveal where they find Him. When Herod failed, like Pharaoh before him, he came out openly and ordered his soldiers kill all the baby boys in Bethlehem. (Matthew 2:16) And where did God send the one boy He rescued to protect Him? It's the same place He sent Moses, Egypt. Is it all just coincidence, or is God repeating His-story so that we will see Him on the throne of Heaven working out His plan in the midst of this world's tragedies. Our Savior has come to draw us out of this world's system into the Kingdom of God. He is the reality of which Moses was just a shadow. (Hebrews 3:3) He draws us through the waters of baptism and through the wilderness of this life into the Promised Land. And He did it in a way we would never imagine, the cross!

Questions
1 How could God allow …?
2 Where is God when tragedy strikes?
3 Amram and Jochabed were people of _____ !
4 How did Moses become a basket case?
5 What insignificant sound changed the course of history?
6 How did God bless Jochabed's faith?
7 Have you read the Manhattan Declaration?
8 How bleak was it for the Israelites?

9 Is our situation hopeless?
10 What was God doing?
11 Why is his name ironic?
12 What did Pharaoh overlook?
13 What is the parallel story in the New Testament?

My Way! Exodus 2:11-15

Thanks to people of faith like Shiphrah and Puah, the midwives who defied the Pharaoh, and parents like Amram and Jochabed who hid their baby in a basket among the reeds in the Nile, Moses is now a 40-year-old prince of Egypt. (Acts 7:22-23) Of course, the people played a small but important role. It was God that gave them the courage and directed their steps. It was God that touched the princess' heart to keep the child. It is God that is fulfilling His word in bringing a savior! (Genesis 15:13-14) Exodus is full of flawed people, but the emphasis is greatness of God!

This is one of those stories in Scripture that point to the glaring lesson of man's ways versus God's. Moses was trained in all the ways of the Egyptians. *Moses was educated in the great Temple of the Sun which was the outstanding university of the day. We underrate what the Egyptians knew and accomplished. Their knowledge of astronomy was phenomenal. They knew the exact distance to the sun. They worked on the theory that the earth was round and not flat. They knew a great deal about chemistry which is evidenced by the way they were able to embalm the dead. We have no process to equal it today.* (—from J. Vernon McGee's Thru The Bible) He was probably even trained in warfare and hand-to-hand combat. What would you do if you were in Moses' place?

Since the discovery of the King Tutankhamen's tomb and the fabulous wealth within, we have a little idea of the opulence and luxury of the ruling class in Egypt. Moses had it made. As far as this world goes, he had it all. And if he could just lay low and wait for his turn, he could rule it all. What a perfect time that would be to change the conditions for his people! God seems to have answered the prayers of the suffering Israelites and will soon put Moses on the throne, just as he had elevated Joseph. Sounds great, doesn't it?

There is a problem with this scenario. God wants to deliver more than the Israelites. God's vision is greater than our vision. He wants to declare to the Egyptians, slaves in Egypt, and even to the Israelites that have begun to adopt Egyptian gods, that He alone is God! (Jude 1:25) He wants to show us His glory, His heart. He wants to paint for us a picture of His power and might, and that won't happen if Moses just tries to influence Egypt to be kinder, gentler, nation.

11 One day, after Moses had grown up, he went out to where his own people were and watched them at their hard labor. He saw an Egyptian beating a Hebrew, one of his own people. There are several important words in the text that give us some insight to what was going on in Moses. "he went out" is the Hebrew word yatza. The same word is used later to describe the Exodus. Remember, Moses is writing this, so he may be giving us a clue to what was going on inside his heart. He had to go out of Egypt before he could lead others out. It is the same challenge that his name represents, "to draw out of". The allure of Egypt dazzles everyone, that is, until we start to see how shallow and mirage like it really is. By going out, *He gave up position, pleasure, and prosperity, and by doing so he rejected three of the world's biggest temptations: narcissism, hedonism, and materialism.* (Preaching the Word - Exodus: Saved for God's Glory) (Hebrews 11:24-25) Moses went out - to where his own people were – and watched...

    The word "watched" *yara* is also significant. It implies to see with emotion. It was used of Hagar when she could not watch her son die. (Genesis 21:16) Moses has broken out of his training of seeing the slaves as mere tools. They are his family. His heart went out to them. He knew that he could have easily been there among them in hard labor, but God had another plan. What was it? Surely God had set him in that position so that he could do something. This is our first reaction when we see injustice. What can I do? How can I change this?

    Now Moses is in a dilemma. Can he wait until he takes the throne? People are suffering every day. Suddenly he heard someone cry out in pain. He went to the sound and saw a taskmaster mercilessly beating a Hebrew slave. The word for beating is the same word for killing in verse 12. We don't know if the taskmaster was beating the Hebrew to death or just punishing him, but Moses was suddenly faced with the need to act. (Psalm 82:3-4)

    12 He looked this way and that, and seeing no one, he struck down the Egyptian and hid him in the sand. The taskmaster died in the struggle. This raises a lot of questions. Was Moses dressed like the prince he was or like a Hebrew? If he was dressed like a prince he could have ordered the man to stop. Was he looking for help or was he premeditating murder? Or did Moses lose his cool and in disgust for the cruelty before him intend to take the life of the taskmaster? Or was it an accident of the fight that ensued. We don't know. We just know Moses took the life of the taskmaster. (Genesis 9:6)

    Could Moses have gotten out of any punishment for this? Perhaps, but he must have been concerned that the current Pharaoh would see it as the beginning of rebellion. He wouldn't have hidden the body if he thought he could justify it and persuade Pharaoh he was loyal to Egypt. Moses probably thought he could get away with it. He was hoping that the Hebrews would now know that the baby taken so long ago had grown up and was sympathizing with their plight. (Acts 7:25)

    The very next day, Moses went out again to watch his people. He saw a Hebrew abusing another Hebrew. The problem isn't just enslavement to the Egyptians. The problem is slavery to sin! Even believers will wrong other believers. Moses asked the man in the wrong, "Why do you strike your companion?" 14 He answered, "Who made you a prince and a judge over us? Do you mean to kill me as you killed the Egyptian?" Then Moses was afraid, and thought, "Surely the thing is known."

Moses probably hoped that the man he rescued the day before would either stay quiet about the event, or rally people to Moses as the leader of their rebellion. Word of the murder somehow spread, and instead, the attitude of the Hebrews seemed to be one of bewildered doubt. The man in the wrong actually did have a point. Moses wasn't assigned to be a judge or overseer by Egypt or the Hebrews. Under what authority was he operating? God hadn't sent him to do this either. If that was the response of the Hebrews, even just some of them, the Pharaoh would surely hear about it.

Now what? There was no longer a chance to stand in between two worlds. His going out, and the rash action that followed, meant he would have to leave both worlds, Hebrew and Egyptian. He tried it his way and failed. He had to flee.

What was God up to? Why didn't He intervene? Have you ever been there? You thought you knew what God was up to, and you stepped out in what you thought was faith. Something went wrong, and before you know it, you have a huge mess on your hands and you're left wondering why God didn't step in and change it all. That's when we usually see that we were operating on our own good intentioned ideas and not the leading of the Holy Spirit. (Matthew 17:24-27)

At 40 years of age, Moses left Egypt and traveled to Midian. It was the ancient land of Shasu, the grazing land of nomadic shepherds. He's a broken man. All his relationships are now in the past. His dreams of helping his people must die. His certainty of being raised as a prince to ease the burden of his people, an idea he must let go. He had 40 years of the world's education. Now he'll have 40 years of God's. He'll be humbled in the desert. Then he'll be ready to hear from God.

24 By faith Moses, when he was grown up, refused to be called the son of Pharaoh's daughter, 25 choosing rather to be mistreated with the people of God than to enjoy the fleeting pleasures of sin. 26 He considered the reproach of Christ greater wealth than the treasures of Egypt, for he was looking to the reward. Hebrews 11:24-26 (ESV) The Hebrews passage seems to indicate that Moses had made up his mind by the time he went out to watch his people. He had seen all that Egypt offered and chose to suffer with the people of God. He knew the pleasures he could experience in the royal court came at the suffering of his own people, but more importantly, he recognized that those pleasures wouldn't last. (1John 2:17) I hope all of us recognize that truth!

I struggled with understanding how Moses could consider the reproach of Christ until I read this commentary on the subject. According to Brevard Childs, this *"phrase indicates an actual participation by Moses in Christ's shame in the same way as the saints who follow Christ later also share."* In other words, as we suffer for Christ we are also suffering with Christ, enjoying what the Apostle Paul termed "the fellowship of sharing in his sufferings" (Phil. 3:10). Such suffering is the inevitable result of being identified with Christ and with his people. Where is our ultimate allegiance? What is our primary identification? If we call ourselves Christians, we must forsake the world to follow Christ, becoming spiritually joined to his people, just as Moses was. (Preaching the Word – Exodus) All believers by faith are a part of the body of Christ. To suffer with them for being unlike the world, whether they lived before the cross, or after, is to suffer the reproach of Christ. How should this connect us with ministry to the persecuted church?

Moses may have passed through the country that is today Sudan. People are still suffering reproach for the sake of Christ in that very same area of the world. Have we chosen to suffer with them or enjoy the pleasures of sin for a season? Our pleasure isn't at their expense as Moses' pleasure would have been, but the Scriptures do command us to love our brothers and to remember those who are mistreated since we are also in the body. (Hebrews 13:3)

The story is also told in even more detail by Stephen in the book of Acts. 23 *"When he was forty years old, it came into his heart to visit his brothers, the children of Israel. 24 And seeing one of them being wronged, he defended the oppressed man and avenged him by striking down the Egyptian. 25 He supposed that his brothers would understand that God was giving them salvation by his hand, but they did not understand. 26 And on the following day he appeared to them as they were quarreling and tried to reconcile them, saying, 'Men, you are brothers. Why do you wrong each other?' 27 But the man who was wronging his neighbor thrust him aside, saying, 'Who made you a ruler and a judge over us? 28 Do you want to kill me as you killed the Egyptian yesterday?' 29 At this retort Moses fled and became an exile in the land of Midian, where he became the father of two sons.* Acts 7:23-29 (ESV)

We have seen that Moses was a foreshadow of Jesus. What can we see of Jesus in our text for today? First, remember that Jesus also learned obedience through the things He suffered. (Hebrews 5:8) Jesus was never guilty of rash disobedience like Moses, but as Moses learned from that mistake to look to God and not do things his own way, so also Jesus realized the same truth without sinning.

Moses identified himself with the people of God for the purpose of saving them from their enslavement. Jesus became one of us, fully identifying with us in order to set us free from enslavement to sin. (Romans 8:2-3) Moses was not ashamed to call the Hebrews his brothers. Jesus is not ashamed to call us brothers. (Hebrews 2:11) Think of that. Even after the Hebrews spilled the beans about what Moses had tried to do for them, he still considered himself of their family. We misrepresent Jesus time and time again and He still calls us family. What grace!

It was a big step down from the palace to the slave pits, but Moses was willing to humble himself and give up the position he held. Jesus took a much bigger step down from the halls of heaven to the world of fallen man to walk among the slaves of sin. (Philippians 2:6-8)

I think Moses knew in his heart that the Egyptian world would not change. Even if he became Pharaoh, the ethnic hatred, the greed that enslaves others, the abuse of man for personal advancement is a deeper problem than mere education or even indoctrination. He really had no choice. If he was going to identify with the people of God, he had to leave the evil influences and mindset of Egypt. He couldn't change Egypt, so he had to leave it behind and draw us out with him. (James 4:4) So also, Jesus isn't changing the kingdoms of men, but drawing us out to be citizens of heaven.

As admirable as Moses goals were, as big a heart that he had for his people, he was guilty of something we all have to deal with, doing it my way. This was Moses declaring himself Savior and going about delivering them in his own wisdom (aided by the most enlightened education of the day), to bring justice to the world. Man's way often sounds great. That is why we so often try it. But if salvation is going to come to these broken, arguing, demoralized Hebrews, it is going to come from God by grace. (Ephesians 2:8-9)

How about your friend or neighbor? Can you save them? Well, I hope no one ends up dying in the process. The lesson here is that God has His way and His time. If you come up with a great scheme to lead them to Christ, you may do more damage than good. Pray! Remember how God won your heart. More than likely it wasn't some plan someone developed in a spiritual war room. (John 15:5) Instead, it was God working through this thing and that person and He brought it all together at the perfect time and moved on your heart. In other words, it was God and his grace. Perhaps God used a Moses, but it wasn't that person's plan; it was God's plan.

Maybe at some time you've come to this place that Moses is at in the story. You've failed. You did what you thought was right and it ended up really ugly. OK, what did you learn? Next time act at His leading. Are there some bodies buried in the sand that testify to your guilt and fear? It is just evidence that it was you and not God. God does have a great plan to deal with that neighbor or loved one. Pray. Watch. Wait, and act at the leading of the Holy Spirit. If you've given up and had to let go of your dreams, good! God has a better one for you, one that you would never have dreamed up on your own. Get ready. Listen. Watch for those burning bushes. Listen to the Word and to that still, small voice. Wait for the Lord! Be strong and take heart and wait for the Lord. (Psalm 27:14)

Questions
1 What would you have planned had you been in Moses place?
2 What does "went out" imply?
3 What exactly was Moses leaving behind?
4 What does "watched" imply?
5 What changed everything? Been there, done that?
6 Why weren't the Hebrews glad to see Moses?
7 How could Moses choose the reproach of Christ?
8 How does Moses foreshadow Jesus in these verses?
9 Why did Moses fail?
10 What should we learn from the story?

11 Did you take home an application?

God's Preparatory Academy Exodus 2:16-25

Our passage today finds Moses starting all over again. He has just murdered an Egyptian taskmaster, and since it became known, he had to flee from the reigning Pharaoh. It is quite possible that Moses was adopted by Hatshepsut who was married to her half-brother, the young Thutmose II. She reigned with him as co-regent until she declared herself the first female Pharaoh. She reigned for 20 years until her other half-brother, Thutmose III, took the throne. There is no record of how she died. Did the situation with Moses cause Thutmose III to arrange her assassination? Had Thutmose III dispatched her years before? No one knows. If Moses was her adopted son, then he was in a very precarious situation in this battle for the right to rule Egypt. The murder of a taskmaster would be just the excuse that Thutmose III needed to eliminate his competition. (Hebrews 11:27)

Moses arrived in Midian as a refugee from Egypt. (Acts 7:29) The Midianites were probably a nomadic people who traveled seasonally to find pasture for their flocks. Our passage last week ended with Moses arriving at a well. His ancestors Isaac and Jacob's wives were both first encountered at a well. (Genesis 24:11; 29:2) This wasn't that unusual as wells were meeting places, but it does remind us of the sovereignty of God in orchestrating the times and places that influence our lives. (Acts 1:7)

Apparently, the shepherd daughters of Reuel had a regular confrontation with another group of shepherds. Reuel expected them at a certain time because of this dispute. It could be that, in the contention over the well, the shepherds would make the women draw water for their sheep before allowing them to draw water for their own. Moses wandered in on this dispute and stood up for the oppressed women. If Moses was being groomed to potentially be Pharaoh one day, he had to learn to lead out in combat. Pharaohs were respected for being warriors. He dispatched the shepherds but exercised a little more control in doing so than he did with the taskmaster. No one died. This is great movie material. If Chuck Norris was a little younger he could play the role.

Moses had begun God's Preparatory Academy. He had learned how to confront injustice without the excessive use of force. He still had a heart for the weak and abused, but he was learning how to react without losing control.

The daughters returned home and Reuel asked why they arrived so early. They answered *"An Egyptian rescued us from the shepherds. He even drew water for us and watered the flock."* They relayed the story of the Egyptian that had helped them by chasing off the shepherds and drawing the water for the flock of Reuel. A man drawing water for women was unusual, but it reminds us of the story of Rebecca who had drawn water for Abraham's servant's camels as he sought a wife for Isaac. (Genesis 24:19) Women were a little more highly regarded in Egypt than in other cultures, but for this prince to humble himself and serve them was another sign that God was changing his heart. Godly leaders must learn humility and service. (Matthew 20:28) We don't have a lot of details about these 40 years of Moses being away from Egypt, so the details that are given are important points in his transformation.

Shocked that these 7 daughters had let such a chivalrous man get away, he asked, *20 "And where is he?" ... "Why did you leave him? Invite him to have something to eat."* The nomadic people are very hospitable even today. But even more importantly, you don't get too many opportunities to find an acceptable suitor wandering around in the desert. Here was a man who in one encounter had showed that he cared for the weak, stood up for the rights of women, and was able and willing to protect them. He's a good catch.

21 Moses agreed to stay with the man, who gave his daughter Zipporah to Moses in marriage. 22 Zipporah gave birth to a son... Moses next lesson in servant leadership was a family. This is God's great training ground for most of us. Some are blessed with the gift of singleness and can devote their whole affections to the Lord. But most of us need a family to help us learn to put others first, to learn to be able to yield our demands to the desires of others. It's where we learn to cooperate and sacrifice. The New Testament speaks of leaders of the church as being men who are married and have obedient children. (1Timothy 3:2-5) They have their house in order. How can they bring order to the household of God if they cannot bring order to their own household? This comes by earning the respect of their family by being a loving servant leader.

Moses named his son Gershom, saying, "I have become an alien in a foreign land." I think we tend to misunderstand this passage. Rather than referring to being an outcast in Midian, he was saying that he had become alien in Egypt. Moses is speaking in the past tense. It would be more accurate to translate the passage, "a stranger I have been there." By associating himself with his people, the Hebrews, he became an alien in the very place he was raised. He joined his ancestors the patriarchs in realizing this world is not our home. (Hebrews 11:13) You may have lived here all your life, but if you are a believer, it's a foreign land. We just can't be comfortable in a world that is fallen and unjust. We can't get used to people abusing one another. We can't ignore the sin that causes such suffering in our world. (2Peter 2:8)

Parenting children is one more lesson Moses will learn in God's Preparatory Academy for it is in facing the selfishness of children that we are faced with our own selfishness. We must learn to discipline in love and guide by example. We learn when to be lenient and when to draw the line. They break our hearts, and they fill them with love. Children are God's gift to help shape us even as we learn to gently shape them. (1Thessalonians 2:7)

But perhaps the greatest lesson of all was just referred to in passing. Reuel was called a priest of Midian. What kind of priest was he? He was descended from Abraham through Keturah. (Genesis 25:4) He was a cousin of Moses. There is archeological evidence that this region to which Moses fled was one of the first to worship Yahweh! This would have been passed down from Abraham. (cf. Exodus 6:3) As a priest of Midian, Reuel would have reminded Moses of the stories that were surely told to him as a child by his mother Jochabed. He would have reinforced the greatness of a God who honors His promises and who made a covenant with their forefather. (cf. Genesis 15) He prepared Moses for Moses' own encounter with the God named Yahweh.

The name Reuel means "the friend of God". Later we will learn that he is also called Jethro. Jethro may be a title similar to "his excellency". His forefather, Abraham, was also referred to as "the Friend of God". (James 2:23) So we see a direct link to Abraham and the likelihood that God sent Moses to this wilderness to be under the tutelage of this priest. God was getting into Moses while getting Egypt out of Moses.

But there is one more factor; Moses became a shepherd. Since the Midianites made their living raising flocks, Moses did what was detestable to the Egyptians. He became a shepherd. (Genesis 46:34b) Many of God's great leaders took this class, Shepherding 101, in God's Preparatory Academy.

People are said to be like sheep in a number of passages. (Psalm 77:20; 78:52; Isaiah 63:11) It is really a humiliating comparison, but so true. Sheep can't care for themselves. They need guidance. They can't discern good plants from poisonous ones. They can't groom themselves. They usually stink unless the shepherd has bathed them. They tend to wander into dangerous situations. They are vulnerable to predators.

Moses spent the next 40 years of his life in the wilderness tending these creatures, caring for his family, learning about YHWH, until the day of his call. It took 40 years to learn the wisdom of the world, and 40 years to put that wisdom in its proper place and learn the ways of God. He went from palace prince to desert wandering shepherd. What a fall! Or was it? God's way up is often down. His lessons are rarely learned in a classroom. They are lessons of the heart and will. They are about the priority of a relationship with God.

An unknown person wrote this paragraph about Moses' decisions to this point in his life. *"Bred in a palace, he espoused the cause of the people; nursed in the lap of luxury, he embraced adversity; reared in the school of despots, he became the champion of liberty; long associated with oppressors, he took the side of the oppressed; educated as her son, he forfeited the favor of a princess to maintain the rights of the poor; with a crown in prospect, he had the magnanimity to choose a cross; and for the sake of his God and Israel, he abandoned ease, refinement, luxuries, and the highest earthly honors, to be a houseless wanderer."* Anon.

Moses will be 80 years old when he encounters YHWH and gets his commission to do what he had long given up on ever achieving. Whenever we are tempted to grow impatient with God's timetable for our lives, we should remember Moses, who spent two years of preparation for every year of ministry. - Preaching the Word – Exodus: Saved for God's Glory. God has a plan for each of our lives. It is probably something far less dramatic than delivering a nation, but it is important nonetheless. Don't forget the importance of Jochabed and Reuel to the life of Moses. We are all in God's Preparatory Academy, learning through life's lessons to be people of humble service and love. (Psalm 25:9)

Moses and all of us, if we are to be useful to God, must come to that place that John Wesley came in this prayer of his: *"I am no longer my own, but yours. Put me to what you will, rank me with whom you will; put me to doing, put me to suffering; let me be employed for you or laid aside for you, exalted for you or brought low for you; let me be full, let me be empty; let me have all things, let me have nothing; I freely and wholeheartedly yield all things to your pleasure and disposal."* John Wesley (1703-1791) [The Methodist Service Book, (London: Methodist Publishing House, 1975), D10 .] –repeat it-

Now we switch gears in one sense to see what is behind God's induction of Moses and all of us into God's Preparatory Academy. *23 During that long period, the king of Egypt died. The Israelites groaned in their slavery and cried out, and their cry for help because of their slavery went up to God.* We need to keep in mind that the Israelites have slowly been adopting the gods of Egypt. It won't be long after their miraculous deliverance that they will want to reproduce one of the gods, a golden calf. (Exodus 32:24) God still heard them. We will find out in a minute why God would hear the cry of idol worshippers. Surely some of them were still faithful to the God of their forefathers, but most had either added other gods or abandoned Him altogether. Should God hear us when we suffer if we worship false gods, or were we just getting what we deserved?

24 God heard their groaning and he remembered his covenant with Abraham, with Isaac and with Jacob. There was one great reason for God to hear them. God had made a covenant with the patriarchs. He had promised Abraham that after 400 years He would bring them out of captivity. (Genesis 15:13-14) He had promised to make them a great nation and give them the land first promised to Abraham. When God hears our cries, he remembers His covenant, His promises.

Now, ask yourself this, "Has God given us promises?" The Scriptures tell us that He has given us great and precious promises. (2Peter 1:4) He has promised that whoever believes in Jesus will have eternal life. (John 3:36) He promises that if we receive Jesus and believe in His name we will become sons of God. (John 1:12) He has promised us that as believers in Jesus we are heirs of the promises to Abraham. (Galatians 3:29)

We cry out to God in our temporary suffering of this life and God remembers the great promises He has made to us because we have accepted the sacrifice of Jesus on our behalf. He remembers because we have been adopted into the family of God. (Romans 8:15)

These four active verbs have become very important to the Jewish people and they should be to us as well. God hears, remembers, sees, and knows. What powerful reminders to cling to in our times of testing. He hears our cries. He remembers His promises. He sees our plight. He knows us personally, intimately.

The NIV misses the translation of the last verse. *25 So God looked on the Israelites and was concerned about them.* The ESV give us a more literal translation. *25 God saw the people of Israel—and God knew.* If I tell you I am concerned about your suffering, it doesn't really give a sense of personal involvement or commitment. In Hebrew, the word "to know" is used of intimate relations. God is not just concerned; He knows what you feel, what you are enduring, and the particulars of your suffering. He feels toward you like you feel for your hurting child, only He knows exactly what you are enduring. He knows that you are His child and He sees in you the righteousness imparted to you by your Savior Jesus Christ. (Romans 3:22) He knows *our light and momentary afflictions are working for us a far exceeding weight of glory.* (2Corinthians 4:17)

If we need to be broken, separated, exiled, humbled to be all we can be for His glory and for our eternal good, then He will walk with us through the process. (Hebrews 13:5) If it takes our whole life, it will be more than worth it for the reward is eternal. This isn't just pie in the sky, it's the righteousness of Almighty God. Cry out! He hears you. (Psalm 34:17) He remembers His promises. He sees your situation. He knows! He knows! No one else may understand, but rest assured beloved, He knows!

This is why we are in God's Preparatory Academy. People are crying out to Him He is preparing you and me to be His voice to them. He wants to lead them out through us.

Once you are delivered from Egypt and know the comfort of God's presence, you can be His instrument in helping others who are crying out. He knows your need. HE KNOWS the need of every soul crying out to Him!

Questions:
1 What may have been a factor in Moses fleeing?
2 What was Moses first lesson in Midian?
3 What was the next lesson?
4 What does the last half of verse 22 mean?
5 Next lesson? Application?
6 Who do we think Reuel worshiped and why?
7 What was the last class in the wilderness? Apply.
8 What was the ration of preparation to ministry?
9 Why is God taking Moses through this?
10 What are the four active verbs describing God? Apply.
11 What does "know" mean in verse 25? Apply it personally.

God Encounter Exodus 3:1-10

Moses is now 80 years of age. (Acts 7:30) He has spent the last 40 years herding sheep in the desert wilderness. He has abandoned his dreams of freeing his people. He is no longer a prince; he is nobody. You are never too old and your training is never too insignificant to be a tool in the hand of

Almighty God. In fact, the more humble you are, the more likely it is that God will use you. (1Corinthians 1:26-29)

Our culture admires youth and the wisdom of man. We desperately try to stay youthful in looks and attitude because this is admired. (Proverbs 20:29) I pluck those old man eyebrow hairs and work out, but time marches on and our days are numbered. No amount of Botox or face-lifts can change that. And as far as the wisdom of man goes, I just can't imagine that the Book of Life has those little letters after our names. What does last, however, is what you did with your encounter with God.

1 Now Moses was keeping the flock of his father-in-law, Jethro, the priest of Midian, and he led his flock to the west side of the wilderness and came to Horeb, the mountain of God. Moses has no sheep of his own. He is still keeping the flocks of his father-in-law. We notice that the father-in-law's name is Jethro. Before he was referred to as Reuel, the priest of Midian. It is the same man. Jethro may be his title, meaning "his excellency" or he may have had two names. In either case, he is called Jethro from this point on.

The location of Horeb is much debated. It probably doesn't matter, for the important point is what happened there. Being called "the mountain of God" is significant. At that time, gods were thought to inhabit specific regions. Apparently, the earliest believers in YHWH thought He inhabited this mountain. Of course, we find later that God is omnipresent. (Psalm 139:7-10) His location can't be fixed and yet He manifests Himself in ways that we can relate in specific places and times. Someone may have had an encounter with God at this mountain before Moses.

2 And the angel of the LORD appeared to him in a flame of fire out of the midst of a bush. He looked, and behold, the bush was burning, yet it was not consumed. Who is the angel of the Lord? The Hebrew grammar (appositional construct) implies that this expression MalakYahweh would better be translated, "the angel that is Yahweh" or "The Angel Yahweh". This manifestation has occurred previously in the story of Hagar, Genesis 16, and in the story of the near sacrifice of Isaac, Genesis 22. He is referred to as Yahweh in all three of these cases. So who is speaking to Moses?

Since God is a spirit and inhabits eternity, mortal man cannot see Him. (John 4:24) But when He chooses to manifest Himself in space and time, He does so in a way that we can relate to Him. He gives us something to look at and listen to since that is how we perceive things. The Apostle Paul tells us that the visible manifestation of the invisible God is Christ Jesus. (Colossians 1:20) For this reason, many of us believe that He was the pre-incarnate Christ that was speaking with Moses. He is both Lord and God.

3 And Moses said, "I will turn aside to see this great sight, why the bush is not burned." During those 40 years in the desert, Moses had likely seen lightning strike a tree or bush and seen it burn up. I've seen lightning strike a juniper tree near my home and watched into the night as it burned. It made me think of Moses. If that tree was still burning in the morning I was going to hike up the mountain to see it. Unlike Moses' bush, the juniper was consumed. Moses' bush just kept burning and burning. God got his attention.

Children of God, remember God knows how to get your attention! Those who sincerely seek after God and long to follow Him with all their heart and soul often wonder if they missed something. Unless you are blatantly sinning, which hardens our spiritual ears, don't worry about having missed something. (Deuteronomy 4:29) God knows how to get our attention. If there is something to be concerned about, it is obedience after we have heard what He is saying. (Deuteronomy 1:43)

The fact that the bush was not consumed points us to God's self-sufficiency. He did not need the bush. He does not need us. He is self-existent. Gregory of Nyssa in the fourth century commented on the bush not being consumed. He wrote, ...what Moses saw in the burning bush was nothing less than "the transcendent essence and cause of the universe, on which everything depends, and alone subsists. (Colossians 1:17)

4 When the LORD saw that he turned aside to see, God called to him out of the bush, "Moses, Moses!" And he said, "Here I am." God (Elohim) called to Moses! God is speaking from a bush that is ablaze with His glory. The word that is used for bush, seneh, means a small bush of only a few feet in diameter. Why would God choose to manifest Himself in a little thorn bush? But then, maybe that is all there was other than rocks and grasses. In the Biblical world, bushes and trees sometimes represented people. I suspect that God may be saying that He can manifest Himself in anything He chooses, even in the life of broken down shepherd who has abandoned his hopes and dreams. Even in people like you and me. You can't be too insignificant for God.

Even if you are just a little thorn bush, you can become ablaze with the glory of God! He can use you to encourage others that God can work through them too. Get in His presence! Let Him light you up, and see how He can bring Himself glory through you.

We must also note that God called Moses to Himself. Providence directed Moses' steps to the place of the encounter. God brings us to Himself. (Proverbs 20:24)

The double use of Moses' name is a term of endearment in the Semitic culture. (Genesis 22:11;Acts 9:4) It implied friendship and affection. Moses would have been put at ease knowing the One in the fire was not there to judge him.

Fire is a very significant manifestation. Many of the manifestations of God involve fire. There was the smoking firepot in the covenant with Abraham (Genesis 15:17), the pillar of fire that led the Israelites (Exodus 13:21), and the fire that came down on Sinai when Moses met with God (Exodus 19:18) to name a few. God is even called a consuming fire in Deuteronomy 4:24. Fire gives light but also consumes. It purifies and it can destroy. John the Baptist predicted that Jesus would baptize with the Holy Spirit and with fire. (Luke 3:16) The presence of God will not abide that which is evil. (Psalm 5:5)

5 Then he said, "Do not come near; take your sandals off your feet, for the place on which you are standing is holy ground." When people presented themselves to Pharaoh, they were required to enter without sandals. God uses our individual cultures to communicate in ways we understand. The mountain of God was not the only place God is, but Moses understood it as a place one encounters God. Taking off your shoes may be symbolic of not bringing the dirt of this fallen world before a pure and holy God, but Moses would have seen it as a sign of reverence and subservience when appearing before one that is vastly superior. No other place in Scripture makes this demand to take off one's sandals.

Even though Moses was addressed as a friend, he was to keep his distance. He is being taught about the holiness of God. God's holiness requires respect and distance. We'll see this again in Exodus 19. Boundaries are set around this same mountain where Moses will again meet with God. No living thing is to cross that boundary. It is the same idea as the veil that was before the Holy of Holies in the Temple. (Hebrews 9:3)

Holy is a word that will appear again and again in Exodus. It is to be separated for Divine purposes. When applied to God, it means His "otherness". It is that distance of Creator to creation. It is the infinite distance between Deity and humanity. (Hosea 11:9; 1Samuel 2:2)

Because of the work of Jesus on our behalf, the veil in the Temple that separated us from God was torn and we can draw near to God. (Hebrews 10:19-22) We still come with reverence and awe, but we no longer need fear the wrath of God upon our sin. Jesus took that upon Himself.

6 And he said, "I am the God of your father, the God of Abraham, the God of Isaac, and the God of Jacob." And Moses hid his face, for he was afraid to look at God. Now we know we are talking about the God that Moses' ancestors encountered as recorded in the book of Genesis. This is the God that made the covenant with Abraham and renewed it with Isaac and Jacob. This is the God that promised to bring them out of bondage after 400 years of being in a strange land. (Genesis 15:13-14)

Moses covered his face. He knew that to look upon the full glory of God would mean the end of his physical life. It is just too much for our earthly bodies to take in. (Exodus 33:20) When people in the Book encounter God, it always comes with the realization of their utter unworthiness to be in His presence. There seems to come over people an understanding that their sinfulness demands judgment. (Isaiah 6:5)

So how will we ever spend eternity in His presence? Again, it is because of what Jesus has done for us that we can stand in the judgment. Our resurrected bodies will be sinless and our souls purified that we might live in His presence. (Hosea 6:2) It is impossible for us to imagine what joy that will be. (Psalm 16:11)

7 Then the LORD said, "I have surely seen the affliction of my people who are in Egypt and have heard their cry because of their taskmasters. I know their sufferings, Here, those amazing words of the last chapter are repeated. God remembers His covenant (verse 6). He sees their affliction and hears their cry. He knows their suffering. What comfort these words should be to every child of God. This is God's self-disclosure of His heart.

Some would say that He is only that way toward His chosen people, the Jews. Well, peek into the future of the Jews and you can see He chose them as an example of unfaithful people. He chose them to show us His enduring and gracious love. He loves the world. (1John 3:16) We saw in John's epistle that He is love. (1John 4:8) He cares about every hurting soul and unhealthy body. He will not always deliver us as He is about to deliver the Israelites, but He always sees. He always hears. He always knows what you are dealing with. You can be sure of that.

Whatever happens in your life, know that God remembers His promises. Know that He sees your situation and hears your cry. Know that He knows all about it, every detail.

8 and I have come down to deliver them out of the hand of the Egyptians and to bring them up out of that land to a good and broad land, a land flowing with milk and honey, to the place of the Canaanites, the Hittites, the Amorites, the Perizzites, the Hivites, and the Jebusites. God was declaring the time had come. The 400 years was over. The sins of the people in the land of Canaan had reached the limit of God's patience. They had passed the point of any possible return. (Genesis 15:16)

To "come down" is an anthropomorphic expression, as if God inhabited some space above us. It means that He is about to act decisively in the affairs of men. It is a declaration that the transcendent God is about be seen in the immanent. He will act to deliver them from the Egyptians and bring them up out of the land.

When God delivers, He not only takes us out of a place and conditions, but He brings us to a new place, a new space, if you will. There is a destination. He delivers us up out of sin and rebellion to loving obedience. He takes us out of our selfish mean-spirited attitudes and into His loving sacrificial Spirit. (Ephesians 5:8) God always delivers from the evil to take us to the good. (1Peter 2:9; Luke 11:24-26)

Keep in mind that this is not the end of trouble for the Israelites. Moses may have imagined a merry jaunt through the desert to the Promised Land, a couple of weeks of joyful caravanning, but that is not remotely close to the reality that was before him. Life is full of trouble. (Job 14:1) But it will be trouble of a different type. It will be trouble with a refining purpose.

9 And now, behold, the cry of the people of Israel has come to me, and I have also seen the oppression with which the Egyptians oppress them. Of course God had heard the cry of the people from the day they were enslaved, but the expression "has come up before me" tells us that it is now time for God to act. There is a time for everything. (Ecclesiastes 3:1) Moses was about 40 years early on his first effort. It was the right idea then but the wrong time and method.

God always sees all things, but now the time has come to deal with the Egyptian abuse of the Hebrew people. (Hebrews 4:13) Now His seeing is inciting action. God's Spirit is always striving with man, but there comes a time when He will strive no more. (Genesis 6:3) A line has been crossed, and there is no longer the openness to change in the heart of those with whom He is striving. That is when God takes action to deal directly with the situation. It is a warning to us to yield to God's conviction so that we don't have to face more severe forms of discipline.

10 Come, I will send you to Pharaoh that you may bring my people, the children of Israel, out of Egypt." Moses is commissioned to do the task he had given up on. Now he can do it God's way. He has been humbled and trained in God's Preparatory Academy for this moment. At 80 years of age, he is about to embark on one of the most remarkable stories in history. We know he is ready because he immediately tries to explain to God why He has the wrong man.

Come, I will send you! It is the call of God to every little thorn bush who is humbled and ready to surrender to Jesus as Lord of their life. It's a call to go to Him. He didn't say, "Go!" He says, "Come!" because He is already there at work in the midst of the pain and suffering. (Matthew 4:19) He will lead us to that sick neighbor, that doubting relative, or that business acquaintance. Come I will lead you to be in this ministry, or serve in that capacity. Do you hear the call this morning? Did you hear it in prayer this weekend? Are you willing to hear it? "Come, follow me to…" let the Spirit fill in the blank.

The Lord isn't looking for a few good men, like in the Marine Corps. He is looking for a few broken people, common little ordinary thorn bushes that are willing to follow His lead, willing to be a vehicle for His fiery glory.

Questions:
1 How did God prepare Moses for service?
2 Why does Reuel have another name?
3 Who is the angel of the Lord?
4 What is significant about God using a bush?
5 Why did God repeat Moses' name? Who else?
6 Why does God appear as fire?
7 Why was Moses told to come no closer? And now?
8 What verbs does the Lord repeat?
9 What do they mean to you?
10 What does "come down" mean?
11 What comes after taking us out?
12 Why does God say "come" instead of "go"?

The Name Exodus 3:11-22

The once proud prince of Egypt is now an 80-year-old shepherd in the wilderness of Midian. The invisible hand of Providence has led him to "the mountain of God", Mount Horeb.

here he encountered the Lord of glory. The Lord told him He had seen the affliction of the Israelites and had heard their cry and remembered His covenant. He knew!

Our text last week ended with God commissioning Moses to come to Egypt and bring the people out. Then he was to guide them to the Promised Land.

Have you ever had an old dream that you had given up on, stir again in your heart, but because of the pain associated with the past failure, you just didn't want to even consider it again? After 40 years of doing what was once detestable to him, Moses must have felt that way.

11 But Moses said to God, "Who am I that I should go to Pharaoh and bring the children of Israel out of Egypt?" "Who am I? Just a broken down nomad with a flock of sheep that aren't even my own. Been there and done that and failed big time! All due respect, but You've got the wrong guy."

That was a sign that God had the right guy. What if we heard, "OK, it's about time. I've been waiting until You saw how all my training made me the perfect candidate for the job"? For an ordinary job that might be a good sign, but for a supernatural God sized job it would be a definite eliminator. (John 15:5) Moses not only knew what he was up against but he also knew who he was. Who am I to do a job like that? (1Peter 1:24)

Before we are too hard on Moses for his lack of faith and hesitation, we should think about that call. A man in Arizona recently went to North Korea to tell Kim Jung Ill to let the people of North Korea go. By the grace of God he was returned alive, but nothing changed. That guy had guts! What if you truly believed that God was telling you to go stand before Ahmadinejad and tell him to end his nuclear program, or worse yet to remind him of his Jewish roots? I would ask, "Why me?" Wouldn't you?

12 He said, "But I will be with you, and this shall be the sign for you, that I have sent you: when you have brought the people out of Egypt, you shall serve God on this mountain." This is the great qualifier. "I will be with you!" At the moment, Moses doesn't know the extent of what that means. Later in the journey, he will tell God, "If you aren't going, then I'm not going!" (Exodus 33:15-16) He learned by experience that with God all things are possible. Without Him, good luck, because that is about all you have. If you are going to do a God sized job, you better be sure God is with you to do the job through you. (Matthew 19:26)

Who am I? Who are you? With God, we are a majority. With God, we can do all things as He strengthens us. (Philippians 4:13) With God there is no obstacle that will not be moved. (Hebrews 13:21) We have so many examples in Scripture of God's call including the phrase, "I will be with you." (Joshua 1:5; Judges 6:16; Jeremiah 1:8) His call is the promise of His presence. Just be sure it is God's call. That is so often our point of failure. Good ideas and God ideas can be worlds apart!

Isn't it fascinating that God gave Moses a sign that would not be seen until after he stepped out in faith. He had to confront Pharaoh before he could see the sign. He had to do the task described, at least in part, before he would see the proof. It's kind of like saying, "Trust me, and you'll be able to look back and know I was there." Why does God so often desire to stretch our faith and make us so uncomfortable? Well, it's because faith pleases Him AND earns you a heavenly reward, which also delights His heart. (Hebrews 11:6)

The sign itself is also something we should consider. You shall serve God on this mountain. Wasn't Moses about to begin serving God in Egypt? And wasn't the destination the Promised Land? What is so special about serving God on the mountain? Well, that is where Moses would receive the Law. For Israel, this is a greater historical moment than the expansion of the physical kingdom under King David. This is the climax of Israel's history until Jesus came. (Galatians 3:24) It affected the entire western world because those laws are the basis of our own. That is the greatest service that man could ever perform, receiving the very words of God for the world. That is why this is such a special sign that would convince Moses that this was truly God with him.

I would have thought that the plagues and the miracle of a nation pulling out of enslavement would have been THE sign. God sees things from a timeless and worldwide perspective. We are caught up in the moment. The receiving of those laws was the greatest sign of the presence of God until the time that the word was made flesh. (Psalm 138:2; John 1:14)

13 Then Moses said to God, "If I come to the people of Israel and say to them, 'The God of your fathers has sent me to you,' and they ask me, 'What is his name?' what shall I say to them?" This is a loaded question. Is Moses really considering disobeying a direct command from Almighty God, "IF I come…" He's not talking to someone with Whom he can bargain. If God tells you to come, you better say, "When I come" not "If I come"!

The supposition is based on a fear of being rejected. "What do I say? What if they don't like me this time too?" (Exodus 2:14) But we don't know anything of the fear of rejection. Right?

The question of the name may be as straightforward as it sounds, but the ancient world, especially Egypt, had very specific ideas about a name of a god. There is evidence that the region of Midian worshiped the God YHWH before the Israelites in Egypt knew the name. The Bible actually tells us that God had not revealed His name to the Hebrews yet. (Exodus 6:3)

The name of a god was thought to describe the attribute or action of that god. Gods had a common name and a secret name. This carries over into many cultures including the Navajo. If one knew the secret name they were thought to be able to wield the power of that god.

Moses was most likely just asking to know the official name of the God of Abraham, Isaac, and Jacob, but the cultural context may imply more. Certainly the Hebrew people see a name as representing character and destiny. Moses had asked, "Who am I?" (verse 11) Now he is asking, "Who are You?"

14 God said to Moses, "I AM WHO I AM." And he said, "Say this to the people of Israel, 'I AM has sent me to you.' " The world of Moses' day considered gods' names to be word plays of their actions. God will reveal His name in the next verse, but the description is one they could relate to culturally. It sounds like the name that was about to be revealed. The verb "to be" in Hebrew is hayah. Much has been written on this. One commentator contends that God was refusing to answer the question. Others say He is declaring that He is self-existent.

As for us, we are who we are from birth. We are who cultures and circumstances made us. We are the sum of our genes and the influences in our life. But God is who He is! He is who He has always been. He makes the circumstances. They don't change Him; He changes them! He alone is who He is. This is the fundamental difference between Creator and creation.

Depending on the vowels, which did not exist in writing at the time, it could be saying, "I am the One who brings things into being." I personally like the description suggesting He is timeless. "I am" includes He is and was and is to be. (Revelation 1:8) He alone did not come into being. He just is and always has been!

The bottom line is that His name is a mystery. Even in the next verse when God uses the form we have come to know, YHWH, we still don't have the vowels or know how to pronounce it correctly. The vowels were superimposed in the second half of the first millennium A.D. to remind Jews to say Adonai (Lord) instead of the sacred name of God when reading the Hebrew text. Translators, not understanding this, created the name Jehovah, a name foreign to Jews.

15 God also said to Moses, "Say this to the people of Israel, 'The LORD, the God of your fathers, the God of Abraham, the God of Isaac, and the God of Jacob, has sent me to you.' This is my name forever, and thus I am to be remembered throughout all generations. Now God goes beyond the major attribute of eternal existence to the very name He is called, YHWH, the LORD. He is the same God that called Abram out of Ur and made a covenant with him. (Genesis 12:1) By describing Himself this way, He is reminding the Hebrews that He will keep His covenant. Time passes, but He is unchanged. (Malachi 3:6) His name remains the same. There is no need for Him to change. There never will be a need for Him to change.

16 Go and gather the elders of Israel together and say to them, 'The LORD, the God of your fathers, the God of Abraham, of Isaac, and of Jacob, has appeared to me, saying, "I have observed you and what has been done to you in Egypt, Notice that Moses is to call the elders. This is that system of leadership we studied in January. Even Moses does not act alone. He works with the elders. (see verse 18) They will go with him to meet with Pharaoh. They are not always right, but they are respected, and they will eventually make the right choice.

Moses is to tell them exactly what he has already heard. The God of their forefathers knows what they are going through. He hears and sees and remembers the covenant.

17 and I promise that I will bring you up out of the affliction of Egypt to ... a land flowing with milk and honey." ' God is going to fulfill the promise He made to Abraham. That land of agriculture and pasture will be theirs as God drives out these wicked nations in judgment.

18 And they will listen to your voice, and you and the elders of Israel shall go to the king of Egypt and say to him, 'The LORD, the God of the Hebrews, has met with us; and now, please let us go a three days' journey into the wilderness, that we may sacrifice to the LORD our God.' The elders will eventually listen. Good thing God didn't add the word "eventually" or Moses might have stayed in Midian. It won't end up like the last time when they rejected him. They will go with Moses to stand before Pharaoh.

Now we have that problem again of deception. Were the elders united in a program of trying to trick the Pharaoh that it was just for 3 days? Personally, I don't think so. I think this was the beginning of a negotiation process. They started off small. "Just let us go worship for 3 days." Pharaoh doesn't want to share his glory with any other gods. The answer to the minimum demand is, "No!" Pharaoh wants all the glory for himself. (Isaiah 42:8) As they get toward the last plague, Pharaoh knows they are leaving for good. He is not deceived. In fact, he will drive them out. (Exodus 12:32) For a awhile, he won't ever want to see them again.

19 But I know that the king of Egypt will not let you go unless compelled by a mighty hand. God is outlining the future that Moses is facing. It is a mystery to me why some Christians think that the future is changeable. God knows the future because He is there now. He tells us what happens because He sees right now what happens. He is declaring what He knows. It will take the hand of God to move the king of Egypt. He will have to be compelled. (Exodus 13:3)

20 So I will stretch out my hand and strike Egypt with all the wonders that I will do in it; after that he will let you go. God is explaining the whole process. (Isaiah 46:10) I don't think that made it any easier for Moses, but at least he knew God knew and it was all in God's hands. Even if God doesn't tell us what is going to happen, we can have the same assurance. He knows what we have to go through, and He will use it for our good and His glory. (Romans 8:28)

21 And I will give this people favor in the sight of the Egyptians; and when you go, you shall not go empty, 22 but each woman shall ask of her neighbor, and any woman who lives in her house, for silver and gold jewelry, and for clothing. You shall put them on your sons and on your daughters. So you shall plunder the Egyptians." "Borrow" is an unfortunate word in the KJV. The Hebrews are asking for and receiving the wealth of their neighbors. It is their pay for the years of slavery. It will be used one day to build the Tabernacle and eventually the Temple.

Plunder is usually from the defeat of an enemy. In this case it is the women that will gather it, not soldiers. When Egypt fights against God, they will be so defeated that they will allow the Hebrew women to plunder their wealth. God is humbling the pride of Egypt and showing that their gods are nothing.

Today we have seen the name of God, I Am, declared to Moses. God identified Himself as the same God that spoke to the patriarchs. About 1500 years later, a man, who when speaking with His critics declared, *"Before Abraham was, I AM!"* (John 8:58) They knew exactly who He was declaring Himself to be and they thought it was blasphemy. It would have been, had He not been the very One that appeared to Abraham on the way to judge Sodom and to Moses in the burning bush. He is the self-sufficient, eternal, Almighty God manifest to us as Jesus Christ.

He had told the crowds, "You will die in your sins if you do not believe I am the One I claim to be. (John 8:24 – emphasis mine) No wonder in the Garden of Gethsemane when He told them that He was I AM, they fell back to the ground. (John 18:6)

We have questions, doubts, and fears like Moses had. Jesus says to go and make disciples. We answer, "Who am I?" And He answers, "Surely, I am with you until the end of the age." (Matthew 28:19-20) The same One who made the covenant with Abram, the same One that went with Moses into Egypt, goes with us as we take the Good News wherever He sends us.

Questions:
1 Why wasn't Moses excited to obey God? Relate
2 How did God reassure Moses?
3 What was the sign?
4 We must know the difference between _____ ideas and _____ ideas.
5 What was the high point of Israel's history?
6 What's wrong with Moses' question?
7 What is the connection with I AM and JHWH?
8 What are the possible meanings of JHWH?
9 What did God promise the elders?
10 What did God neglect to tell Moses?
11 Why did God ask them to plunder the Egyptians?
12 How does the name relate to Jesus?

Why You Can! Exodus 4:1-17

We continue the account of Moses before the fiery presence of the Angel JHWH in the burning bush. Moses is barefoot and his face is hidden because he is on holy ground. Considering the other encounters with the glorious Presence recorded in Scripture (Isaiah 6:5; Daniel 10:7-8), we can surmise that Moses is trembling, and probably on his face in the dirt. The awareness of God's holiness accentuates Moses' shortcomings. I believe that Moses' initial excuses are not so much defiance as they are his understanding how incapable he is of doing what God is asking. In other words, Moses knows himself, his weaknesses, and the size of the task to which God is calling him.

God's answer to his concern is, "I will be with you!" (Exodus 3:12) God is our sufficiency for whatever task He assigns us to do. So Moses next concern is the Israelites. "OK, You will be with me, but what about the people; what if...?

1 Then Moses answered, "But behold, they will not believe me or listen to my voice, for they will say, 'The LORD did not appear to you.' " Moses didn't have a great reception the first time he tried to liberate them. (Exodus 2:14) He's wondering why they would be receptive this time. In fact, he sounds like he may still harbor some bitterness and is certain that they won't believe him. After all, he was raised Egyptian. He's been gone for 40 years. Suddenly he is going to show up and say God appeared to him, like He did to their forefathers. Why would they believe him? But God said they would! (Exodus 3:18) Moses was considering his past experience to be more reliable than the revelation of God. Be careful not to make the same mistake.

2 The LORD said to him, "What is that in your hand?" He said, "A staff." This is the voice of YHWH speaking to Moses. God could have just skipped this verse and gone right on to verse three. Why ask what He already knows? Why not just say throw your staff on the ground?

We have seen that Moses' own abilities and own ideas were a disaster. That does not mean that God is not able to sanctify ordinary things and use them for His purposes. What is in your hand? This passage will go on to talk about supernatural gifts and abilities, but God can also take the ordinary and use it in extraordinary ways, like the little bush that is ablaze with His presence. (James 1:17) What is in your hand? Name it right now in your mind. What are the natural things that God has given you? Will you let Him sanctify them for His use? Will you let them become signs, as God uses them in extraordinary ways, to draw people to believe?

God showed Moses how to use it as a sign. He had him throw the staff on the ground and it turned into a snake. It frightened Moses. You'd be frightened too, if you threw down a stick and it turned into a rattler or some other venomous snake.

The snake was worshiped in Egypt as a symbol of wisdom and healing. The spitting cobra was a sign of sovereignty, deity, and authority and was worn on the Pharaoh's headdress. The Pharaoh's scepter was often in the form of a cobra. This miracle of the snake declared that God is the real sovereign deity, even over Pharaoh, and greater still, over the ol' serpent, Satan. (1 Corinthians 15:27)

Apparently, God knew the people would need a sign to help them believe. How gracious of God to give the unbeliever not one sign, but as we shall see, three! And is He any different toward the rest of mankind? Doesn't His desire to see that none perish cause Him to give signs to each and everyone to help them believe, if they are willing to receive it? (2Peter 3:9) I know He was faithful to deliver me from accidents, to arrange incidents, and to bring godly influences at the time I needed them the most. I bet you can say the same.

What is that in your hand? May God use it as He wills 5 "that they may believe that the LORD, the God of their fathers, the God of Abraham, the God of Isaac, and the God of Jacob, has appeared to you."

But just because God uses that thing in your hand as a clear sign, don't expect people to fall on their knees and give their life to God. We humans can be pretty obstinate. So God gave Moses a second sign, the leprous hand. Stick your hand in your robe, pull it out, and it looks like you have the awful disease of leprosy. Put it back in and take it out, and it is normal again. Why this sign? Leprosy was a dreaded disease. If we won't take the first sign God gives, He has to make His warning a little more severe. Notice that these signs are things people fear. Signs to wake up the unbeliever of necessity need to be fearful.

I know a number of people that came to the Lord when they heard in their spirit the voice of God tell them that He was not giving them any more chances. The sign is a warning of judgment, but also of the ability to heal what was considered incurable.

It may also have been a picture of how the Hebrews felt as a nation and of their desire to be whole. They surely felt leprous as they were daily abused. God may have been declaring through the sign that they can continue in that condition or be made whole by the hand of God. (Isaiah 1:18)

9 If they will not believe even these two signs or listen to your voice, you shall take some water from the Nile and pour it on the dry ground, and the water that you shall take from the Nile will become blood on the dry ground." The Nile was one of Egypt's most revered gods and considered to bring life. This miracle showed that God could take the life right out of it.

Blood should remind the Hebrews of the covenant with Abraham. (Genesis 15:10-11) When God promises, God delivers. He can't deny His word. He promised to give Abraham's descendants the land, to make them a great nation, and to bless the world through them. (Genesis 15:5-6)

What is more important, the blessing of the Nile that regularly watered their fields and pastures and gave them some sense of security, or the promises of Almighty God? Psalms 46:4 (ESV) *4 There is a river whose streams make glad the city of God, the holy habitation of the Most High.* John 7:37b-38 (ESV) Jesus stood up and cried out, *"If anyone thirsts, let him come to me and drink. 38 Whoever believes in me, as the Scripture has said, 'Out of his heart will flow rivers of living water.' "* Which river will you choose? The worldwide blessing promised in that covenant with Abraham is the blessing of Jesus, the source of living water. (Acts 3:25-26) He is the river that makes our hearts glad. It was His blood spilled upon the ground that is our real security and provision. (Revelation 1:5)

I don't think the Hebrews understood all this in that miraculous sign. It was enough for them to remember the blood covenant with Abraham and the promises of God. (Genesis 15:13-14)

God gave three gracious signs full of meaning and warning. Together they declared that the people better listen to Moses, because he is the spokesman for Almighty God.

10 But Moses said to the LORD, "Oh, my Lord, I am not eloquent, either in the past or since you have spoken to your servant, but I am slow of speech and of tongue." "Let's say the people are convinced by the signs, what about my stuttering problem?" I'm surprised God didn't say, "That's why I picked you!" (1Corinthians 1:28-29)

One of the greatest American preachers was D.L. Moody. When he was young, he tried his hand at preaching. One of the elders talked to him afterward and told him that he just did not have that gift and that he should find some other way to serve the Lord. Well, most of you know the rest of the story. He went on to hold great revivals, and was in great demand in Scotland and England. It wasn't so much his eloquence as it was the power of God that came with his words. (Acts 7:22) It was same with Moses as well as the Apostle Paul. (1Corinthains 2:4)

Moses' questions were beginning to cross the line from lack of self-confidence to the lack of God- confidence. You can discern that in the way God answered him. *11 Then the LORD said to him, "Who has made man's mouth? Who makes him mute, or deaf, or seeing, or blind? Is it not I, the LORD?* Most of you know that my grandson was born with a cleft lip and palate. It is a fairly common deformity that affects about 1 in 600. I remember not long after his birth reading this passage. I had held the opinion that all such problems were just the result of living in a fallen world. But this passage indicates that God is the One behind these problems. Deformities and handicaps do not make us any less a person. They give the individual more to deal with, or, in some cases, less to deal with. In His wisdom, He makes, or at least allows, the differences for His own reasons.

It was a relief for me to understand this, because I thought we were dealing with the results of the fall, when in reality, God declares here in this verse that He is behind it. If God is behind it, it will surely be one of those blessings in disguise. (Psalm 30:11)

That is what God was saying to Moses. "I made your mouth the way it is for my own purposes." We humans are so arrogant that we think God owes us a perfect body or perfect health. It's all about God, not you or me. His love for us may be expressed in a difficulty because it is what we need. (Psalm 119:71)

According to Jesus, some afflictions are the result of sin (John 5:14), and others are for the glory of God to be manifest. (John 9:2-3) You can't put all problems down to the same cause.

I can only guess that the purpose for Moses' problem with speech was that God would get the glory and people wouldn't overrate Moses and his abilities. (1Corinthians 4:7) This deliverance of the Israelites has little to do with Moses. Moses didn't come up with the miracles and plagues. God does it all. It's all the grace of God, like our own deliverance.

12 Now therefore go, and I will be with your mouth and teach you what you shall speak." God already promised to be with Moses, but now God specifically says He will be with his mouth. Not only will God help Moses to overcome his handicap, but He'll teach him what to say. God is pretty much saying that He'll do everything if Moses will just obey and go.

13 But he said, "Oh, my Lord, please send someone else." Now he has crossed the line. God promises to do it all, and Moses is still trying to get out of it. Moses is uttering that great oxymoron, "No, Lord!" (Acts 10:14) If

He is your Master, you don't say, "No!" No and Lord just don't go together. If He is Lord you say, "Yes!", to whatever He asks. "No", means He isn't Lord.

In survey after survey, the number one fear of the average person is public speaking. For most of us, it is the fear of saying something stupid or embarrassing ourselves in front of a lot of people. I've done it so many times that I found out it isn't deadly. It looks like Moses had a fear we all share, but he also may have had the fear of being executed by the current Pharaoh. (Proverbs 29:25)

I'm so glad that the Bible tells us stories about people like us. Isaiah said, "Here am I; send me." (Isaiah 6:8) But most of us are more like Moses. "Oh my Lord, please send someone else." If you don't want to face God's anger, may I suggest that you humbly follow the Isaiah model.

14 Then the anger of the LORD was kindled against Moses and he said, "Is there not Aaron, your brother, the Levite? I know that he can speak well. Behold, he is coming out to meet you, and when he sees you, he will be glad in his heart. Moses was more worried about talking to Pharaoh than Almighty God. If you want to get God riled up, just tell Him you don't think He can do it. After looking at the wonder of the human body, and the stars in the sky (Psalm 19:1), the beauty of flower, and any number of the wonders of creation, God expects us to understand that nothing is too hard for Him. (Genesis 18:14)

God can see that Moses will not place his faith in God's ability, so he points to Moses' brother. Apparently, God knew the Moses respected his brother's ability to give a speech. God told Moses what he needed to hear to get him to start cooperating. God knew Moses will do most of the speaking, but at this point Moses just needed to have the assurance that he wouldn't HAVE to speak.

Aaron will be glad to see him and know he is alive after a 40 year separation. He will speak if Moses doesn't, but God is really helping Moses take the first step by lowering the bar of expectation about what he has to do.

I think the Lord is angry because it is an insult to our mighty Creator when we refuse to believe He can do what He promises to do. Faith pleases God. (Hebrews 11:6) Lack of faith can anger God. Heed the warning!

15 You shall speak to him and put the words in his mouth, and I will be with your mouth and with his mouth and will teach you both what to do. 16 He shall speak for you to the people, and he shall be your mouth, and you shall be as God to him. That sounds like what happens when we share Jesus with others. If we just won't fear and will look to God, He'll put the words in our mouths and teach us what to do. We will be the voice of God to the unbeliever.

17 And take in your hand this staff, with which you shall do the signs." When you see the busts of the Pharaoh, you see crossed over his chest a whip in one hand and a shepherd's staff in the other. It symbolically represents that he punishes and guides his people. God anointed the shepherd's staff in Moses' hand to be the real staff of sovereign power.

It is no coincidence that God chose his staff to be the instrument of miracles. It was saying to Pharaoh that the authority over people belongs to God. God is the Great Shepherd. When Jesus declared He is the Good Shepherd (John 10:11), He reminded us that He is the true guardian and guide of all mankind for our good.

What is in your hand, fellow believer? Look at a few good examples in our fellowship of people that used what was in their hand. Thelma sows, so she makes dolls for the Christmas boxes and parachutes to drop Bibles into guerilla controlled areas of Columbia. Jane is gifted with design and theater, so she and Lynne do Potter's Hand Productions. Don is gifted with financial savvy, so he helps with Young Life. We could go on and on.

What is that in your hand? How does God want you to use it? If you are worried about your inability, let God reassure you of His ability and willingness to work through you. (Matthew 4:19) Are you expressing a lack of faith in God? Let Him send along someone to help, but don't be surprised if you end up doing what you thought you could never do. Do you still say, "Send someone else"? What is that in your hand? Trust in God's ability to anoint and use it for His glory. That is the only reason why you can!

Questions:
1 What was Moses' fear? Application?
2 Why was it wrong headed?
3 How can we relate to verse 2?
4 Explain what the first sign meant to Egyptians? Hebrews?
5 What was sign 2 and meaning?
6 What was sign 3 and meaning?
7 What was Moses other excuse? Ours?
8 What can we learn from God's response?
9 What made God angry?
10 Why use a staff for signs and plagues?
11 What is in your hand?

My Deliverer is Coming Exodus 4:18-31

Moses had just given God every excuse he could think of, and God answered every one. What Moses didn't realize was that God picks imperfect people. Noah was a drunk; Job went bankrupt; Abraham was too old; Isaac was a daydreamer; Jacob was a liar; Leah was ugly; Joseph was abused; Gideon was afraid; Sampson was a long haired womanizer; Rahab was a prostitute; Jeremiah and Timothy were too young; David had an affair and was a murderer; Elijah was suicidal; Jonah ran from God; Naomi was a widow; John the Baptist ate bugs; Peter denied Christ; the disciples fell asleep while praying; Martha worried about everything; The Samaritan woman was divorced, more than once; Zaccheus was too small; Paul was too religious; Timothy had an ulcer...AND Lazarus was dead! So what's your excuse! (1Corinthians 1:26-29)

Maybe if Moses had come a bit later in Biblical history he would have realized that if you don't want the job, just tell God how qualified you are. Our excuses just encourage God to use us so He can display His power. The real danger is in telling God, "No!" Moses tried when he said, "Send someone else." That will incur the anger of the Lord and cause us problems as God deals with our unwillingness. But finally after God saying He would do it all and give Moses a helper, Moses agreed.

18 Moses went back to Jethro his father-in-law and said to him, "Please let me go back to my brothers in Egypt to see whether they are still alive." And Jethro said to Moses, "Go in peace." Moses apparently didn't have the faith to tell Jethro what he was really doing. I can't blame him. Would you have said, "I'm going to Egypt to single handedly deliver my people, with God's help of course." God sized tasks are hard to explain. It takes faith to present them to others.

Moses did the courteous thing and asked leave of his employer, father-in-law, who was also the priest of Midian. Just because God directs us to do something doesn't mean we can leave common courtesy behind. Moses showed us how to put God first but be courteous and thoughtful as well. (2Corinthans 6:3)

19 And the LORD said to Moses in Midian, "Go back to Egypt, for all the men who were seeking your life are dead." The LORD again addressed Moses' fears and ordered him to go. It seems like this verse may have been added because Moses was stalling. God already sent him once. (Exodus 3:16) Sometimes we know what the Lord is asking but we keep stalling, excusing ourselves by saying it is not yet God's timing. How patient of God to address our concerns and to not give up on sending us.

20 So Moses took his wife and his sons and had them ride on a donkey, and went back to the land of Egypt. And Moses took the staff of God in his hand. Now he has more than one son. This is important to what follows. He took what is now called, "the staff of God." It was once his staff, but now it is God's. I think we can apply that to our own gifts and possessions. If we give them to God, they are no longer our own.

21 And the LORD said to Moses, "When you go back to Egypt, see that you do before Pharaoh all the miracles that I have put in your power. But I will harden his heart, so that he will not let the people go. God is preparing Moses' heart for the rejection he would face so that he does not prematurely give up. We'll discuss the hardening of Pharaoh's heart when we get into the plagues.

22 Then you shall say to Pharaoh, 'Thus says the LORD, Israel is my firstborn son, 23 and I say to you, "Let my son go that he may serve me." If you refuse to let him go, behold, I will kill your firstborn son.' " This is the first time that God refers to Israel as His firstborn son. Moses now knows that God is going to give Pharaoh a choice of either releasing the Hebrews or losing his son. God is letting Pharaoh know the seriousness of His relationship with the Hebrews. The pharaohs had been killing God's son. That's a dangerous thing to do. (Zechariah 2:8) If this Pharaoh would not let them go, he would reap what he has sown. (Job 2:8)

The New Covenant has so many parallels to what is happening here. As the firstborn son, Israel failed to represent God to the world. Jesus, a member of that firstborn son, Israel, did faithfully represent God throughout His life as God's only begotten son. His sacrifice in our place makes it possible for us to be sons of God. (Romans 8:29; Galatians 3:26) Look how serious God is about liberating His sons and daughters! We see in God's intense desire to deliver the Israelites, the same intensity to deliver us through the cross of Calvary. (1John 4:9-10)

The next part of the story is a very enigmatic portion of Scripture. I'll give you my interpretation with the warning that commentators are all over the place with this one. We may have to wait till heaven to get the full and certain meaning.

24 At a lodging place on the way the LORD met him and sought to put him to death. 25 Then Zipporah took a flint and cut off her son's foreskin and touched Moses' feet with it and said, "Surely you are a bridegroom of blood to me!" 26 So he let him alone. It was then that she said, "A bridegroom of blood," because of the circumcision. The covenant of circumcision was made with Abraham, Moses' ancestor. (Genesis 17:10) All the descendants of Abraham were to be marked in this way. It was a symbol of their special relationship with God indicating that their hearts were sensitive to Him. (Deuteronomy 10:16)

Apparently, the Reuel side of the family did not follow the ritual. Moses knew that when he returned, if he was going to say he was in a special relationship with God, he and his sons would have to bear the mark that his family bore as a sign of covenant.

My guess is that Zipporah was reluctant to allow Moses to carry out the surgery because of the suffering the child would endure. What mother wants to hear their child scream in pain? I think they had been having an ongoing argument, and Moses was giving in to his wife's demand that their youngest son not be circumcised. The other son was probably already circumcised for "son" here is singular. That former experience may have so upset Zipporah that she said, "Never again!"

It sounds as if Moses became ill and was about to die if their son was not circumcised. Perhaps God used this to force Zipporah to do what she would not allow Moses to do to her son, to circumcise him. She thought she had to, to save Moses' life. She called Moses a bloody husband because of the demand that her sons be circumcised.

Why was circumcision such a big deal? Listen to what God told Abraham in regards to circumcision. *14 Any uncircumcised male who is not circumcised in the flesh of his foreskin shall be cut off from his people; he has broken my covenant."* Genesis 17:14 (ESV) If Moses came to lead God's people out of bondage and to deliver the Law to them but personally could be disobedient to the covenant God made with Abraham and his descendants, how could he ever deliver the Law to them? How could he expect them to live in accord with the Law while he justified disobedience? How could he lead the nation when he did not have his house in order? This became a New Testament requirement for elders, that they lead their family to follow God. (1Timothy 3:4-5) If Moses could not exert his authority in his home, how could he exert his God given authority over the nation?

The lesson is a timeless truth. When God calls us to service and promises His presence, the first step is our own personal obedience to God. He calls us to clean up our act before we go out to call others to follow. He touched Isaiah's lips with the coal from the altar before he could be sent to deliver a message to people of unclean lips. (Isaiah 6:5-7)

If we are going to speak to a people of sensuality and lust, we better examine our own behavior first. If we want to speak to others about a relationship with Jesus, we'd better be taking time for our relationship with Him. We can ask others to go where we have not gone, but it will carry very little weight of conviction. The power comes when we are living examples of our message. (Philippians 4:9)

Jesus told the crowds to listen to the Pharisee's message, but not to follow their example because they didn't live what they preached. (Matthew 23:2-3) This would have been true of Moses had he gone into Egypt to set the nation free while he was in denial about keeping the covenant God made with Abraham that promised them freedom and a land of their own.

27 The LORD said to Aaron, "Go into the wilderness to meet Moses." So he went and met him at the mountain of God and kissed him. I find it interesting that Moses went back to the mountain of God before he went to Egypt. It was probably on his route to Egypt, and he may have wanted to share the experience with his family.

Was he looking for one more encounter? If he was, the encounter came in a different form. It came as the confirmation through Aaron's visit. (Exodus 4:14) God had told Moses that Aaron would be sent to help him, and now, here he was just as God had said.

We never see a repeat of the burning bush in Scripture. God seems to delight in different expressions so that we don't neatly box Him up and write a book on the seven signs of a true manifestation of God. You might address the generalities, but the specifics are unique every time.

I call this visit by Aaron a double confirmation. Sometimes we believe we have God's leading, but then someone comes along with the same message and confirms that we heard correctly. Like the signs, Aaron was a confirmation that Moses was not crazy, but that he really heard from God. What are the chances that the brother you haven't seen for 40 years shows up right after God tells you he's on his way to help you? When God confirms a call like that, we should sit up and take notice.

28 And Moses told Aaron all the words of the LORD with which he had sent him to speak, and all the signs that he had commanded him to do. A faithful messenger speaks what God has spoken and shows what God has shown him or her. We'll see later that when Moses' tries to speak and act on his own, he is severely penalized. (Numbers 20:12) Jesus told his followers, "If you love me, you will obey my commands." (John 14:21) Moses is now in the obedient servant mode and that means that God can work powerfully through him.

29 Then Moses and Aaron went and gathered together all the elders of the people of Israel. 30 Aaron spoke all the words that the LORD had spoken to Moses and did the signs in the sight of the people. Aaron begins as the spokesman just as Moses had requested and as God had promised, but watch as the story progresses how Moses gains confidence in God's ability regardless of his own inabilities. (Exodus 10:25) They faithfully conveyed to the people what God had spoken and the signs that were given.

Imagine the awe the Hebrews must have felt as they watched and listened. They knew the promise God had given Abraham to set them free after 400 years, and it was now 430! (Genesis 15:13; Exodus 12:40-41) They were probably on the verge of giving up on the promise ever being fulfilled when Moses and Aaron came with hope. God had not forgotten.

The rod becoming a snake declared that the real authority was in God's hands not Pharaoh's. The leprous hand cleansed said that God could afflict, and He could make well. (Isaiah 45:7) Though they had been afflicted, God could restore them from what was considered an incurable condition.

The last sign challenged them to look to God as their source of living water, not the Nile. (Jeremiah 2:13) Though the Egyptians saw the Nile as the giver of life, God was the true Giver of Life. The blood poured out on the ground reminded them God could not forget the covenant he made with their forefather Abraham. (Genesis 15:10) They were powerful signs with powerful messages.

31 And the people believed; and when they heard that the LORD had visited the people of Israel and that he had seen their affliction, they bowed their heads and worshiped. Revival! Hope is restored. Worship is renewed. The message of God has been spoken and received. The people believe that God sees, hears, remembers, and knows! They are not abandoned. (Exodus 3:7)

The phrase, "the Lord had visited the people of Israel" doesn't mean that He ever left them. It means that He was about to fulfill His promises in a tangible way. He had seen their affliction from the beginning, but now they have let go of their doubt about God not seeing. They believe He is who He had declared Himself to be to Hagar, the God who sees. (Genesis 16:13) Doubts and fears were released and had been replaced with hope and courage.

This is a pattern throughout history. This is definitely His story. We get bogged down in this fallen world. We wonder if God sees. Does He remember the promises in His word? Does He really know what I am going through? Faith is displaced by doubts and fears. Our focus turns to the trials and pain in our life.

Then God sends us a messenger. It may be the Word that comes to life as we read it. It may be from the lips of a brother or sister in Christ. It may be a word on Christian radio, and we believe. We let go of the doubt and fear and we grasp hold of hope and courage. We are renewed and excited that God is going to act. We know the Lord has visited us and seen our affliction, and we bow our heads in reverent worship.

Oh how He loves you and me. We wonder why He loves us, how He could love us, and then we remember, it is because His firstborn died for our sins. He set us free from slavery to sin and from the despair and hopelessness of unbelief. (Galatians 5:1)

Let us remember this morning the many times the Lord has come and visited us and made us know He has seen our affliction. If you are in that place this morning, listen and believe, and together let us all bow our heads in reverent worship of our God who has remembered His promises and come and redeemed us. He has kept His promise to bless the world through the seed of Abraham in Christ Jesus. (Genesis 22:18)

Questions
1 What good is an excuse for not serving God?
2 Why did Moses ask Jethro for permission?
3 Why didn't he tell Jethro the truth?
4 Who is God's firstborn? What was the threat to Pharaoh?
5 What happened at the Inn?
6 Why was it important? Gen 17:14 Application?
7 What did Aaron's arrival mean?
8 How would the Hebrews have felt upon seeing the signs?
9 How is our journey similar to the Hebrews at this point in the story?

God, Why? Exodus 5:1-23

We are returning to our study in Exodus. Moses had met with some success. The people believed the signs that God gave him and were convinced that God had seen their misery and was about to fulfill His promises to Abraham. They were moved to worship as their faith and hope were restored. But just because God is in something, doesn't mean there won't be some major bumps in the road, at least from our human perspective. Think of them as speed bumps to keep us from getting ahead of God. God already told Moses that Pharaoh's heart would be hard and that God would have to compel him to let the people go. Moses was forewarned, as we are. (Acts 14:22)

They had success with the Hebrews, now they are going to their first encounter with the Pharaoh. *1 Afterward Moses and Aaron went to Pharaoh and said, "This is what the LORD, the God of Israel, says: 'Let my people go, so that they may hold a festival to me in the desert.'"* They did it! Moses had tried so hard to get out of this. I wonder if they were shaking as they spoke? Did Aaron do the speaking? They had cast their life into the Lord's hands, stepped out in faith, and done what God had asked. Now, will they die? Will Pharaoh yield? Will God intervene? They had to be wondering what was next?

2 Pharaoh said, "Who is the LORD, that I should obey him and let Israel go? I do not know the LORD and I will not let Israel go." We have to hear this in the cultural context. We don't know if this is the first time

Pharaoh had heard of YHWY as the God of the region of Midian, or if Moses had just told him the name for the first time. Moses identified YHWH as the God of the Hebrews. So Pharaoh is saying that he doesn't recognize this God. He has Ra, Osiris, Horus, the Nile and many others, but who is YHWY? "I don't know him, and I won't take orders from him!"

That is a great question. "Who is the LORD?" (John 17:3) God is about to reveal who He is. He will show Pharaoh that He alone is God. He will show that He is all-powerful, and can do as He pleases and none can stand against Him. (Job 23:13)

It's a fair question. After all, if someone came to you in the name of some god, and told you that this god orders you to do something, it would be prudent to ask who the god is. If He is the Creator of heaven and earth, to whom you owe your very existence, then you better obey.

It is a question that every living person must ask when confronted by the conviction of the Holy Spirit. Who is the Lord? Is He the figment of someone's active imagination, or is He the One who brought everything into being, the architect of time and space, the beginning and the end? (Revelation 22:12) It is the ultimate question. (1John 5:20)

However, I don't think Pharaoh is really asking a question. I think he is making a statement. Kind of like, "Who do you think you are? Don't you know that you are talking to a god?"Pharaoh declared that he did not know YHWH, and he will not let Israel go. God says, "Let them go!" Pharaoh answers, "Heck no!"

Oppose a command of God and you will pay for your disobedience. It's not as if God wants to show who is boss, but He's telling you to do what is in your best interest. If Pharaoh would have just said, "Yes", consider the loss and pain that he would have been spared.

It is the same with every command. (Deuteronomy 10:13) After Jesus gave the new command to the disciples, He said, *"I have told you these things so that my joy may be in you and that your joy may be complete."* (John 15:11) His commands are for our good. So when we say, "I will not", we are setting ourselves up for a time of extra difficulty and pain. (Ezekiel 20:13)

3 Then they said, "The God of the Hebrews has met with us. Now let us take a three-day journey into the desert to offer sacrifices to the LORD our God, or he may strike us with plagues or with the sword." I don't think the Lord was being deceptive in asking for three days, rather He was revealing how hardhearted Pharaoh was. There are records from that era of slaves being given permission to leave work for a short time of worship. This wasn't that unusual a request, but the whole work group at one time may have been unprecedented. Pharaoh wasn't willing to share his glory with God, even for just three days.

There is no record of God ever saying He would strike the Hebrews with plagues or sword. Was Moses using "us" as one who was raised Egyptian? Possibly? Or maybe he was relating the motivation for Egyptians' worship of their gods to that of the Hebrews for the sake of Pharaoh understanding the urgency of the request. Either way it was a warning that

Pharaoh is going to be impacted if he will not yield to the demand. Either he will be plagued or his work force will be. He would never be able to say he wasn't warned of the consequences of saying no to God.

Remember, this was just the beginning of the bargaining between God and Pharaoh. Moses doesn't even call God the God of the whole earth, but simply the God of the Hebrews. How gently God begins this negotiation. God asks for a little deference, and Pharaoh says he will give none whatsoever. In fact, he is irritated at the gall of these Israelites to ask to worship any other god than him! (Daniel 5:23)

4 But the king of Egypt said, "Moses and Aaron, why are you taking the people away from their labor? Get back to your work!" 5 Then Pharaoh said, "Look, the people of the land are now numerous, and you are stopping them from working." Though the text isn't clear, it sounds like the nation was standing behind Moses watching and wondering what was about to happen. I can see Pharaoh pointing over Moses' shoulder, "Look at all the labor that is being lost! You are a distraction! Quit wasting my time and theirs!"

6 That same day Pharaoh gave this order to the slave drivers and foremen in charge of the people: 7 "You are no longer to supply the people with straw for making bricks; let them go and gather their own straw. 8 But require them to make the same number of bricks as before; don't reduce the quota. They are lazy; that is why they are crying out, 'Let us go and sacrifice to our God.' 9 Make the work harder for the men so that they keep working and pay no attention to lies." What they may have feared came to pass. The conditions were made even worse than before. The Hebrews were responsible for making bricks for Pharaoh's building project, and some other people provided the straw. Pharaoh had to dissuade the people from listening to Moses, so he made the workload greater and blamed it on Moses. "If they have time to listen to Moses' fantasies, they have too much time on their hands. They can find their own straw for the bricks."

There is some very detailed information in the text that is completely accurate historically. The bricks of that era were made with straw. The oversight was exactly as described. The Egyptians worked though Hebrew overseers. There is even a portion of Pithom that is one of the store-cities that the Hebrews built that doesn't have straw in the brick. The Bible is historically accurate even when addressing a story over 3500 years ago.

We should note that the word Pharaoh used in this verse for "work" has the same root as the word for "worship" in 4:23. Pharaoh is saying, "If they want to worship another god, make them worship me even harder." In the first verse Moses declares, "This is what the Lord says…" and in verse 10, Pharaoh says, "This is what Pharaoh says…" as if he were a god. Pharaoh is setting up a competition between himself and the Hebrew God. Who is really in charge? Whose staff is the real symbol of authority? (1Chronicles 16:31)

If you relied totally on "open doors", on God making the way easy, to assure of God's favor, then you'd think that Moses was deceived. After all, if God were in this, if He saw our misery, why would things get worse? We have a tendency to think that if we are in God's will, everything will fall into place.

In 1813, one of America's first missionaries went to Burma. His name was Adoniram Judson. It took years to learn the language and translate the Gospel of Matthew. His first few converts came only after years of self-denial. When war broke out with the British, he was suspected of spying and imprisoned. He was sometimes left hung by shackled feet with his head and shoulders touching the ground. His wife begged for his release. She had given birth to their first child. Before his release she and the baby had died. His second wife also died of a fever as well as three of their children. Who ever said God's will is easy? In his later years, because he had pulmonary disease, he had to whisper the message to someone who could preach it. But before he died, there was the Gospel of Matthew in Burmese and many Christian churches.

God doesn't promise clear sailing, but He does promise to see us through to our destination! (Acts 27:23-26) Moses first storm had just hit. When the brick quotas weren't met, the Hebrew foremen were beaten. Remember that this is a confrontation about who is God. When the foremen were beaten did they cry out to God? They had just worshiped God who saw their misery, but when their misery increased where did they run, …to Pharaoh. Three times in verse 15 and 16 they refer to themselves as "your servants." (Matthew 6:24) Why didn't they go to Moses whom they had recognized as one who met with God?

17 Pharaoh said, "Lazy, that's what you are--lazy! That is why you keep saying, 'Let us go and sacrifice to the LORD.' 18 Now get to work. You will not be given any straw, yet you must produce your full quota of bricks." The implication is that if they keep asking, they will just make it harder on themselves. From Pharaoh's frame of reference, that was a smart thing to do. Now they won't listen to Moses and will blame him for their troubles.

You do realize that this is Satan's well- worn tactic. Blame God for your troubles. If you face difficulties in serving God, Satan suggests you quit listening so that you won't have to face more trouble. Reality is that life is full of trouble regardless of whether you are with God or living selfishly. (Job 5:7) Trouble is a part of living in this world. You can walk through it with the God of all Comfort or you can face it on your own. (2Corinthians 1:3-4)

At the end of my first year at Wayside, I was tempted to throw in the towel. Complaints and discouragement can become overwhelming. We were growing, but some were leaving. Someone said, "We'll never have children here." Someone else said, "You are chasing all the older people off with that guitar music." Well, seven years have passed since those comments, and we are three times larger, sending out missionaries, ministering in a number of different outreaches and small groups, the web site is reaching over 4000 every month, books published and we could go on and on. But you have to weather the storms and persevere by the grace of God. He'll only give us what we can handle with His help. (1Corinthians

10:13) I'd never have survived what Adoniram Judson went through, so God put us in this easy place with difficulties that are trivial. (2Corinthians 12:9)

The Hebrews fell for Pharaoh's tactic and blamed Moses. *20 When they left Pharaoh, they found Moses and Aaron waiting to meet them, 21 and they said, "May the LORD look upon you and judge you! You have made us a stench to Pharaoh and his officials and have put a sword in their hand to kill us."* Moses and Aaron were waiting to see the results of the meeting of the overseers with Pharaoh. Pharaoh seems to have won this battle. They looked on Aaron and Moses as the source of their new problem. They even asked that the God whose name had been revealed to them by Moses judge Moses.

We can't be too hard on them. I've had something similar, where I was just doing as I knew the Lord was leading and had someone ask God to judge me. I think they honestly believed they were in the right and believed I was wrong. What do you do when people have the truth so twisted that they are convinced that wrong is right? (Isaiah 5:20-21)

Those people did see the signs. They did believe it at the time and worshiped God. They rejoiced that God had heard their misery. But now, they see Moses as the source of increased misery. They've been beaten. They have to work even harder than they have in the past. You have to feel sorry for them.

I imagine Moses felt like he had failed, and yet his conscience was clear. He had done what the Lord asked and he knew that it was only a matter of time before the Lord did what He had promised. God would keep His word and compel Pharaoh with a heavy hand. (Exodus 3:19)

That doesn't lessen the sting of rejection from these leaders of Israel. (Galatians 1:10) He probably flashed back to the first rejection and back to the bush and how he tried to get out of being put in this position. Those situations where you end up cursed by people if you do and cursed by God if you don't are the toughest of all. It seems no matter which way you turn it's painful. (2Tim 4:16) But God has a plan and has promised it will end differently, so you persevere in faith. (Revelation 3:21) You have to. If you love the Lord you have no other choice. (John 6:68)

This is a very hard place in which Moses finds himself. It is a place every follower of God will eventually face in one way or the other. It is a place where faith grows strong and sinks its roots deep. (Ephesians 3:17) We are going to leave Moses there, but know this, his response to this trial is to run to God in prayer and honestly lay it out like he sees it. (Mark 14:36)

22 Then Moses turned to the LORD and said, "O LORD, why have you done evil to this people? Why did you ever send me? 23 For since I came to Pharaoh to speak in your name, he has done evil to this people, and you have not delivered your people at all." "Why did you ever send me?" He didn't try to sound religious or spin it in a good light or even say that he had faith. He just poured out his heart to God. Moses expected things to go smoother even though God had told him they wouldn't.

Sometimes we get an idea in our head of how God should get something done. He often warns us that it won't go that way, but we imagine how we think it should go. And then, like Moses, we run whining to God with our complaint. (Psalm 62:8) God is so patient! He will answer. He will continue to have patience with Moses and you and me. He will be glorified, and we will be in awe. (Psalm 18:30)

Questions:
1. Why does God give us speed bumps?
2. What did Pharaoh mean in verse 2.
3. Why does God insist on obedience?
4. Why did they just ask for 3 days?
5. Why was Pharaoh's response clever?
6. Should we expect God to clear a path for His will to be done?
7. Who does Satan like us to blame in our difficulties? Why?
8. Who got blamed? How did he feel?
9. What was the catch 22 for Moses? Why is it so difficult? Relate.
10. What do you think of Moses' prayer?

I Am the Lord Exodus 6

We left Moses discouraged and doubtful that God could accomplish the task through him. The people's extra burden of increased labor turned them against Moses, just as Pharaoh had planned. (5:21) It seemed like the wisdom of Pharaoh had prevailed, but then Moses prayed. Prayer changes things, but more often it changes our attitudes instead of our circumstances.

We hold up certain prayers in Scripture as model prayers. This is certainly one that is never cited, but it is a model that we all resort to by default. "What's going on? Why me? Nothing is going according to my understanding of what I think you told me. Woe is me! Can I just forget the whole thing?"

If you haven't prayed that prayer in some form or another, your day is most likely coming. We all seem to have to go through that place of discouragement, where God challenges us to have faith in Him and just believe. (Hebrews 11:6)

God could have rebuked Moses for his doubts, for not listening to what God had already said. After all, God appeared in the burning bush and warned him that Pharaoh would not listen. God promised that He would compel Pharaoh to yield with wonders done by His mighty hand. "Only then", God warned, "will he let you go." (3:19-20) Did Moses forget so quickly, or did he just prefer to forget that part? Or did he remember, but prefer to not experience that hardship, and so is now whining about it.

Judging by my own human nature, I'd say it was the latter. He remembered it well enough to record it for posterity. What Moses recorded about himself makes him look rather bad. That is integrity. Even if you think someone else wrote it, they are writing about their hero. Yet, like all the Bible characters, they are so much like us. There is an authentic ring to Moses' complaint. He is just like us.

The God of all grace and comfort answered Moses' whining. He'd rather hear your honest heart than some nice sounding religious words. (Luke 18:13) Remember, He already knows what's in your heart. You can't fool God. (1Chronicles 28:9)

1 But the LORD said to Moses, "Now you shall see what I will do to Pharaoh; for with a strong hand he will send them out, and with a strong hand he will drive them out of his land." Allow me to paraphrase this. "You see Pharaoh's stubbornness and clever dealing now, but the day is coming when you will see how I cause him to drive you all out of the land."

The difficult initial encounter was necessary to appreciate the extent of the miracle. If Pharaoh had just acquiesced, God would not have been glorified, and the people of Egypt would not have a revelation of the true God. Israel may have been grateful, but they would have been tempted in an even greater way to return. This difficulty was a necessary opening act, and so are many of the difficulties we face in life. (Romans 5:3-5)

Don't always interpret problems to be a sign of a wrong direction. They may simply be the prelude to a greater victory. (Hebrews 11:39-40)

Trials help us learn and grow. We learn to have faith in God. We give Him greater honor and praise when He turns the situation around. In many cases we are strengthened against temptation because of the consequences we know we would endure if we gave in to them. We learn a little more about the amazing God we serve. We learn to listen and trust what He has said, even when things seem to go from bad to worse. We turn our eyes from this world, to God. (2Corinthians 4:18) This is what Moses was doing, in spite of his doubts. And God said, "Now you shall see..."

2 God spoke to Moses and said to him, "I am the LORD. God is saying, "In case you are wondering if I made a mistake, remember that I am already in the future." The eternally existent God never has to look back and say, "Whoops! I should have done that differently!" (Numbers 23:19) When you are perplexed about how things are turning out, remember, God isn't. He knows. He knew before He directed you. He sees the results. He is the I AM. (Ephesians 2:10)

That is enough of an answer for all of Moses' doubts and ours as well. He is! If we could just grab hold of that concept, what a difference it would make in how we interpret the seeming setbacks of life. (Romans 8:28)

That alone was enough of an answer, but God continued, *3I appeared to Abraham, to Isaac, and to Jacob, as God Almighty, but by my name the LORD I did not make myself known to them.* The patriarchs may have had an excuse because God had not revealed this aspect of His nature. They called Him El Shaddai, the all-sufficient or Almighty God. But God had revealed His name to Moses, and with that name came an increased understanding of God. With that understanding comes and expectation that we should see life in the light of that new knowledge. (Exodus 34:6) Do we?

What is your reaction when you get in Moses' situation? You had an expectation, and not only did it not come to pass, but things got worse. You can then blame God or trust God. Which you do, and the attitude you choose are determined by what you really believe about God.

God reminded Moses that He had appeared to the patriarchs. In seeing the burning bush Moses joined that elite group, but with revelation comes expectation. For the most part, they obeyed. Now Moses is expected to obey as well. (John 14:23)

4 I also established my covenant with them to give them the land of Canaan, the land in which they lived as sojourners. What Moses is about to do is connected with that earlier covenant made with his forefathers. (Genesis 15:7) God cannot lie. He is there in the past, present with Moses, and there in the fulfillment. God isn't going to let Moses down, even if Moses does doubt and fear. God can't let him down, because it is about fulfilling the promises He has made. This deliverance is going to happen! (Jeremiah 1:12) These are all reasons for Moses to have faith. He's the Lord. He appeared to them. He made promises.

5 Moreover, I have heard the groaning of the people of Israel whom the Egyptians hold as slaves, and I have remembered my covenant. This is now the third time God has told Moses that He has heard their groaning. Perhaps this time there is implied the additional groaning of the new burden of gathering the straw. If the groaning was heard before, the increased groaning must be heard even more. God remembers the covenant with Abraham, the promise to bring them out after 400 years. (Genesis 15:13-14)

Though most of this was said before in chapter 3, now, in the midst of the trial, Moses needed to be reminded. Don't we need a reminder of things we already know when we react to trials with fear? (Romans 15:16) Sometimes we just need someone to speak those old familiar verses to us to help us get our eyes off the problems and on to the truth of God's word. Don't feel you are being condescending when you remind someone of a verse they already know by heart. We all need an occasional reminder. Moses then received his next instructions. The instruction is to speak again to the Israelites. It is a series of "I will…" declarations framed with "I am the LORD!"

6 Say therefore to the people of Israel, 'I am the LORD, and I will bring you out from under the burdens of the Egyptians, and I will deliver you from slavery to them, and I will redeem you with an outstretched arm and with great acts of judgment. God wants the people to understand what He is trying to get Moses to understand. God does what He does because of who He is. We can believe Him no matter how things appear because He is the eternal One. (Revelation 22:12-13)

So first, Moses must again proclaim that God is the Eternal One, and then the vow of God to bring them out, deliver them and redeem them. This is full of Gospel connotations. The Hebrews heard it as freedom from the burden of slavery. How? It will be by God's outstretched arm.

This is one of the many places when God is speaking on multiple levels. There is what the people hear. There is the reality of its fullness in their lives both physically and spiritually, and there is the greater truth to which the Old Testament shadows point. (Hebrews 10:1)

A slavery greater than that of Egypt began in Genesis chapter three. Jesus called it slavery to sin. (John 8:34) He said that anyone who commits sin is enslaved by sin. That's all of us, just in case you weren't sure. That enslavement means we need redemption and deliverance. How did God say He would do that? It's with His outstretched arm. And who did Isaiah say was the arm of the Lord? He is the suffering Servant of Isaiah 53. "Who has believed our report and to whom is the arm of the Lord revealed. He grew up before Him as tender shoot..."and later in the song, "he shall bear their iniquities" and "he bore the sin of many." Isaiah 53:1, 11d, 12c Jesus alone delivers us from enslavement to sin.

He is the eternal God. He has the big picture in mind, the ultimate fulfillment of the covenant to bless the world, not just Israel. (Genesis 12:3) God has a greater cry in His ears, and greater deliverance in mind, the cross of Jesus. (Revelation 13:8)

God continued, *7 I will take you to be my people, and I will be your God, and you shall know that I am the LORD your God, who has brought you out from under the burdens of the Egyptians.* God was making them a special group of people, His own, adopting them. When it all came to pass, they were to solidify the reality of who God is in their hearts and minds. Notice that God speaks as if taking them out is inevitable because of His eternal perspective. (Ezekiel 12:25)

The New Covenant application for us is that God has made us a part of the family of God. He has adopted us and grafted us into the trunk of these ancestors of faith. (Romans 11:19-20) He has become our God and we are His people. The burden of guilt and of fitting in with the world has been lifted off our shoulders. We should know that He is the eternal God. That should affect the way we see every trial and difficulty, good times and bad.

God summed it up with this, *8 I will bring you into the land that I swore to give to Abraham, to Isaac, and to Jacob. I will give it to you for a possession. I am the LORD.'* " The final "I wills" are to bring them into the Land of Promise and give it to them. He brings us out to bring us in. We aren't meant to die in the wilderness. Then, for the fourth time in this short declaration, God said, "I am the LORD!" If He says it, that settles it.

The first hint of trouble and the Israelites will utterly contradict what God has told them they need to fix in their hearts and minds. They'll start whining about being brought into the desert to die because there wasn't enough room in Egypt to bury them. (Exodus 14:11) Can you believe it?

I can, because I look at how I act when the heat is on. Burdens start to pile up. God allows them to refine me and test my faith, and I start whining like the Israelites.

Did He not deliver us? Does He not remind us that He is the LORD, the eternal One? Was our redemption possible any other way? Then why didn't we get in our hearts and minds that He is the LORD? The fact that I'm whining shows I missed the lesson. If I got the lesson, I would be praising God in every circumstance because He promised to use it all for my good. (1Thessalonians 5:18) He promised to refine my character. He promised to get me ready for heaven. (James 1:3-4)

If God can redeem my soul and bring me out from under the burden of the world, then I should know that He can take care of any other situation in life! I should know He is the LORD, YHWH, the eternal One, who is mighty to save! I should be laughing and singing not whining and moaning. (James 1:2) Amen?

Let's go over these "I wills" that are not only for them, but for all that God calls. I will bring you out the world system, deliver you from enslavement to sin, redeem you from the enemy of your soul, make you my own child, be your God, bring you in to the family of God, and give you heaven. What promises! He is the LORD.

9 Moses spoke thus to the people of Israel, (and they praised God again! NO?) *but they did not listen to Moses, because of their broken spirit and harsh slavery.* What a sad verse. Their spirits were so broken by Pharaoh, that they dared not have any hope. Sometimes the world can be so difficult, and sin can be so destructive, that we just give up. But that does not mean that God gives up on us! (2Timothy 2:13) He already said "I will". And brothers and sisters, He already said what He will do in us. Remember, He is the LORD! Don't forget the implications!

God sent Moses back to Pharaoh to make the demand again. *12 But Moses said to the LORD, "Behold, the people of Israel have not listened to me. How then shall Pharaoh listen to me, for I am of uncircumcised lips?"* The broken spirit of the people had settled in on Moses as well. He reverted to his old excuse. He didn't want to bear the blame for increased hardship. Moses still didn't understand why God wants to use the ones who know they can't do it. He still hasn't learned that excuses just encourage God to use you. (1Corinthians 1:26-29)

The next verse looks forward to the pep talk God has in the next chapter with Moses and Aaron. 13 But the LORD spoke to Moses and Aaron and gave them a charge about the people of Israel and about Pharaoh king of Egypt: to bring the people of Israel out of the land of Egypt. It is mostly a repetition of the talk they already had. God already dealt with Moses' excuses. He already told him it was going to be an effort and take time. He already told him the eventual outcome. He just needed a reminder, like most of us occasionally do.

The rest of this chapter is the family tree of Moses and Aaron, so we know exactly who these people are. Lineage was especially important to the Hebrews because of the promises to Abraham to bless his descendants. (Genesis 18:17-18) It has winners and losers, people of great faith and power-hungry politicians. It has names like Baldy and Clumsy, as well as heroic names like Great Expectations. People just like us. God knows our names but the point of the chapter is that He calls us all to know His. When He says He is the LORD, He wants us to grab hold of all that means for our lives. He wants to infuse our daily life with faith and confidence, with trust and peace. He is the LORD!

Questions:
1 Why was it necessary for to begin with such resistance?
2 How does difficulty help us mature?
3 What should, "I am the Lord" say to Moses? and to us?

4 How should we look at the seeming setbacks of life?
5 How can people see what we really believe about God?
6 Why do we need to be reminded of what we already know?
7 Who is the outstretched arm of the Lord?
8 Go over the "I wills" and relate to today?
9 What can make the difference between praising and whining?
10 Do you live like He is the LORD?

Supreme God Exodus 7

We left Moses complaining before God about his inability and God's lack of action during the first encounter with Pharaoh. In verse 13 of the last chapter, we are told that God renewed His charge to Moses. Chapter seven is an account of that command and of Moses' obedience by faith.

1 And the LORD said to Moses, "See, I have made you like God to Pharaoh, and your brother Aaron shall be your prophet. God had already said this in 4:16. But now God is telling Moses to "see" that what God has said has come to pass. It is another command of God to walk by faith and then see that what God says is reality. (2Corinthians 5:7) The only way Moses is going to see it is if he obeys God and goes back to Pharaoh again. He escaped with his life last time, and his people suffered for the exchange. But God says His word is reality, not how Moses was interpreting the conditions around him at that time.

Did it look like Moses was God to Pharaoh? No way! It looked like Pharaoh made a fool of Moses. But God was saying that is only how it appeared. God's perspective is reality. Moses' perspective is just a snapshot in time. Believe God!

It reminds me of when Ida left us. The shell looked as if life was fading but the Word tells us she was entering into everlasting life. I could believe my eyes at the moment or I could believe the never failing Word of God. (John 11:25) See, *"death where is your victory; where is your sting?... thanks be to God who gives us the victory through our Lord Jesus Christ."* (1Corinthians 15:54-56) Believe God!

God told Moses he would be God to Pharaoh. The word "like" is not in the Hebrew text. Of course, God is not saying that Moses is divine, but rather that God is at work in Moses. Pharaoh thinks he is the incarnation of a god. God is beating Pharaoh at his own game by being God in Moses.

Though this terminology is not used again in Scripture, the New Testament calls us God's ambassadors. (2Corinthians 5:20) We represent God to unbelievers. They may have been avoiding an encounter with God, but when they encounter our love and concern, they are encountering God's love and concern. The ultimate example of this was Jesus Christ who is divine and actually is God with us. (Colossians 1:15)

To be God's ambassador is a big responsibility! We must carry it out the way Moses did, by faithfully doing what God instructs us to do in demonstration of the fruits of the Spirit. (Galatians 5:22-23) And just in case you think you are too old to start down this road, remember Moses was 80 and his brother was 83!

In verse two God told Moses that he is to go back to speak to Pharaoh. Moses sounded like he was trying to use his inabilities to get out of the task, and God simply said, "You shall do this!" It is the same with us. Ephesians 2:10 tells us God planned in advanced the good works we will do. There is that mystery of free will and the sovereignty of God.

Well, Moses could have packed it up and headed back to Midian and lived out his years as a shepherd, maybe even taken his father-in-law's role as the priest of Midian. But he heard God's command and he believed God when God said, *3 But I will harden Pharaoh's heart, and though I multiply my signs and wonders in the land of Egypt, 4 Pharaoh will not listen to you. Then I will lay my hand on Egypt and bring my hosts, my people the children of Israel, out of the land of Egypt by great acts of judgment.* God had told him this before, but Moses needed the reminder that God was still going to do all He promised. Fellow believer, we can count on His promises, no matter how things appear at the moment. (Joshua 23:14)

I'm not saying we should ignore the facts around us. Sometimes the evidence around us shows that we are in error. I am saying that when God's word is clear on an issue, you should believe God and not your temporary circumstances. (2Corinthians 4:18) God will complete what He has started. He will deliver His people from the land of Egypt. He will deliver us from the bondage of sin. He will present us faultless before God's throne. (Jude 1:24) He will because He cannot lie. What He says is reality!

There is another reason that God has chosen this course of action. 5 The Egyptians shall know that I am the LORD, when I stretch out my hand against Egypt and bring out the people of Israel from among them." God is delivering His people so the Egyptians will know the true God is YHWH, not Horus, or Isis, or Pharaoh or the Nile, but YHWH! The word used here "to know" is not just knowledge but experiential knowledge. God wants us to experience Him! God so loved the world that gave His Son. (John 3:16) We tend to think that the Old Testament is all about God and Israel. It is, only so far as Israel was supposed to become a nation of priests for the world to know the true God. (Exodus 19:6)

The Old Testament is really a book that reveals God and His desire to restore the marred image of God in mankind. God is not just bringing Israel out of Egypt, but bringing all who are seeking the true God out of Egypt. A great number of people that were not of Israel will depart with Israel because God is going to prove that He alone is sovereign. (Exodus 12:38)

I have wondered why Moses didn't use the signs God gave him to convince Pharaoh at the first encounter. If you read chapter four carefully, you will see the signs are for the Israelites to believe. (Exodus 4:1; 5) The next verse is the first time God told Moses to use the signs before Pharaoh. Moses was faithful to do only what God instructed. That is why God picked him. That is the kind of people God is seeking. The person who runs off using God's gifts to show their greatness loses the assignment. Pride will disqualify them from service. But the humble servant who only obeys is given more to do. (Luke 16:10)

9 "When Pharaoh says to you, 'Prove yourselves by working a miracle,' then you shall say to Aaron, 'Take your staff and cast it down before Pharaoh, that it may become a serpent.' " Now he has the green light to use the signs before Pharaoh. But notice that Moses must wait for Pharaoh to ask. This is the basis for the Jews' encounter with Jesus, asking Him for a sign. (Matthew 12:38) They believed that if the One like Moses came to deliver them, He would perform miraculous signs like Moses. Jesus did! (Deuteronomy 18:15) They just didn't accept the healings as a sign. In doing so, those who opposed Jesus were putting themselves in the same category as Pharaoh, people with a hard heart.

11 Then Pharaoh summoned the wise men and the sorcerers, and they, the magicians of Egypt, also did the same by their secret arts. 12 For each man cast down his staff, and they became serpents. But Aaron's staff swallowed up their staffs. Remember that the staff was a symbol of authority. The shepherd's staff in particular was the symbol of the one that ruled the people. That is why you see busts of pharaohs holding a shepherd's crook.

This is a confrontation of who has the right to rule. Pharaoh insists that he is a god, the very incarnation of Ra and Horus, and that all must obey him. God gave him a reasonable request and Pharaoh has refused to share his glory with God.

There are accounts, even today, of a snake in Egypt that can become stiff when a nerve is pinched in its neck. Moses was performing a miracle. The magicians were doing a trick.

God was declaring that He was the true authority in the staff, and the only wise God and deity for that is what the snake represented to the Egyptians. That authority, wisdom and power was in the hand of Moses, God's instrument.

The magicians represented Pharaoh. They did their trick that declared symbolically that Pharaoh was the one who has authority with many gods. But then something happened that must have really shaken them. Moses' staff swallowed up their staffs. Notice the text didn't say snake but staff. That's because the emphasis is on who has the authority. The magicians couldn't duplicate that!

The Egyptians saw the act of swallowing something as taking on its attributes. What was symbolically declared was that the God, YHWY, is the only sovereign Lord. All power and all authority come from Him! (Job 12:13) That was a powerful statement! It must have infuriated Pharaoh. But what could he do? It was a miracle. *13 Still Pharaoh's heart was hardened, and he would not listen to them, as the LORD had said*.

Pharaoh had been warned. The sign was clear, but Pharaoh refused to yield. When God gives someone a clear sign and they refuse to yield, He must then do something more forceful to get through their hard heart. It was time for the first plague. All of the plagues came as a judgment on one of the things that Egyptians worshiped. (Exodus 12:12)

The Nile was considered a god that brought life. It watered the fields with its annual flood. It provided fish in abundance. The act of throwing babies into the Nile when Moses was born may have been an act of worshiping the Nile. (Exodus 1:22)

God told Moses to go down by the Nile and wait for Pharaoh to come. Pharaoh most likely came each morning to observe a religious ritual of worship to the Nile. Upon Pharaoh's arrival Moses was told to tell him, ...so far, you have not obeyed." *17 Thus says the LORD, "By this you shall know that I am the LORD: behold, with the staff that is in my hand I will strike the water that is in the Nile, and it shall turn into blood. 18 The fish in the Nile shall die, and the Nile will stink, and the Egyptians will grow weary of drinking water from the Nile."* God even wants Pharaoh to know that He is the LORD!

Right then and there Pharaoh could have yielded, but his heart was hard. The LORD does give us warnings. He often tells us what the consequences will be if we continue to harden our heart. (Proverbs 28:14)

Did you notice that it is Moses that is speaking? God told Moses to say these things. The man who complained that he couldn't speak is now speaking the very words of God. God's power is perfected in our weakness. (2Corinthians 12:9)

Aaron took the rod of God and stretched it out over the land and then struck the river with it. The water turned to blood. The Egyptian magicians also did the same. Some people believed they were using demonic forces. It may be, but it's my opinion that they were just tricksters. They could cote the tip of their staff in a clear chemical that would turn water red, but could they turn a whole river into blood?

Egyptian records describe these magicians as students of the magical arts found in the "House of Life", a special section of some Egyptian temples that housed records of magical arts, spells and charms. They were considered to be theological experts.

In the 1950s, Greta Hort gave a natural explanation for the plagues that were described in the Bible. She believes that a single cell organism (flagellates) came down river from Ethiopia and under certain conditions multiplied to the extent that the water turned red. The abundance of these organisms upset the oxygen content in the water causing the fish to die. On very rare occasions this does happen.

The Bible, however, says it turned to blood. Is that just descriptive or was it actually blood? Even if it was caused by a natural phenomenon, the miracle would then be that God told Aaron to dip the rod in the water at just the time these organisms were about to explode numerically. That's just as big of a miracle. It's interesting that those who feel the need to explain away the miracles of the Bible don't see that they've simply described a miracle in different terms.

Only today, with microscopes and the knowledge of microbiology, could someone predict an explosion of an organism. Even then, they would have great difficulty predicting the moment of the color change in a body of moving water. That would be nearly impossible even with modern science.

Egyptians believed the Nile was the god Osiris' bloodstream, the god that caused it to flood each year providing fertility for crops. It was ironic that God turned it to blood. The Egyptians sang songs to river praising its sweet smell and gift of food. Now it stinks and the fish are dead. It was God's revelation to the Egyptians of the futility of worshiping the creation rather than the Creator. (Romans 1:22-25)

God showed that the Nile was not the Giver of Life. God alone is the source of living water. He is the well that never runs dry. He is the only One that satisfies our spiritual thirst. (John 4:14)

There was a cultural factor in the plagues that we must understand. Pharaoh had the responsibility of keeping order in Egypt. The world outside of Egypt was considered to be in a state of chaos. Pharaoh was believed to keep the gods pacified so that catastrophic events did not occur, so that chaos did not invade Egypt. When the water turned to blood, Pharaoh would have been concerned that the perception of the people would be that he had not done his job, or that the gods were angry with him.

One description of chaos from 2000 B.C. speaks of blood everywhere. "Verily, the heart is horrified, For affliction pervades the land, Blood is everywhere… Verily, the river is blood, but one drinks from it…" Just as Pharaoh had caused the Israelites to blame Moses, now God has turned the table and the Egyptians will be blaming Pharaoh for this invasion of what they saw as chaos.

God was showing everyone in Egypt that He alone brings peace and order. The Hebrew word is shalom. What are you looking to for peace and provision in your life? Has God struck you 401k to show you it is not god? Does God need to bring more judgment on our gods so that we will see that He is our only source of peace and provision?

23 Pharaoh turned and went into his house, and he did not take even this to heart. Moses survived again. He did what God commanded, and though Pharaoh didn't take it to heart, the Egyptians had to consider it. The God of the Hebrews had proven His authority over their god, the Nile. The one that they thought gave life, now stunk of death.

The only way for the people to get water was to dig along the shore. Every time they went for water that week, they knew the God of the Hebrews was greater than Osiris and the Nile.

The plagues were revealing the glory of the God of Israel, not just to the Egyptians, but to Israel, and to the whole earth. God is working in every life, even in the lives of the hard-hearted ones. They will bow the knee to Him or die in rejection of the One they know in their heart of hearts is the Lord of all.

God is doing the same today through the message of Jesus, the Gospel. When we hear the Gospel record, we know there is none like Him. We either bow in surrender or we harden our heart to the point of no return. (Proverbs 29:1)

We look at the everyday miracles around us and we decide to admit Jesus is Lord, or like Pharaoh, we go into our house and allow our heart to be hardened. How many signs do we need? Is your hard heart causing God to be more forceful with you? All authority belongs to God. The sooner we yield the better! We must see Him and Him alone as our only source of provision and peace.

Questions:
1 What was God's answer to Moses' prayer?
2 What did God instruct Moses to do?
3 What was God's heart behind the plagues?
4 Why didn't Moses show the signs at the first encounter with Pharaoh?
5 What was the meaning behind the Moses' staff swallowing the others?
6 What did the Nile mean to Egyptians?
7 What was Pharaoh's reaction? Why?
8 What did it say to the Egyptians about Pharaoh?
9 What did the plague reveal? NT?
10 How are we like Pharaoh at times?

A Hard Heart Exodus 8-9:7

God had shown Pharaoh through Moses' staff that the God of the Hebrews is the God of all authority. The staff of Moses swallowed up the staffs of the magicians. Then God had Moses confront the source of the Egyptians security, the Nile, believed to be the bloodstream of Osiris. Ironically, the water turned to blood which made the river stink of dead fish. Pharaoh was unmoved. His heart was hardened.

Don't you wonder if Pharaoh really believed his own religion? When he, as the incarnation of Ra and Horus, went into temples to appease the many gods of Egypt, did he really think of himself as a priest? Or did he know it was all a way to control the people? When he saw these miracles take place, did he really believe that his gods were as powerful as the God of Israel?

My suspicion is that he knew or at least came to realize in time that the God of the Hebrews is the God over all. Yet Pharaoh could not relinquish his power or his pride and give in to God's commands. (Proverbs 21:24)

Does that sound familiar? How many unbelievers know the God of the Bible is real, all-powerful, directing the course of history, and yet they will not yield to His command to know Him and be saved. (John 17:3) How many believers know He is God and yet will not come out of Egypt by living in compromise? (1Peter 1:15-16) I suppose to some extent we have all experienced that condition of a hard heart.

Who hardened Pharaoh's heart? I believe Pharaoh did as is clearly stated at the end of the next plague. Later we will see the text state clearly that God hardened his heart, but not until the sixth plague. (Exodus 9:12)

God had shown His power to be greater than the temples' magicians, and greater than the god Osiris (Lord of the Dead, God of Resurrection, One who causes the Nile to flood). We saw how that symbolized things we look to for security other than God. The people of Egypt were no doubt shaken by this first plague and what it said about Pharaoh's ability to appease the gods and keep their world at peace. (John 16:33)

Since he would not yield, a second plague was in order. Yet, God first gave a warning and a chance to change his mind. *1 Then the LORD said to Moses, "Go in to Pharaoh and say to him, 'Thus says the LORD, "Let my people go, that they may serve me. 2 But if you refuse to let them go, behold, I will plague all your country with frogs.* God was saying, "Let my people go and worship someone other than you, Pharaoh! Let them serve me!" God was demanding. He has a right to demand. He is Creator. We ought to serve Him. Notice again that worship and service are interchangeable. To truly serve God is to worship Him and vice versa.

God warned of the severity of the plague. This wasn't just a few frogs, but frogs in everything, in pots and pans, in their beds, everywhere! Heqet was a frog headed woman goddess that was worshiped as the goddess of fertility. Amulets of little green frogs have been discovered from this era in Egypt that were supposed to help women become pregnant.

Apparently Pharaoh was unmoved by the warning and refused to let the people go, so God had Moses proceed. The frogs they loved to worship were everywhere. The abundance was disgusting. God is showing the Egyptians that their false gods are a curse, and not a blessing.

7 But the magicians did the same by their secret arts and made frogs come up on the land of Egypt. How did they do that since it was already happening? Perhaps they just took credit for something already taking place. Whether it was demonic power or deception, Pharaoh believed his magician priests could do the same. The difference was that the magicians couldn't get rid of the frogs.

8 Then Pharaoh called Moses and Aaron and said, "Plead with the LORD to take away the frogs from me and from my people, and I will let the people go to sacrifice to the LORD." Pharaoh said, "I give up. Go! Just ask the LORD to take away the frogs." But when the LORD did, Pharaoh changed his mind. The pressure was off, so his commitment was off.

Isn't that typical? "Lord, if you'll just heal me, if you'll just save me from this financial crisis, if you'll just help my kid get off drugs... or whatever is the immediate 'plague' then I'll do the thing you've been asking that I've been avoiding. God, just let up and I'll get serious about serving You." God takes the pressure off and we slowly go back to our old ways.

9 Moses said to Pharaoh, "Be pleased to command me when I am to plead for you and for your servants and for your people, that the frogs be cut off from you and your houses and be left only in the Nile." God was so gracious to Pharaoh as to even let him pick the time. God knew Pharaoh would go back on his word, but God still gave him every chance to know Him.

10 And he said, "Tomorrow." Moses said, "Be it as you say, so that you may know that there is no one like the LORD our God. The magicians couldn't get rid of the frogs or they would have already done it. Pharaoh is given grace to see the power and greatness of God even though he will not change. God is the same with everyone. (Acts 10:34) There will not be a soul in hell that did not harden their heart time and time and time again. Not a soul there will say, "If I only knew…?" They can say it, but let God be true and every man a liar. (Romans 3:4) God reveals Himself to the godly and the wicked. (John 1:9)

God did what Moses asked. The frogs died and the Egyptians piled them in heaps. The rotting frogs made the land stink. Again, chaos had invaded the false sense of peace in the land of Egypt, and the people would have seen Pharaoh as the one to blame.

15 But when Pharaoh saw that there was a respite, he hardened his heart and would not listen to them, as the LORD had said. He hardened his heart! He refused to listen. This is the curse of the sin nature. (Isaiah 6:10) We tend to think that the pressure on us is perhaps just a natural phenomenon, just a part of life and not the Lord dealing with us. This refusal to listen was the indictment against Israel in their last days. (Jeremiah 7:27) It isn't just a problem with Pharaoh's ears.

Mankind has the same problem. We want to listen to our own whims. We want to do it our way. We want to stay in control. We don't want to bow the knee and give anything up. We want to save our life and we end up losing it. (Luke 9:24) It's no surprise that Pharaoh did this. We all do it. Our only hope is the life of Jesus in us. We all have a hard time listening because we know that if we hear, we will have to let go of our will and ways.

There was no warning for the third plague. Out of the dust came gnats or in some translations lice. The Egyptians worshiped Geb as the god of the earth. Instead of blessing them with goodness from the land, it brought forth another annoying pestilence. Whether gnats or lice, they covered man and beast, creating an unbearable annoyance. Only the land of Goshen was exempt, which showed God was in the midst of His people protecting them. (Psalm 91:7)

I wonder if the plagues that did not harm Goshen were ones that the Israelites had not allowed to creep into their religious worship. The workers on the tombs, some of whom were Hebrews, had a temple that included all these gods. The Hebrews had been influenced by Egyptian gods, as we will see later.

The Egyptian magicians were unable to reproduce this miracle. *19 Then the magicians said to Pharaoh, "This is the finger of God." But Pharaoh's heart was hardened, and he would not listen to them, as the LORD had said.* They called it "the finger of God". God had invaded the present in breaking the normal cycle of things and manifested his wrath against these false gods. Of course these idols were nothing. Yet, behind them are demons that accept the worship of man and encourage the continuation of idolatry. (1Corinthians 10:20)

Jesus used the phrase "finger of God" when speaking of how He cast out demons. He described it as the kingdom of God having broken into the routines of life doing the miraculous. (Luke 11:20)

Pharaoh again hardened his heart and refused to listen to God's demands. What would it take? How much do we as individuals have to see before we humble ourselves and submit to God? How much do we as a nation have to endure before we recognize our punishment is from God to turn us from our idolatry? What will it take for us to listen with our heart?

20 Then the LORD said to Moses, "Rise up early in the morning and present yourself to Pharaoh, as he goes out to the water, and say to him, 'Thus says the LORD, "Let my people go, that they may serve me. God again is gracious enough to warn Pharaoh, in spite of Pharaoh's hard heart. Apparently Pharaoh is still worshiping his false god the Nile each morning, even after the first plague. It has always amazed me how people can be shown a false god is detrimental to them and yet continue worshiping it. (Isaiah 46:6-7)

The demand was made again, and a warning was given. "Let my people go, or else…" The next plague is called a swarm. This may be mosquitoes, scarabs or it may be a blood sucking fly or even a mixture of flying pests. (Psalm 78:45) We have a blood sucking fly in our area. When I used to swim in the creek, I remember how I hated them. They would try to land where you couldn't swat them and bite into your flesh. Imagine great swarms of them biting you all the time. It would drive you mad! This could have been addressing the god Khepri, Egyptian god of creation and movement of the sun. His image was of a man with the head of a fly. Egyptians also worshiped Baalzebub that is mentioned in the New Testament (Luke 11:15), Lord of the Flies, who was to keep swarms of flies out of Egypt. God is again showing the gods of Egypt to be a curse rather than a blessing.

Once again the plague was not going to touch Goshen. Verse 23 literally says that God put "redemption" between my people and yours. Redemption is what saves people from judgment. It was to be clear to Pharaoh that this was from God, and that God was protecting His people. (Leviticus 20:24)

Pharaoh tried a compromise. *25 Then Pharaoh called Moses and Aaron and said, "Go, sacrifice to your God within the land."* Moses explained that their sacrificial animals were worshiped by Egyptians and it would create conflict, possibly even the stoning of the Hebrews by the Egyptians. Rams and cows were sacred to Egyptians. Imagine a barbeque in front of a Hindu temple. It sounded like a possible compromise, but it wasn't what God had asked. God wants us out of Egypt altogether, not a compromised worship with one foot in both worlds. You have to leave Egypt to get to the Promised Land.

28 So Pharaoh said, "I will let you go to sacrifice to the LORD your God in the wilderness; only you must not go very far away. Plead for me." Pharaoh knows what is about to happen. He doesn't want to lose his labor force. He relents to get rid of the flies, but again, when the pressure is gone, he'll go back on his commitment.

29 Then Moses said, "Behold, I am going out from you and I will plead with the LORD that the swarms of flies may depart from Pharaoh, from his servants, and from his people, tomorrow. Only let not Pharaoh cheat again by not letting the people go to sacrifice to the LORD." It's as if they both know they have more rounds to go. Moses is saying, "You better not be cheating!" Pharaoh knows when the flies are gone he'll go back on his word. Back and forth they go. Meanwhile, god after Egyptian god is being declared to be powerless at best, and at worse a curse.

32 But Pharaoh hardened his heart this time also, and did not let the people go. This is getting to be like Charlie Brown and Lucy with the football. She promises not to move it. When Charlie goes to kick it, she moves it every time. Pharaoh keeps promising and reneging. (Matthew 5:37)

God graciously warned Pharaoh again. This time God gave him another chance to listen and a warning of what will come. It is the warning of a disease that will destroy the livestock. Pharaoh's wealth was largely in livestock. Once again, Goshen was to be spared. (Mal 3:16-18) Once again, Pharaoh can see there is none like YHWH! (2Samuel 7:22)

Horses and cows were sacred animals to the Egyptians and highly valued. The cow god, Apis, represented Pharaoh's courage, strength, virility and fighting spirit. The cow goddess Hathor was depicted with cow horns, with the sun between them. She was thought to nourish the Pharaoh and was the goddess of love and glamour.

God gave Pharaoh a night to reconsider. It's hard to imagine, even experiencing plague after plague he just will not yield. He fit the description from the poem Invictus, "His head is bloody but unbowed." Pharaohs prided themselves in determination. God called this stubbornness and a hard heart. Determination can be good, bad or neutral, but a hard heart is always a selfish heart. (Philippians 2:3)

By morning Pharaoh was still unwilling to yield. The plague struck. Pharaoh had to wonder why his gods had let him down again. He sent someone to see about the cattle in Goshen. Not one of them had died. The message was crystal clear! The evidence is undeniable. What will it take?

7bBut the heart of Pharaoh was hardened, and he did not let the people go. The Egyptians believed that when a person died, their heart would be weighed. The feather represented what is right and just. If their heart was heavier than a feather, they would be consumed by the creature Ammit (devouress or swallower). Every time the heart is described as hardening, the Egyptians would read it as being heavier. The guilt of Pharaoh was piling up. The assurance of judgment was getting more certain with each plague.

The miracles we see around us may not be as great a sign as those in the Exodus, but we do see signs that require us to either yield our heart or harden it. Some of the greatest signs for me were not afflictions but the deliverance from the affliction. It's the goodness of God that leads us to repentance, if we are willing to receive it. (Romans 2:4) It was the lifting of each plague that should have caused Pharaoh to repent.

God shows our gods to be nothing but a curse, and we must make a choice. We will carry on and harden our heart, or we will yield and rid our lives of those gods. (Matthew 4:10)

We don't have the bizarre gods of Egyptian mythology, but we have the gods they represent, security, power, sex, prosperity, etc. We don't call them gods. At times we sing to them. We believe in and trust them just like the Egyptians trusted their gods. We think our gods are beneficial and blessing our life, when really they have become a curse. We get on that hamster wheel of making more money or gaining respect or pleasing our self in some way. It looks like it is satisfying, but it ends up being a never-ending cycle of destruction. (Ephesians 4:19)

The real God comes along and smashes them right before our eyes. We have to make a choice. Will we still believe in them even when we have discovered that they are powerless to save us, when the satisfaction is temporal and even harmful? Will we harden our heart like Pharaoh? Or will we let the love of Jesus soften and break our heart until we serve and worship Him alone?

Questions
1 Do you think Pharaoh believed he was really two gods incarnated?
2 Why did God send a plague of frogs?
3 Why did God allow Pharaoh to pick the timing for the frog removal?
4 Why did Pharaoh harden his heart in verse 15? Relate?
5 Why did God exempt Goshen?
6 What did the magicians call plague #3? How did Jesus use the term?
7 How did God reveal the gods of Egypt to be a curse rather than a blessing?
8 What is the difference between stout-heartedness and hard hearted?
9 How did the Egyptians read "hard hearted"?
10 Why do you think Pharaoh sent someone to check on Goshen?
11 How can we relate to the gods of Egypt?
12 Consider Malachi 3:16-18 in reference to our text.

The God Hardened Heart Exodus 9:8 –10:29

The Nile turned to blood, frogs covering the land, gnats covering everyone, and then biting flies; the livestock in the field died, and proud Pharaoh has stood defiant. His heart is rock hard. He relents for a moment and then his pride kicks in and he goes back on his word. What will it take? (Isaiah 46:10)

Ravi Zacharias was at ASU recently. A student asked him to comment on the hiddenness of God. It is a theological argument that questions why a God that loves mankind would stay so unseen and seemingly unrevealed to so many.

Part of Ravi's answer included that God is working through dreams and visions to cause tens of thousands to come to Christ in Muslim countries where the Gospel is banned. He told the story of one man who for seven years had the same dream night after night. Jesus appeared to him in his dream and invited the man to trust in Him and be made right with God. After seven years of the same dream every night he finally accepted God's invitation and became a Christian.

Is there any limit to which God will not go to reveal Himself to man? (John 12:46) I would flip the argument on its head and say the Bible is hands down the most translated and distributed book in the history of the world. Is this not proof that it comes from the God who loves mankind and wants them to know Him?

Look at the extent to which God was going in Egypt so that the Israelites, the Egyptians, and Pharaoh might know that He is the LORD! Pharaoh's hardening of his own heart only gave God more opportunities to display the folly of the gods of Egypt (Numbers 33:4) and the glory of God Almighty.

Half the plagues are over. Pharaoh hardened his own heart each time, yet God had promised that He would harden Pharaoh's heart to show His mighty power. It is my conviction that Pharaoh had passed the point of no return. God could see that Pharaoh was determined not to allow his heart to be changed. (Jeremiah 26:4-6) Pharaoh will not yield to God. He may be forced to give in to His demands, but he will never yield his heart to know Him as LORD. Now God will begin to harden Pharaoh's heart to show the gods of Egypt are worthless.

Plague number six was boils on everyone in Egypt. In obedience to God's command *10 "...they took soot from the kiln and stood before Pharaoh. And Moses threw it in the air, and it became boils breaking out in sores on man and beast.* The plagues are now very personal. Chaos seems to have invaded Egypt to an extent that they had never been witnessed before. The gods of healing Im-Hotep and Sekhemet were proven to be powerless. God alone is the Great Physician. Every Egyptian individual and animal was afflicted. It reminds us of Job's affliction. Unfortunately, they did not respond like Job did. (Job 2:7-10)

It was another action full of irony, for this is the same action the priests would make with sacrificial ashes to pronounce a blessing on the people. God was turning the action into a curse. And if the soot was from the brick kilns of the overworked Hebrews, it was even more meaningful. The Egyptians were reaping the suffering they had sown. (Job 4:8)

Pharaoh kept asking his magicians to imitate the plagues with their tricks. They failed before, and now they can't even stand before Moses to try to perform their tricks. 12 But the LORD hardened the heart of Pharaoh, and he did not listen to them, as the LORD had spoken to Moses.

The Lord stepped in and hardened Pharaoh's heart. That tells me Pharaoh would have given in. He would have let them go out of desperation, but his heart would not have changed. God was not done. Does God have a right to harden the heart of the unrepentant? Of course He does! (Job 23:13) He is not willing that any perish, but He knows that Pharaoh will never turn to God. God is revealing Himself to Pharaoh and to Egypt. If hardening Pharaoh's unrepentant heart brings a greater revelation, so be it! (See verse 16)

God said, *14 For this time I will send all my plagues on you yourself, and on your servants and your people, so that you may know that there is none like me in all the earth.* God is warning, "Now I'm really going to let you have it with plagues on your heart!" Translators should just leave it "heart" instead of "you yourself" (ESV) Egyptians believed the heart of Pharaoh was the foundation of their society and the source of human progress.

The hardening of Pharaoh's heart speaks to the hiddenness of God question. The hardening of Pharaoh's heart revealed God's power and authority to the world. This is happening so that the world may know there is none like God in all the earth. (1Samuel 4:8) Bow your knee Pharaoh! Worship God all you ends of the earth! He'll have no other gods before Him! (Exodus 20:2-3)

But is that fair? Here is what is fair: 15 For by now I could have put out my hand and struck you and your people with pestilence, and you would have been cut off from the earth. Fair would be for God to say, "This evil man won't stop abusing my children, so he and all his children are dead!" That's fair! How dare Pharaoh exalt himself above God! How dare he refuse a command of God again and again! (Joshua 23:16)

God goes on to say, *16 But for this purpose I have raised you up, to show you my power, so that my name may be proclaimed in all the earth.* God is having mercy and patience upon Pharaoh in not obliterating him so that God's might and power, mercy and love, may be proclaimed in all the earth, so that God is not hidden, so that men might know and revere Him.

We read this story today and if we are honest we see the same tendencies in us that we see in Pharaoh and his advisors: Is it really history? Did it really happen just like that? Maybe it was some natural phenomenon? Give me a break! God revealed Himself in the plagues of Egypt. Let us not harden our hearts or God may end up hardening them further to reveal His glory through our stubborn refusal to believe! He is God Almighty. Get used to it because that fact will never change! (Malachi 3:6)

Plague number seven was hail like they had never seen. God is now giving the Egyptians a chance to show their fear of God and to begin to pull out of their culture. This was a plague on the sky goddess Nut who was the mother of the sun god Ra. She was supposed to protect Egypt from destruction that came from the heavens. *19 Now therefore send, get your livestock and all that you have in the field into safe shelter, for every man and beast that is in the field and is not brought home will die when the hail falls on them." ' "*

That must have really angered Pharaoh. God is really asking people to make a decision between God and the Egyptian gods including Pharaoh. Pharaoh can't order his servants and animals in or it would show his inability to do anything about the plagues. He was caught in his own trap and had to plead with his gods as a last resort. (Deuteronomy 4:7)

Skeptics ask where the animals came from if they all died in plague five. Plague five says all the animals in the field died. The ones that were in shelters would have lived and may now be in the fields, not to mention the ones they may have purchased from the Hebrews.

The hail wiped out everything but didn't fall in Goshen. Pharaoh called for Moses. How did Moses get to the palace? Did he walk in divine protection?

27 Then Pharaoh sent and called Moses and Aaron and said to them, "This time I have sinned; the LORD is in the right, and I and my people are in the wrong. 28 Plead with the LORD, for there has been enough of God's thunder and hail. I will let you go, and you shall stay no longer." One of Egypt's worship songs declared their Sun god Right and that he fought against Wrong. Pharaoh was confessing he was on the wrong side! This is what we call a false conversion. Just because a person says the words does not mean that their heart has been changed. You can say the right words until the cows come home (pun intended). In this case they aren't coming home. The hail killed them! Pharaoh's heart is unchanged.

Moses said he would stop it so that Pharaoh "might know that the earth is the LORD's". Even in the stopping of the plagues at God's timing showed God is sovereign over all things. (Romans 2:4) The ending of the plagues was just as instructive as the plagues. God allows chaos and creates peace, not Pharaoh!

Then Moses declared that even though he is stopping the plagues, he knows Pharaoh and his servants don't yet fear the LORD. Why? The next verse tells us. Two kinds of wheat had not yet sprouted. Pharaoh could still see a way out. There was hope the nation wouldn't starve. He is still stupid enough, hard hearted enough, to think he can go on resisting God because there is another crop yet to come up.

Now you may think, I wouldn't have been so dumb, but just think how many times and ways the LORD had to get your attention before you finally surrendered your heart. Maybe you weren't as bad as me. I had to get hit over the head with a 2x4 again and again and again. Even then I had to see it illustrated in others' lives over and over so that I really began to sense the fear of the Lord. Still, pride and the flesh tempt me to think I might be able to slide in this area or that and the Holy Spirit has to remind me of how stupid it is to even consider those thoughts for a moment. (John 16:8) Thank God that He is not hidden but constantly pursues us to save us from this fallen world! (Galatians 1:4)

34 But when Pharaoh saw that the rain and the hail and the thunder had ceased, he sinned yet again and hardened his heart, he and his servants. God let up the pressure, and Pharaoh hardened his heart. It's as if God gave him one more chance to reconsider. God didn't do it this time. Pharaoh again hardened his heart. He is beyond hope.

He had crossed that line. Now listen to what God declared. *1 Then the LORD said to Moses, "Go in to Pharaoh, for I have hardened his heart and the heart of his servants, that I may show these signs of mine among them,* From here on out every plague will end with God hardening Pharaoh's heart. God will finish showing all the signs necessary to prove to Egypt and the world that He is the LORD.

God went on to tell Moses that the other purpose is that Moses may tell his descendants of the greatness of God. (Deuteronomy 4:9) That is what we are doing right now. We are seeing there is none like God. God wanted Moses to know with total conviction that He is Almighty God.

Moses and Aaron went before Pharaoh again to announce the eighth plague. But they have a question from the LORD for him. "How long will you refuse to humble yourself before me?" That is the question that confronts every unbeliever and every backsliding Christian. Sin is exalting our self above our Creator. It is declaring that we have a right to call the shots. Like so many people, Pharaoh just can't admit that he isn't god. He's hoping against hope that he can somehow pull off this confrontation with God.

The eighth plague is a locust swarm that will devour everything not destroyed by the hail. Some of the largest locust swarms have been estimated to be as large as 10 billion insects. A swarm can be as big as 1000 square kilometers and rise a kilometer into the sky. Each one eats their weight in plant material every day. Pharaoh had a night to think it over, but his officials didn't want to take the chance.

7 Then Pharaoh's servants said to him, "How long shall this man be a snare to us? Let the men go, that they may serve the LORD their God. Do you not yet understand that Egypt is ruined?" This was a desperate plea as they could have suffered for suggesting Pharaoh was not able to stop Moses or any god. They had seen enough. They cost was too great. They didn't surrender their hearts, but their heads told them they were doomed if they resisted further.

Pharaoh had an idea that the Hebrews would not be returning. The request was no longer for three days, but to let them go. So Pharaoh asked who was going. (Joshua 6:25) Moses answered, "All of us!" Pharaoh demanded that only the men leave to go worship. Time for the locusts to descend! They covered the ground and ate every green thing. The locust headed god, Senehem was shown to be a vain thing to worship.

Once again Pharaoh pleaded for mercy and promised to let the people go. Once again he went back on his word. The LORD hardened his heart. It was time for plague number nine.

The most revered of all Egyptian gods was the sun god, Amon-Ra. Pharaoh was said to be his son, even his incarnation. Songs of praise were lifted to him for bringing light to each day. *21 Then the LORD said to Moses, "Stretch out your hand toward heaven, that there may be darkness over the land of Egypt, a darkness to be felt."* For three days no one could see a thing. What does it mean that the darkness could be felt? Sounds like a line out of a horror movie. No light of any kind shone for everyone was forced to stay where they were for the duration. (Genesis 1:3-4) That is supernatural! For the Egyptians, this was the most unsettling plague yet!

24 Then Pharaoh called Moses and said, "Go, serve the LORD; your little ones also may go with you; only let your flocks and your herds remain behind." He made one last attempt to make sure his slaves would return by asking that their flocks and herds stay behind. Moses didn't budge.

Pharaoh is in no position to bargain. *27 But the LORD hardened Pharaoh's heart, and he would not let them go.*

Pharaoh made a last ditch effort to end the cycle of plagues and demands. *28 Then Pharaoh said to him, "Get away from me; take care never to see my face again, for on the day you see my face you shall die." 29 Moses said, "As you say! I will not see your face again."* Earlier, Moses may have feared that warning, but now he knows it is merely Pharaoh sealing his own fate. If he would not see Moses, he could not ask for mercy from God. (Proverbs 27:22)

We can't avoid God's demands on our life. We can avoid his messengers. We can refuse to read the Bible. We can avoid time in prayer, but His demands are still there. He must have first place. His children must worship and serve Him. They must come out of the world. They must make a journey through the wilderness of life to the Promised Land. (1Peter 2:9) If you really think God is hidden, I'd challenge you to ask in sincerity that if He is real, that He reveal Himself to you, only do not harden your heart when He answers that prayer.

Questions
1 Is God hidden?
2 Who hardened Pharaoh's heart in the first five plagues?
3 Why was ash used in plague 6?
4 Why did God harden Pharaoh's heart? Is that fair?
5 What was changing in plague 7?
6 What is a false conversion?
7 Why did God stop the hail?
8 How are we tempted to harden our heart?
9 What god did darkness address? Implications?
10 Why was Pharaoh's threat self-defeating?

Final Plague Exodus 11; 12:29-32

Blood, frogs, gnats, flies, pestilence, boils, hail, locusts, darkness! Egypt was devastated. With crops and animals destroyed, starvation loomed. The gods of Egypt were shown to be a curse rather than a blessing. Pharaoh was shown to be powerless to keep "chaos" from the land. And all this had come through the hand of a stuttering shepherd and his common, yet God empowered, staff. What a mighty God we serve!

Through it all, Pharaoh had remained hard hearted. He would give in, even plead for relief, but when the pressure was off, he immediately turned back and refused to yield to God's demand to "Let my people go!" He hardened his own heart the first five times. Then God began to harden Pharaoh's heart to show His wonders in Egypt that God's name might be proclaimed in all the earth. (Exodus 9:16)

1 The LORD said to Moses, "Yet one plague more I will bring upon Pharaoh and upon Egypt. Afterward he will let you go from here. When he lets you go, he will drive you away completely. God would not immediately harden his heart this time. Pharaoh would yield to the demand, but he wouldn't yield his heart. It will be hardened again. (Exodus 14:6-8)

It happens in lives today. God puts the pressure on, and finally people do what they know God is demanding them to do but without yielding their heart. We only have to look back to the full churches after 9/11 to see how fear can cause us to surrender to God's demand while refusing to yield our hearts. (2Chronicles 25:2) There is a difference between doing what God requires because you know it is in your best interest, and yielding your heart to God. One is the worship of self. The other is the beginning of a relationship with God. (Deuteronomy 4:29)

2 Speak now in the hearing of the people, that they ask, every man of his neighbor and every woman of her neighbor, for silver and gold jewelry." When God called Moses at the burning bush, He told Moses they were going to plunder the Egyptians. (Exodus 3:21-22) The back wages for their years of slavery would be collected. God used the term, "to plunder", as when an army was defeated. God defeated Egypt's gods, and to the victor go the spoils, but God gave the spoils to the Hebrews.

They simply asked their neighbors for clothing and precious metals, and because of the power of the plagues, and the respect they had for Moses and his God, the Egyptians readily yielded to the request. The wealth of Egypt went with God's people so that they could build the Tabernacle at God's instruction. When God's hand is in something, we never need to worry about the cost. The wealth of the world is His. (Deuteronomy 8:18)

We saw that with the building of Hope Cottage. It was a two million dollar project. We thought that was pretty ambitious, especially during the economic downturn, and yet by faith we helped start it off with our little gift. In a few years, the mission that had been in the red, opened their multi-million dollar facility to care for homeless women and children and to share with them the Gospel. Much of that money and labor came from unbelievers. That's amazing! The wealth of the world belongs to God. We just get to manage a portion of it for God's glory. (Psalm 24:1)

The time had come for the final plague. *4 So Moses said, "Thus says the LORD: About midnight I will go out in the midst of Egypt, 5a and every firstborn in the land of Egypt shall die,* Pharaoh had said in the last chapter (which was an earlier part of this conversation) that if he saw Moses face again he would kill Moses. (Exodus 10:28) Moses agreed, but God turned the threat to Pharaoh's firstborn. Moses, who had been so timid and unsure of himself, now boldly ignored the death threat and proclaimed the word of the Lord. What happened to him?

He had seen the hand of God. He gained confidence in the power of YHWH over all the powers of this world. He quit looking at himself and his inabilities and looked to God and His omnipotence. He came to the place we all need to come, total confidence in the Word of the LORD. (Psalm 119:42)

The last plague was the hardest thing a human being can endure, the death of your own child. How could God do such a thing? Does God end lives? Yes! He gives life, and He takes life. (Deuteronomy 32:39) While

Egypt thought Osiris was Lord of the Dead, God would prove otherwise. There is a time to live and a time to die and those times are determined by the sovereign God of the universe. (Ecclesiastes 3:1-2)

The Egyptians were reaping only a portion of what they had sown. They had thrown the Hebrew babies to the crocodiles of the Nile. Justice was being served. They had enslaved generations of Hebrews and worn them out like tools. They had afflicted God's children, now God would afflict theirs, just as He had warned. (4:22-23) Now it was time to pay in wealth and blood.

When we demand that God soften His judgments, it is really our own recognition of our fear of justice. We don't want others to suffer for their actions, because we don't want to suffer for ours. In making that kind of a demand, we are asking for God to compromise His righteousness. We see it in our own progressive judicial system of today. If God did what man desired, we would hate Him for being unjust and rightly so. If He does what His perfect nature demands, we should fear Him and seek His mercy. (Pslam 33:18) Do you really want an unjust God? Think that through!

Remember, God already told Pharaoh He could have easily wiped the Egyptians from the face of the earth (9:15) and been perfectly justified in doing so. God's just wrath is measured with mercy. It doesn't have to happen. Pharaoh could have humbled himself. The Egyptians can seek refuge with the Hebrews. God even told Pharaoh the very hour that it would take place. Still, Pharaoh would not yield.

I would imagine the word spread throughout Egypt very quickly. Again, a choice had to be made. Would they call on the gods of Egypt or flee to Goshen and find refuge in a Hebrew home? It's another chance to make a choice.

6 There shall be a great cry throughout all the land of Egypt, such as there has never been, nor ever will be again. Those words must have struck terror in the hearts of the officials that heard it. There would be some serious soul searching that evening about what they truly believed. How would they interpret all the plagues?

7 But not a dog shall growl against any of the people of Israel, either man or beast, that you may know that the LORD makes a distinction between Egypt and Israel. Osiris assistant was a canine headed god, Anubis. You see his image in hieroglyphs of embalming the dead. He guided the dead into the afterlife. That may be the reference to "not a dog shall growl".

They had seen the distinction before. The Hebrews were God's people. They were set apart to serve and worship Him. They did not belong to Pharaoh. Shalom (peace) was not the product of Pharaoh's intercession with the gods of Egypt. Shalom is the presence of God in the midst of His people. (John 14:27) He is the only source of true peace.

This is the distinction or difference today as well. It's not just because you go to church. It's not because you don't do things that they do. It is because God has made His home in the heart of the redeemed. (John 14:23) He has set you apart for His purposes. He manifests His very nature in you. The unselfish love, mercy, grace, peace, and joy are not your own.

They are His very own attributes manifest through your life. The world will always be a place of chaos when the Lord is not invited to be present. Where He is, there is peace. (1Corinthians 14:33) That is how the world knows there is a difference.

We would like the difference to be in programs or activities. That takes the pressure off and doesn't demand that He be Lord of every area of our life. But the difference is seen in the presence of God in the individual life, and that only comes when we die to our self and yield our life to Him. (2Corinthians 4:10)

Remember, these are the words of the Lord through Moses to Pharaoh. *8 All these officials of yours will come to me, bowing down before me and saying, 'Go, you and all the people who follow you!' After that I will leave." Then Moses, hot with anger, left Pharaoh.* Everyone will bow their knee before God. That does not mean that everyone will yield their heart to God and know Him as LORD. They will bow because they must. Some will gladly bow in joy. Many will bow with gritted teeth. (Philippians 2:9-11)

Everything God said through Moses had come to pass. Why would this be any different? Pharaoh would rather hang onto his pride than his own son!

Moses went out from Pharaoh's presence in hot anger. It was the righteous indignation of God within him. It was God's anger that this mere mortal would really think he could stand against Almighty God that gives him his every breath.

9 Then the LORD said to Moses, "Pharaoh will not listen to you, that my wonders may be multiplied in the land of Egypt." 10 Moses and Aaron did all these wonders before Pharaoh, and the LORD hardened Pharaoh's heart, and he did not let the people of Israel go out of his land. There are still wonders to be seen, the conversion of many, and the parting of the Red Sea. God is not done. Why? That the world may know that He is the LORD and that there is none like Him.

Egyptians that did not find refuge with the Hebrews would have called on their gods. Everyone must have been up that night watching their firstborn. The breathing was normal. There was no fever. 11:59 and no signs of poor health. They thought, "Maybe Moses was wrong this time. Pharaoh is a god. His firstborn son is a god that will take his place." Midnight! The last breath exhaled and ... no other breath followed. The fulfillment of the Word of the Lord came. *29 At midnight the LORD struck down all the firstborn in the land of Egypt, from the firstborn of Pharaoh who sat on his throne to the firstborn of the captive who was in the dungeon, and all the firstborn of the livestock. 30 And Pharaoh rose up in the night, he and all his servants and all the Egyptians. And there was a great cry in Egypt, for there was not a house where someone was not dead.*

Pharaoh should have been furious with his own heart, but that is rarely the case with the unredeemed. Instead their anger is turned to God, the just Judge, who has warned them, given them sign after sign, and chance after chance. Instead of repenting and pleading with God for forgiveness for the fruit of their sin, they curse God and accuse Him of the things of which they are guilty. Accusations like, "Unfair!" Yes, Pharaoh was unfair in treating the Hebrews as he did, especially after God had used Joseph to save and enrich the nation. "Hardhearted!" Yes, Pharaoh was hardhearted. "Merciless!" Yes, Pharaoh had been merciless. Sin so distorts reality that it accuses God of the things for which it is guilty. (Psalm 50:21)

This moment makes me think of the damned entering hell. The curses that will be hurled toward God, and the accusations aimed at Him will be an accurate description of their own heart. (Revelation 16:21) In voicing their anger toward God they will be announcing the very reason for their sentence. The wail will go up for all that they lost, that which was never theirs in the first place, but which they selfishly claimed as their own, to do with as they pleased. Their cry is a declaration of disappointment that they are not the sole reason creation exists. That is the heart of unredeemed man. (Jeremiah 17:9)

31 Then he summoned Moses and Aaron by night and said, "Up, go out from among my people, both you and the people of Israel; and go, serve the LORD, as you have said. 32 Take your flocks and your herds, as you have said, and be gone, and bless me also!" The Word of the LORD came to pass. Pharaoh has another "false conversion". He is pressured into letting the people go. Finally, he gave an unconditional release of the Hebrews, something he could have done from day one if he had not been the hardhearted man that he was. He finally lets them serve another god, the true God.

His request that Moses bless him shows us he is convinced, for the moment, that YHWH is all-powerful. In a pantheistic culture, one can ask for the blessing of another god, even if that god is not the one they worship. It is a kind of superstitious request wanting good to come to oneself from the unknown spiritual realm. It's like the unknown god that Paul addressed on Mars Hill. (Acts 17:23)

It won't be long before Pharaoh thinks he has made a big mistake. God does harden his heart again, just as He said, and lures him to his doom in the waters of the Red Sea. (Psalm 136:15) Pharaoh is an example of the evil that lurks within the heart of man and the end result of that evil.

Meanwhile, God has shown Himself to be just, the avenger of the downtrodden, the rescuer of the oppressed. He has turned the words of the most powerful man in the world back on him while his wizards declare it is but a finger of the mighty God YHWH. (Exodus 8:19) He has shown the gods of Egypt to powerless and converted a great number of those in Egypt, even when the testimony of his own people, the Hebrews, was almost non-existent. He has kept the promises to the Patriarchs, because His word cannot fail. God has shown the world that there is none like Him.

Today God still brings plagues upon prideful man to humble him and turn him. Will we listen? Will we harden our hearts and look for some other way to save us? Or will we learn from this record that has come down as a warning to us and yield our very hearts to the King of kings and Lord of lords? Will we truly acknowledge that there is none like Him and surrender our hearts? Will we join with those who leave Egypt, those who God has made separate through the blood of Jesus, or will we face His just wrath on our sins as we scream our cursing accusations at God of the sins for which we are guilty?

The greatest plague to face mankind has been announced by God. "The soul that sins must die!" (Ezekiel 18:1) There is but one escape. We stand at the crossroads between Egypt and Goshen. Why would you wait to see if God's unfailing word will come to pass? Why not flee now to the safety of the house of faith? Midnight approaches. Where will you be when the moment arrives?

Questions:
1 Will Pharaoh yield to God? Explain.
2 Did the Hebrews rob the Egyptians?
3 What gave Moses new boldness?
4 What is wrong with getting God to compromise His justice?
5 How can the world see the difference God can make in a life?
6 How could Egyptians escape?
7 Who do the unredeemed blame for the consequences of their sin?
8 How would Pharaoh's life been different if he submitted to God on day one? Application?
9 What does Pharaoh's life picture?
10 Describe how the sense the Hebrews would have had of God?
11 What is the greatest plague? How can we escape?

Passover Exodus 12

In the last chapter we covered that fateful night of the last plague from Egypt's perspective. The warning of the death of the firstborn was given. Even the time it would occur was announced. Pharaoh would not humble himself before God. His pride was more precious to him than his own son. Midnight struck and a wail went up throughout Egypt.

In the land of Goshen it was a completely different set of events. We will now hear the account from the Hebrew perspective. It is preparation for and celebration of the first Passover. It was a new beginning for the nation. In fact, from now on, this would be the beginning of the year. It came at the full moon in the month of Abib (our March/April). Because the Hebrews used a lunar calendar, it varies from our Easter celebration.

First, Moses described how they are to celebrate Passover in the future: *3 Tell all the congregation of Israel that on the tenth day of this month every man shall take a lamb according to their fathers' houses, a lamb for a household.* Each family was to select an unblemished yearling male sheep or goat. Because they were going to eat the entire animal, a smaller family could join together with another small family for the celebration. I love the fact that this richly symbolic celebration is to be done as a family. Since it so strongly points to salvation, we can be encouraged that God's heart is for our entire family to be saved. (Joshua 6:25; Acts 16:33)

They were to keep this lamb until the fourteenth day of this month, when the whole assembly of the congregation of Israel shall kill their lambs at twilight. They lived with this lamb for five days. This was to be sure that it was indeed unblemished. Defects might not be readily visible on first inspection. It surely made them attached to the lamb as well. You can't care for any kind of baby animal for five days and not get somewhat attached.

I raised rabbits for a time while I was in Japan. I had to quit because I just couldn't kill them. The implication is that our redemption is precious and should rend our hearts to see the price that must be paid. If an animal becomes precious to us, how much more the Son of God! (1Peter 1:19)

When the lamb was slain, its blood was gathered in a basin. This word for basin was derived from an Egyptian word, sap, meaning threshold. The Egyptian thresholds were like a trough in front of the door to keep water from flowing into the home. It is also used as translated in your text in verse 22 as "bowl". The rest of the descriptions in verse 7, however, are parts of the entryway into the home. This leads me to believe the animal was hung in the doorway and the blood drained into the trough in front of the threshold.

Then they were to take a bundle of hyssop, dip it in the blood, and touch the doorframes and lintel. (John 19:29) This would have blood on all four sides of the doorway.

They then roasted the whole lamb, took it into the house, shut the door, and enjoyed the barbeque without breaking one of the animal's bones. (see verse 46) God warned them, *22c None of you shall go out of the door of his house until the morning.* They were to eat the lamb *11b with your belt fastened, your sandals on your feet, and your staff in your hand. And you shall eat it in haste.*

It is the LORD's Passover. YHWH's pesah. As is so common in the Hebrew Scriptures, the word for the feast is connected with the key word in passage. Yes, God will pass through Egypt and execute judgment on all the gods of Egypt, even the god they looked to for the future, Pharaoh's son. But God calls it His pesah because He is going to pass over (pasha), His people. (John 3:36)

Like many words it has several meanings. The obvious is to skip, or pass over something, which was derived from an earlier form meaning to limp. In this case it is the homes with the blood on the door. But it can also mean to defend or protect. I've found that one of the amazing things about God's word is that when there are two meanings, that unless one cannot fit the context, they are both applicable. In the execution of judgment, God skipped over the homes with the blood marked doorway, while He also protected them. I'll explain in a moment.

God declared that He would execute judgment on Egypt's gods and take the life of the firstborn. Then He again declared, "I am the LORD!" In other words, I am the Eternal One. I am the Judge. I am sovereign. I will do as I will. (Isaiah 46:10)

13 The blood shall be a sign for you, on the houses where you are. And when I see the blood, I will pass over you, and no plague will befall you to destroy you, when I strike the land of Egypt. Notice that the blood is a sign for "you", not the Lord. Just as God said that when He saw the rainbow, He would remember His promise not to destroy the earth with water (Genesis 9:16), so He now says that when He sees the blood on the door He will not enter to destroy. They are His children, but that is not the reason He will not enter in to judge them. He will not bring a destructive plague because of the blood on the door.

Verses 14 through 20 describe the Feast of Unleavened Bread. Because of the urgency in departing, they did not have time to put yeast in the bread to make it rise. When they celebrated this great deliverance, they were to rid their homes of all yeast and for one week, the 14th through the 21st, they were to have no yeast in their homes and eat nothing with yeast. God was so serious about it that He ordered that anyone caught eating yeast would be cut off from Israel.

When God orchestrates our deliverance from the world, we are not to dally. We need to make haste. Yeast is a picture of sin. (1Corinthians 5:8) Every bit is to be removed from our homes. Seven is a number of completeness. (Revelation 1:4) The seven days is symbolic of the whole of our life. To not follow this ritual was to be cut off from Israel. God was showing how serious He is about removing sin from our lives and our homes. The same seriousness is seen in the blood of the lamb. (Leviticus 17:11)

To this day, there is a ceremony on the 14th of Abid in which the house is searched for yeast. One little bit is left to be found, ceremoniously swept up, and disposed of outside the house.

That was the description for future Passover celebrations. Then, in verse 21, Moses told the elders to go ahead and pick a lamb for each clan and kill it that evening and put the blood on the doors. They didn't have the five days for each family to watch their lamb on this first Passover. That would be done in the future. This night was the night the firstborn would die at midnight.

23 For the LORD will pass through to strike the Egyptians, and when he sees the blood on the lintel and on the two doorposts, the LORD will pass over the door and will not allow the destroyer to enter your houses to strike you. Here we see that sense of the verb pasah in defense or protection. It is used in Isaiah of a mother bird hovering over her chicks to protect them from predators. (Isaiah 31:5) The LORD passed through to strike the Egyptians, but He protected the marked doors to keep the destroyer out. This wording is not a mistake. God protects us from His own judgments.

The same idea is repeated in verse 27 where the LORD commands the people to tell each successive generation about this night. (Exodus 10:2) This is not to be forgotten. There is something about this that is critical for people to remember. 27 you shall say, 'It is the sacrifice of the LORD's Passover, for he passed over the houses of the people of Israel in Egypt, when he struck the Egyptians but spared our houses.' " And the people bowed their heads and worshiped.

The people did as the Lord commanded. I wonder how many Egyptians imitated the actions of the Hebrews. It would have been a real act of faith if any Egyptians did kill their sacred goat or left their home to stay with the Hebrews. It would have said to their neighbors that they had abandoned the gods of Egypt and were siding with the Hebrew God. (Joshua 24:15)

Midnight struck. A wail went up. Every house that did not have blood on the door saw their firstborn die. The future Pharaoh was dead. Pharaoh was defeated. He pleaded with the Hebrews to go serve their God. He's been forced to allow them to serve another god, the true God. 33 The Egyptians were urgent with the people to send them out of the land in haste. For they said, "We shall all be dead." They took their unleavened dough in the kneading bowls and carried it on their shoulders. They asked for the wealth of their neighbors in clothing, gold and silver. 36 And the LORD had given the people favor in the sight of the Egyptians, so that they let them have what they asked. Thus they plundered the Egyptians.

When the Hebrews left, they did not leave alone, for God had convinced many of the Egyptians that their gods were no gods at all. *37 And the people of Israel journeyed from Rameses to Succoth, about six hundred thousand men on foot, besides women and children. 38 A mixed multitude also went up with them, and very much livestock, both flocks and herds*. A mixed multitude went up with them. I love that line because it tells us salvation is for all who will believe. (Romans 10:13) Slaves from other nations as well as Egyptians were a part of this mass migration. God not only did what He had promised Moses, and Abraham before him (Genesis 15:14), but He did more than either of those great men could have imagined. He brought the humble souls of other nations out with them, making them one with Israel. (Genesis 12:3)

In the closing verses of the chapter God told them how the people of other nations could participate with them in the celebration of Passover. As long as the males were circumcised, they could participate fully with the Hebrews and be considered as one of them. That was the sign of entering into a covenant with the God of Abraham. (Genesis 17:10)

What a picture that must have been! If there were 600,000 men, then there must have been a total of over two million people! Archeologists argue that Egypt's largest standing army was only 20,000. It may be that the word *elef*, translated thousand, may mean "clan" or "military unit". Nevertheless, along with the mixed multitude it would have been an historically major mass migration. All were following the stuttering shepherd Moses and the staff of God. What an amazing record of God's faithfulness to keep His word and expose the lie of the culture in Egypt! But is there more? Oh is there!

Pharaoh was a real character, and Egypt was a real place. These are real events, but they picture something far greater. Pharaoh is a picture of man's opposition to God, setting himself up as God. God would say something and Pharaoh would say the opposite. It was a struggle for power with which we are all too familiar.

Egypt and its false gods symbolize the world and the oppression of sin. Sin enslaves. It is a hard taskmaster. Jesus clearly used this kind of language warning us that whoever sins is the slave of sin. (John 8:34) Jew and Gentile alike are enticed to believe that false gods of prosperity, glamour, pride and power can fill our empty hearts. They promise peace but leave us in chaos.

At just the right time, God sent a deliver. (Romans 5:6) Moses said that God would raise up a prophet like him, in other words, a humble deliverer that would lead us out of captivity. (Deuteronomy 18:15)

The plagues are God's judgment on the gods of this world. We see them in our own day as the things that man trusts in fail. Then God offers to take us out. Pharaoh/Satan does not want to let us go, but God forced his hand.

Yet, when judgment comes to this world, why should we be spared when we have done the same things as the rest of the world? We worshiped the same gods. Why can the just Judge of all the earth pass us over? Why should He as one that is lame hop over us, and protect us?

Long before the Exodus took place God foretold that the heel of the Seed of the woman would be struck by the serpent (Genesis 3:15), and yet, this male offspring of the woman would crush the serpent's head. Why does YHWH limp over the homes with blood? Why is the blood on the door a sign for us? His heel was struck on the cross. He took our punishment upon Himself so that He could be just and yet righteously merciful.

You see, on the 10th of Abid 30 A.D., when everyone was choosing their lambs, Jesus presented Himself, the Lamb of God that takes away the sins of the world, the unblemished lamb without defect. (John 12:1, 12) We call it Palm Sunday. And though the crowd seemed to choose Him, they later rejected Him. (Mark 15:14) But that didn't stop Him. He who declared Himself to be the door, the door we must enter in to be saved (John 10:9), allowed Himself, the perfect lamb, to bleed from His head, hands and feet. He became that blood-marked door.

He invites your family into this place of safety. When He comes as the just Judge to give to every man according to what they have done, He sees you safely within the blood stained door. His own blood stands between you and judgment. He looks at His own blood shed for you and passes you by. To the world, He is the destroyer. To you, He is your protector and Savior.

He is the lamb of which we partake. No wonder He said that unless we eat His flesh and drink His blood we do not have life. (John 6:54) He is the word made flesh. (John 1:14) If we have entered that blood-stained door, we will partake of the Lamb who shed His blood for us. We will be hungry for His word and Spirit. We will be freed from the bondage of this world symbolized by leaven.

And so, the Apostle Paul tells us, *7 Cleanse out the old leaven that you may be a new lump, as you really are unleavened. For Christ, our*

Passover lamb, has been sacrificed. 1Corinthians 5:7 (ESV) We know the truth and the truth has set us free. (John 17:17)

Now as a great mixed multitude (talk about unbiased toward ethnicity! Revelation 5:9-10) we leave our tools of slavery behind and we are free. We get up to leave and join the crowd (Hebrews 12:1) of those who follow the Shepherd, not the shepherd Moses. He was just a picture of the One to come. Our shepherd is the Great Shepherd, Jesus. He's the Shepherd, the door, the lamb that was slain, and the blood upon the door. He leads us out of the world into the freedom of the Spirit.

In the time, between our choice of Jesus as the Lamb and the fullness of what His sacrifice means to us, we become increasingly attached to Him. Our hearts are broken at the price He had to pay for our sin. That's why it is with great gratitude that we leave the bondage of the world behind, forsaking sin, and walking in the freedom of the Spirit. His rod and staff comfort us, for we've seen the power of His judgments on the false gods of the world. (Psalm 23:4) We know it is this power that will lead us through the wilderness of life and to the Promised Land.

The Exodus is the story of every follower of Jesus. It is a blueprint for the ages to follow. It foreshadows the Great Tribulation. Because our hearts are circumcised (Deuteronomy 30:6), we have been grafted into Israel. (Romans 11:17) We've entered that blood-stained door. We've gotten rid of the sin represented by leaven, and we partake of the Passover Lamb. We are freed! All glory to God!

Questions
1 What did Jews do with the Passover lamb?
2 What are the two meanings of pesah?
3 What kept the destroyer from the Hebrew homes?
4 What did yeast symbolize?
5 From what did God protect them?
6 What requirement was there for foreigners to eat the Passover?
7 What does Pharaoh picture for us?
8 What does Egypt, hard taskmasters, and the false gods picture?
9 Why does YHWH limp over the houses of the Hebrews?
10 What happened on the 10th of Abib 30AD?
11 Who is the blood-marked door?
12 Are you a part of the mixed multitude?

Remember Exodus 13

Passover, our subject for last week, is the first day of the Feast of Unleavened Bread. It was a weeklong feast in which leaven was removed and not used in the making of bread. Our chapter today deals with three issues: the Feast of Unleavened Bread, redemption of the firstborn males, and the Presence of God that led them in a pillar of cloud by day and fire by night. Each of these is a picture of spiritual issues, and each has much to say to us today.

First, lets look at redemption of the firstborn males. Though the final plague did not say that it was only the firstborn males that died, I assume that is the case because of the description of the redemption of the firstborn in Israel is only that of the males. The firstborn male had the right of inheritance. He was to lead the family after the father died. The firstborn male represents the whole family.

Jewish men were to explain to their children the sacrifice of the firstborn animals in this way: *15 For when Pharaoh stubbornly refused to let us go, the LORD killed all the firstborn in the land of Egypt, both the firstborn of man and the firstborn of animals. Therefore I sacrifice to the LORD all the males that first open the womb, but all the firstborn of my sons I redeem.'* It is as if God had said, "All firstborn males should have died. The blood of the lamb on the door caused me to pass over you, but you are as guilty as the Egyptians. You worship false gods. You have doubted my word so I am claiming all firstborn males as mine." (Numbers 3:13) It reminded them that every family belongs to the Lord for His service.

The Hebrews were to sacrifice every firstborn male animal to the Lord to remind them of when God spared their firstborn. A donkey could be redeemed with a lamb. When a calf or lamb was eight days old, it was to be given to the Lord. (Exodus 22:30) A male child could be redeemed with five silver shekels. (Numbers 18:16)

A short time later, the Lord swapped the firstborn males for the whole tribe of Levi. An accounting showed there were more Israelite firstborn males than Levites so the balance redemption price was paid on the surplus males that were not of Levi. (Numbers 3:36-48) *14 "Thus you shall separate the Levites from among the people of Israel, and the Levites shall be mine. 15 And after that the Levites shall go in to serve at the tent of meeting, when you have cleansed them and offered them as a wave offering.*

To redeem means to buy back. These firstborn male animals God claimed as His own, just as He did the firstborn boys. They were set apart for God, consecrated, holy. You could buy back the donkey, or other unclean animals, but the clean animals, the sheep or ox were to be sacrificed to the Lord. When you raise an animal, that firstborn that comes along is special. It is precious to you. The children would naturally ask why it must be sacrificed? That was the time you remembered what happened in Egypt, the mighty power and justice of God. A father could tell his child the whole story, reminding them that they were a chosen people, redeemed by God.

In Luke chapter 2, Mary was offering the sacrifice of the poor to redeem Jesus, her firstborn child. (Luke 2:23) That is when Simeon and Anna gave the prophecies over Jesus concerning the role He was to fulfill in the saving of mankind. (Luke 2:30-32)

If you've been with us on Wednesday nights, you have seen how the line of Messiah went from Eve through the Patriarchs, through Judah, and through David. Another piece of the Messiah puzzle is that He had to be a firstborn male for the firstborn male is holy to the Lord. That matches the

Hebrew wordage in Genesis 3 that first predicts the coming Messiah points to a male child born of a woman. (Genesis 3:15)

That is why in the days of Jesus the Jews had careful records of the descendants of David. Women in that lineage were praying that they would be the one to be the mother of Messiah. They hoped their first child would be a male.

Redemption of the firstborn males is still a religious ceremony performed by Orthodox and Conservative Jews. It is called Pidyon ha Ben. A special silver coin was minted by Israel so that 5 of them would total the prescribed amount (117 gr.). Incidentally, the silver dollars before 1936 also contained sufficient silver so that five of them amounted to a little more than the redemption weight in silver. The Kohens and Levites do not redeem their firstborn males as they are the Lord's and are to be available to serve in the coming Temple. (Numbers 3:45)

The redemption of the firstborn was to remind each generation of the great deliverance of their ancestors as it does even to this day. It was to point to the fact that the blood of the lambs did cause God to Passover them, and yet they still needed to be redeemed. It also reminds them that every family is the Lord's.

Ultimately the sacredness of the firstborn points to the fulfillment of the first promise of a Savior. He is the male seed of Eve that would crush the head of the serpent and provide complete redemption for all who will receive it. It is redemption not from sacred service, as is thought today, but rather to it.

Now we move to the Feast of Unleavened Bread. In the ancient world, each family kept a small batch of dough that had risen in a damp cloth. It would be used to transfer the yeast to a new batch of dough. After the new batch had risen a small portion would be taken and kept for the next batch. The yeast in your bread that day may have come down from many generations earlier.

Last week we saw that yeast was a picture of the old nature we inherited from Adam. (1Corinthians 5:8) It infects each new generation and puffs them up, which is a picture of the chief sin, pride. Sin is passed down not only in our very nature inherited from our parents, but in the patterns of life that we learned from them. (1Corinthians 15:22) Many men have learned to deal with stress by becoming angry. That is how their father reacted to frustration, and we learn how to react to life by watching how our parents deal with life. (Exodus 34:7)

If we had a promiscuous parent, we think the solution to difficulty in marriage is divorce or another relationship. The patterns move from parent to child to grandchild. Some call them generational curses. (Deuteronomy 28:18) Those patterns are very hard to break.

The Hebrews had developed some very evil patterns in Egypt. We will see them as they journey in the wilderness. They developed a pattern of complaining about their situations. (Numbers 14:29) They incorporated the worship of the Egyptian gods. (Joshua 24:14) They developed a taste for certain foods and looked to them as a source of soul satisfaction. (Numbers 11:5)

What does all this have to do with unleavened bread? hat which had been passed down from generation to generation that puffed up but did not increase the substance needed to be cleansed from their homes. Each home was responsible to see that the leaven was out of their home before they started this new beginning. (2Corinthians 5:17)

The picture is very clear. As believers in Jesus, we come out of the bondage of sin and are delivered from worldliness. We must be sure our households are free of sin. The old patterns must be broken. The compromises with evil must end. What was once acceptable is no more.

8 You shall tell your son on that day, 'It is because of what the LORD did for me when I came out of Egypt.' When your children ask you why you don't do things that the world does, when they don't understand the restrictions you put on their lives, you have a chance to tell them that you live your life in gratitude to the One who redeemed you and gave you a new life. You can tell them how sin enslaved you and was destroying you and how Jesus became the blood-stained door through which you entered and were saved. You can tell them how death has passed over you, for you have been given eternal life. You can tell them how God showed you the gods you once worshiped were powerless to help you and were really a curse. Imagine the impact on your children when you spell out your redemption to them. (1Peter 3:15)9 And it shall be to you as a sign on your hand and as a memorial between your eyes, that the law of the LORD may be in your mouth. For with a strong hand the LORD has brought you out of Egypt. Your salvation was no less a miracle than that of the Israelites. Your testimony should be always with you. Scholars argue whether or not this was to be a physical object like the phylacteries (Matthew 23:5) we read about in the New Testament or if the word is metaphorical. Either way, we are told to remember so that God's word will be in our mouth. It is to be in our minds and in our actions for we have been set free by God's strong hand.

Today we know the strong arm of the Lord is Jesus. (Isaiah 53:1) We know that our deliverance is from something far more oppressive than Egypt and Pharaoh ever were. We were in a greater bondage and our deliverance came at a greater price than the firstborn of Egypt. It came at the price of God's only begotten Son. (Galatians 3:13) How much more then should our actions show it (sign upon our hand). How much more should our minds be filled with it (a memorial between our eyes), so that His word might be in our mouth? It was with a strong hand (Jesus) that God brought us out of the worldliness that once controlled our life.

Some of us had such dramatic conversions that this concept is very clear. Even if you grew up in a Christian home and can't remember the day you placed your faith in Jesus, the deliverance is just as powerful. It was still the strong arm of the Lord (Jesus) that paid for the sin nature you inherited. It is still the power of the Holy Spirit that enables you to sweep the leaven from your home. There is still the need for you to remember the great price that was paid so that it might be in your actions and on your mind and in your words.

If you've lost the sense of this great deliverance, I want to ask you to get alone with the Lord and ask Him where you would be if it wasn't for His mercy and grace. I'll say again, that God chose to have some of us grow up in the USA in a Christian home and forced to go to church as children because He knew we were so weak we would never have made it in any other place or age. (Acts 17:26) He chose this time and place because it's the only way we would have come to Him. The great deliverance also includes time and circumstance.

Thank God you are His. Every day praise Him for your salvation! Get a renewed sense of what it cost and how much God loves you to pay that price. Then you'll want to be sure your home is swept clean of the leaven of sin. Then you'll want to tell your children when they ask why you live the way you do.

Remember you were redeemed. Remember that sin is supposed to be purged from your home. This was to be a lasting festival because we forget. I think we'll even be doing it in heaven to keep refreshing in mind and heart what God has done for us. (Zechariah 14:16)

Finally, God led them. *17 When Pharaoh let the people go, God did not lead them by way of the land of the Philistines, although that was near. For God said, "Lest the people change their minds when they see war and return to Egypt."* If they had gone north along the Via Maris, what was then the Way of Horus, there were numerous Egyptian military outposts. It would have only taken a few short weeks to go that route. But God knew their hearts. He had to prepare them for what they would face. There were lessons to be learned.

19 Moses took the bones of Joseph with him, for Joseph had made the sons of Israel solemnly swear, saying, "God will surely visit you, and you shall carry up my bones with you from here." How did Joseph know? The prophetic words to his great-grandfather Abraham had been passed down. (Genesis 15:16) They knew it would be 400 years before they left Egypt, but Joseph showed faith in the prophecy by asking them to take his bones with them to the Promised Land. God made a covenant with his forefathers to give them the land of Canaan. Joseph knew God was faithful to keep His word. I wonder if his command was as much to remind the people of the promise as it was to see his bones buried with his ancestors?

I want you to picture this huge crowd coming out of Egypt, overflowing the roads. There would have been herds and carts loaded with family possessions. The elderly and small children probably road on animals and carts while the rest walked. The men were probably armed and took positions on the perimeter.

There before them rose a giant column of cloud. They were no longer just following Moses. Now they had a visible manifestation of the presence of God going before them. *21 And the LORD went before them by day in a pillar of cloud to lead them along the way, and by night in a pillar of fire to give them light, that they might travel by day and by night. 22 The pillar of cloud by day and the pillar of fire by night did not depart from before the people.* That first evening as the sky began to darken that great column became ablaze and lit the night sky. What a nightlight! The Lord Himself! The psalmist tells us that cloud shaded them from the sun during the heat of the day. (Psalm 105:39)

The lesson is clear in this last point as well. God must guide us! If we are ever to make it to our Promised Land of heaven, we must follow His lead. We don't have a cloud to follow; we have something even better, the Word of God and the indwelling Holy Spirit. (John 16:7) He guides us in the details of life, teaching us what to say and how to say it. (John 12:49) He guides where we go and what we do. He has become the Word on our hand and on our foreheads.

Let's review the lessons. The firstborn was to be redeemed. Never forget you are redeemed. Remember what Jesus did for you. It is your testimony! Tell your children.

Get rid of the leaven. Sin must go! If you are going to start a new life, sin must be purged, not just from your life, but from your entire home. Remember, it is our grateful response for our redemption.

And lastly, His presence will guide you. If you got the first two points, you know the need for the third. We can't go back to following our old desires. We must let God lead us all the way to the Promised Land. We are redeemed to be sanctified to follow where God leads. That is the record of what God did for them, and it foreshadowed what God is doing for you today. Remember, you were redeemed to serve, so get rid of sin, and follow where God leads. Three simple lessons, rich in significance, that we are to remember and pass on to our children. Have you? Will you?

Questions
1 Why does God claim the firstborn? Implications?
2 What is the connection with Jesus?
3 What is Pidyon ha Ben?
4 What is the source of sin in our lives?
5 What patterns of sin had the Hebrews developed?
6 How does God describe how important these points should be to us?
7 How were you redeemed?
8 Are you ready to tell the story?
9 How were they led? Application?
10 What was the cloud?
11 Go over the lessons of chapter 13.

Obedient Waves Exodus 14

8 And the LORD brought us out of Egypt with a mighty hand and an outstretched arm, with great deeds of terror, with signs and wonders. Deuteronomy 26:8 (ESV) That is Moses' own summary of what had happened to this point in our study. This great mixed multitude was following the Angel in the cloud and boldly went out in plain sight, even armed for battle. The LORD had defeated the gods of Egypt. Pharaoh and his officials drove them out of the land, just as God had foretold. (Exodus 6:1)

The locations of the names of the places are very uncertain today. We can't be sure of the exact route or of where they crossed, though there is a fascinating video of a land bridge in the Red Sea with what appears to be coral encrusted chariot wheels on the ocean floor. One problem is the name "Red Sea" in Hebrew, Yom Suph, means Sea of Reeds. Wherever it was, it was location that appeared as if this great band of refugees were cornered.

When we were redeemed, we may have thought we would step right into a land of milk and honey. Instead God led us into a wilderness to build our faith. Sometimes it even looks like He has led us to our doom. "I was trying to follow You, God. Now look where You have led me!" We don't realize that this is the best place for our faith to grow.

God predicted, *3 For Pharaoh will say of the people of Israel, 'They are wandering in the land; the wilderness has shut them in.'* As I have explained before, God is outside of time. He knows our thoughts before we think them. (Psalm 139:2) If He says it will happen, then it will.

God went on to tell Moses, *4 And I will harden Pharaoh's heart, and he will pursue them, and I will get glory over Pharaoh and all his host, and the Egyptians shall know that I am the LORD."* One last time, God will harden the heart of this unrepentant king. He gave in to God's demand, but not because he was yielding his heart. He was afraid of the consequences.

Later, Nehemiah will tell us that in spite of all the signs and wonders, Pharaoh acted arrogantly against God's children. (Nehemiah 9:10) God was making a name for Himself by humbling one of the proudest men on earth. We've seen how Pharaoh is a warning to all prideful men. Isaiah tells us that a day is coming when every prideful and lofty man will be brought low, and the LORD alone will be exalted. (Isaiah 2:11) That is good news to the humble children of God, but ought to strike fear into the heart of every prideful man and woman.

Remember that definition of insanity? Doing the same thing over and over and expecting different results. Well, here goes Pharaoh again. *5 When the king of Egypt was told that the people had fled, the minds of Pharaoh and his servants were changed toward the people, and they said, "What is this we have done, that we have let Israel go from serving us?"* "What did we do?" You did the only sane thing you could do! You gave in to all-powerful God's demand. You recognized He could wipe you out if you persisted. Pharaoh had a temporary lapse of sanity, but that has passed.

It happens to us too. We give the Holy Spirit a chance to speak to our heart and do something by faith instead of by sight. Then we start reasoning out our action and trying to make sense of it and decide it wasn't a good decision. "Why did I pledge to support Young Life?" OR "Why did I say I would go on that mission trip?" We reason our way out of the blessing of walking by faith. (Hebrews 11:6)

Pharaoh and his officials started thinking about losing all that labor and decided they had made a mistake. They called the cavalry divisions up and headed out after the Israelites.

10 When Pharaoh drew near, the people of Israel lifted up their eyes, and behold, the Egyptians were marching after them, and they feared greatly. And the people of Israel cried out to the LORD. They had just seen God deliver them and prove the gods of Egypt were powerless, but they were afraid. My guess is that we would have been as well. They had weapons, but the Egyptians have chariots and horses and are trained soldiers. Women and children might die in the confrontation. On top of all that, there was nowhere to flee. It would have to be a head on confrontation. The impossible situation is the opportunity for great lessons of faith.

"Is it because there are no graves in Egypt that you have taken us away to die in the wilderness? What have you done to us in bringing us out of Egypt?" We'll hear this repeated when things get difficult. (Exodus 17:3) It's the expanded version of "Why me God?" "I gave my life to God and now I have to deal with – ". You fill in the blank. Why do we think following God will be easy? The Bible never says that it will be. We are to give thanks in every situation because we know God is for us. (Romans 8:28) What they couldn't see in the midst of their whining was that this predicament was actually going to finish off their enemies. (Psalm 53:5) In fact, it would become a point in their history that they will always look back on as very special, for God is about to reveal His greatness again. (Ezekiel 20:9)

It is a hard lesson to learn because it goes against our natural senses. Bottom line is this, where is your faith placed? In what do you trust? Pharaoh trusted in his chariots and horses. (Psalm 20:7) But what Pharaoh can't see, and what the Israelites aren't seeing is the invisible realm. *17 The chariots of God are twice ten thousand, thousands upon thousands; the Lord is among them...* Psalms 68:17a (ESV) There was the frightened servant of Elisha who saw an army after the two of them. *17 Then Elisha prayed and said, "O LORD, please open his eyes that he may see." So the LORD opened the eyes of the young man, and he saw, and behold, the mountain was full of horses and chariots of fire all around Elisha.* 2 Kings 6:17 (ESV)

What is your battle? What are the odds? If it's God's battle, why are you fearful? Remember Gideon with his 300 against a multitude of Midianites, or Jehoshaphat against that confederation of armies? (2Chronicles 20:1-2) Or how about David versus Goliath (1Samuel 17:4-7), or Jonathan and his armor bearer against the Philistines? (1Samuel 14:6) The odds don't matter if it is God's battle. God is always the superior force. May the force be with you or maybe we should say, "May you be with the force", because He always wins! Even when it looks like we lose, we win, for we are more than conquerors! (Romans 8:37)

The people then reminded Moses of their sin, as if they were right when they told Moses to leave them alone. *12 Is not this what we said to you in Egypt, 'Leave us alone that we may serve the Egyptians'? For it would have been better for us to serve the Egyptians than to die in the wilderness."*

Obviously, they haven't yet grasped all that God had done to liberate them. They couldn't blame God because they desperately needed Him, so they blamed His messenger. They'll resort to this numerous times. (Numbers 16:3; 12:1) They did the right thing in calling out to God. But they did the wrong thing in blaming His servant Moses. That was rebellion against God. (Psalm 106:7-8) They were crying out for God to save them, and He was saving them through Moses!

Yes, this too is a tendency of fallen man. I frequently hear the complaints about pastors. "Why don't they preach on this or that? Why aren't they for that or against this?" No man is perfect, but maybe the humble question should be this, "If God's ordained leaders are or aren't led the same way I'd like to see them go, then what am I missing? What is my blind spot?"

If there is one thing they should have feared, it wasn't the army of Egypt, but the LORD. He is the One that just demonstrated His power over and over. He's the One that is leading through Moses. They were spared from many of the plagues even though they were guilty of many of the same things as the Egyptians. (Isaiah 8:13)

Now listen to this amazing response from Moses. Sounds to me like he just got a Holy Spirit download. *13 And Moses said to the people, "Fear not, stand firm, and see the salvation of the LORD, which he will work for you today. For the Egyptians whom you see today, you shall never see again.* Moses was encouraging them to have faith in God, not to fear man, and stand firm and see God's salvation. This is exactly what we need to tell ourselves and remind one another when the trials of life overwhelm us. Don't fear man or the situation. God is on the throne of heaven. Worry and fear won't help. Perfect love casts out fear. (1John 4:18) Hold your ground in faith. Believe God and wait and watch for Him to act. They had been redeemed from Israel by the hand of God. Now they must realize that their wilderness journey is just as dependent on God. Your salvation was all of God. Your journey is by the grace of God as well!

But there was one more word of advice from God. *14 The LORD will fight for you, and you have only to be silent."* Let God do the fighting. Ask Him to defeat the enemy. When you don't know what to say, be silent. If you are tempted to blurt out all your complaints and blame someone, just be silent. (2Chronicles 20:17) Watch God work.

15 The LORD said to Moses, "Why do you cry to me? Tell the people of Israel to go forward. 16 Lift up your staff, and stretch out your hand over the sea and divide it, that the people of Israel may go through the sea on dry ground. "What are you crying about Moses, get the people moving! Part the sea!" And then God promised the Egyptians would follow them and be drowned. Twice in the chapter we are told that they will know that *"I am the LORD."*

People complain that God doesn't make Himself plainer, more easily seen. When He does they just excuse it and rebel against Him, which makes them even more accountable on Judgment Day. (Matthew 12:36-37)

The wind blew and the former slaves began to pass through the sea. When they saw God at work again, their fear left. Another amazing thing helped them to have faith. (Hebrews 11:29) The cloud that had led them went around behind them and separated them from the Egyptians. It was utter darkness again for the Egyptians, while it lit their way through the Red Sea. (NIV interpretation of the wording) This Angel who is in the cloud, and who is the Presence of the LORD, is in my opinion none other than Jesus. (Colossians 1:15) He is our light and our salvation. Whom shall we fear! (Psalm 27:1-2)

The last of them arrived on the far shore at dawn. The cloud lifted and let the Egyptians pursue them. What is utterly amazing is that they were belligerent enough to go between those walls of water! (Psalm 78:13) *23 The Egyptians pursued and went in after them into the midst of the sea, all Pharaoh's horses, his chariots, and his horsemen.* It reminds me of a quote from Solomon. *3 This is an evil in all that is done under the sun… the hearts of the children of man are full of evil, and madness is in their hearts while they live, and after that they go to the dead.* Ecclesiastes 9:3 (ESV) Madness was surely in the heart of Pharaoh. There is no other explanation. He was going to recapture them or die. Man versus God. Pharaoh was telling God, "They are mine! And You can't have them!"

God knew this was Pharaoh's heart from the beginning. God raised him up for this very event, to show through him the stubbornness of man and the greatness of God. (Romans 9:17)

24 And in the morning watch the LORD in the pillar of fire and of cloud looked down on the Egyptian forces and threw the Egyptian forces into a panic, 25 clogging their chariot wheels so that they drove heavily. And the Egyptians said, "Let us flee from before Israel, for the LORD fights for them against the Egyptians." Something happened as they got out in the middle of that sea. The wheels began to freeze up (LXX) or fall off (Hebrew). They realized that of the two options, catch the Israelites or die, the latter was becoming more likely. By then it was too late.

God told Moses to again stretch out his hand over the sea. *28 The waters returned and covered the chariots and the horsemen; of all the host of Pharaoh that had followed them into the sea, not one of them remained.* The army of man followed Pharaoh, and the army of God followed Moses and the cloud.

6 At your rebuke, O God of Jacob, both rider and horse lay stunned. 7 But you, you are to be feared! Who can stand before you when once your anger is roused? 8 From the heavens you uttered judgment; the earth feared and was still, 9 when God arose to establish judgment, to save all the humble of the earth. Selah 10 Surely the wrath of man shall praise you… Psalms 76:6-10a (ESV)

What an incredible night! It was the baptism of Israel. (1Corinthians 10:2) It was another opportunity to believe and allow their heart to be changed. *31 Israel saw the great power that the LORD used against the Egyptians, so the people feared the LORD, and they believed in the LORD and in his servant Moses.*

The Scriptures declare that God did this for four reasons. God despised Pharaoh and his army. Man that rejects God after God reveals Himself over and over and over is a pompous fool. (Psalm 14:1) That kind of a person delights in leading others to rebel against their Creator. Nothing can be done to turn them. God despises those given over to evil. (Psalm 7:12-13)

God also did this because He loved Israel. Even though they murmured and doubted. He set His love upon them because of Abraham and the promises He made to their forefathers. (Psalm 86:13; 136:13; Deuteronomy 7:7-8) Remember that you have been grafted into this tree and become a recipient of the promises because of your faith in Christ Jesus. (Romans 11:17)

Probably the most important reason is that He was revealing His name. It was for His name's sake. This event would shake the surrounding nations. The Egyptians will know He is the LORD. (Ezekiel 20:9) The Apostle Paul tells us God raised up Pharaoh so that the name of the LORD would be proclaimed in all the earth.

God also wanted the riches of His glory to be revealed to us. (Romans 9:23) That is difficult for us to understand but think of it like this: glory is the revelation of the heart of God. In our passage today He showed His heart is to deliver those who cry out to Him, even when they aren't perfect. His heart is to judge the arrogant oppressor. His heart is to show us His saving power that we might put our trust in Him. (Romans 10:13)

One day over 1500 years later, the disciples of Jesus sailed into a storm. They had to wake Jesus up because they feared they might drown. Jesus rebuked the wind and the waves and there was a great calm. *The disciples marveled, saying, "What sort of man is this, that even winds and sea obey him?"* Matthew 8:27 (ESV) What sort of man? A man like Moses, only infinitely greater, who gives orders to the winds and the waves. A man to whom we are commanded to listen. (Deuteronomy 18:15) A man who leads the rebellious followers that He loves to the Promised Land and calls down the judgment of God on those who consistently resist Him.

Just as He led them out of their dilemma and saved them, so He will save us if we will cry out to Him. Just as He brought victory when they calmly obeyed and walked in faith with their eyes on Him, so will He bring us through to victory if we will do the same.

Just as the redemption from Egypt was followed by the victory over their enemies in the sea, sealing forever their deliverance, so the redemption of Jesus on the cross was followed by resurrection. Resurrection sealed forever the victory over the enemy of our soul. Our salvation has been by grace through faith and now our journey continues the same way. Every step is a step of faith by the grace of God.

Questions
1 What encouraged Pharaoh to go after the Israelites?
2 Relate Isaiah 2:11 to Pharaoh and to us.
3 Describe the emotional roller coaster of the Hebrews. Relate.

4 Was the battle lopsided? Psalm 68:17 What about ours?
5 Who was fighting the battle? Who fights your battles?
6 What were the people asked to do?
7 How many warnings did Pharaoh have?
8 Why did God raise up Pharaoh?
9 Why did God rescue the Israelites?
10 How does this bring us to Jesus? Mark 4:39; Deuteronomy 18:15

Redeemer Healer Exodus 15

The people that left Egypt had just been on an emotional roller coaster. The mighty hand of God's judgments upon their oppressors freed them. Then they appeared destined for slaughter as Pharaoh's army had them boxed in at the Red Sea. The sea parted and they went through on dry ground. Pharaoh's army recklessly pursued and God released the waters drowning every soldier.

They had probably wondered if they were really free until the moment those waves collapsed upon the soldiers. Now they knew their redemption was complete. There was no longer a reason to fear! God had conquered the army of Pharaoh right before their eyes. If God could do that, is there anything He could not do to bring them into the Promised Land? (Isaiah 43:2-4)

In that moment of great victory there was such a relief, that they had to sing. (Psalm 106:9-12) It is a song that primarily extols God for His greatness. "I will sing to the LORD, for he has triumphed gloriously; the horse and his rider he has thrown into the sea. It was solely the Lord's victory. He didn't need their help. He didn't just triumph; He triumphed gloriously! The song doesn't even mention Moses. How unlike the world's songs of victory!

As we go through this song, there is a way that you, as the redeemed of the Lord, can relate. You were redeemed from the slavery of sin. Sin was a hard taskmaster, but the judgments of God fell on Jesus instead of you, and you were redeemed. (Isaiah 53:5) But so that you might not have to look over your shoulder on the way to our Promised Land, wondering if the enemy was going to overtake you, Jesus rose from the dead. (Romans 5:25) That act was the defeating blow to the enemy of your soul. Jesus conquered death. He triumphed over the forces that were against you. They are defeated once and for all. Is there anything God cannot do to bring us into the Promised Land of heaven? (Romans 8:32)

Yes, there is still some mopping up action to be done. (Hebrews 10:12-14; 1Corinthians 15:28) The enemy is still out there fighting his guerrilla warfare, but the mission is accomplished. The war was won. The rest is just clean up and training to prepare you for eternity. Resurrection was the defeat of Satan's army, and it's something to sing about! (1Peter 3:22)

We need to exalt God in song too! We sing of the Savior's victory that He won single handedly. Jesus triumphed gloriously. That is, He showed the attributes of God on the cross and in the resurrection. Glorious! (1Peter 1:21) We just stood still and watched the salvation of God.

2 The LORD is my strength and my song, and he has become my salvation; this is my God, and I will praise him, my father's God, and I will exalt him. The Lord is my strength, my spiritual strength. The Israelites weren't strong enough to fight Egypt's war machine. The Lord was their strength and continued to be so. We couldn't fight Satan. (Romans 8:3) The Lord had to be our strength and continues to be so!

YHWH is our song! He is the song they sang. (Psalm 118:14) It was all about Him. And He is the song that we sing. I love the songs that focus on Jesus. There's Just Something About That Name; Sweetest Name I Know; Praise the Name of Jesus; Jesus is All the World to Me; His Name is Wonderful; and so many more. He is our song!

He has become my salvation! They were saved from Pharaoh and from slavery. We were saved from Satan and the slavery of the flesh and sin. He has become our salvation! Jesus (Yeshua) means salvation of the LORD! (Matthew 1:21)

He may have not been your father's god like He was for these Israelites, but as our father of faith is Abraham, we can join with that mixed multitude in claiming Abraham as our father too. (Galatians 3:29) Since God is our strength, our song, our salvation, and our father's God, we will praise and exalt Him! We better praise and exalt Him.

If you have the KJV you have a slightly different translation. Instead of "I will praise Him", you have "I will prepare him an habitation". *Nawa* is a Hebrew word that means to rest, as at home, and contains the idea of beauty. It can mean to keep at home or prepare a habitation. The implication is praise but the word is much richer. It's to rest in the Lord as if He's at home with you as you praise His beauty. That's a great description of how we should regard our salvation. (Psalm 27:4; John 14:23)

3 The LORD is a man of war; the LORD is his name. War isn't politically correct anymore. We are so shocked at the horror of war and the cost in life that we have distaste for war. But it's because the Lord is good that He is a warrior against evil. He is at war with the oppressor. He is a man of war against all wrong and injustice. He won't let evil go unpunished. (Proverbs 11:31) He defeated Pharaoh and He defeated Satan through the cross and resurrection. Thank God He is a man of war or we'd be in big trouble.

8 At the blast of your nostrils the waters piled up; the floods stood up in a heap; the deeps congealed in the heart of the sea. The deeps congealed sounds like the wall of water was like Jell-O. God changed the consistency of the seawater so that it stood up in walls on each side of the path through the sea until Pharaoh's army was in the middle of it. Then it returned to its normal state and with all their armor on, they sank like stones.

The victory over the enemy of our soul was no less complete. Just as Pharaoh was out for blood (9b I will draw my sword; my hand shall destroy them.') Satan is out to destroy you and me! (John 10:10) They both thought they were about to gain a final victory when it ended up being their demise. You see, God can even forecast what He will do and the enemy is still helpless to change the course of events. (Job 9:10-12) What a mighty God!

11 "Who is like you, O LORD, among the gods? Who is like you, majestic in holiness, awesome in glorious deeds, doing wonders? Who indeed! There is no one like our God. Even the descriptions of other so-called gods don't come close to the majesty and splendor of our holy God. Their deliverance from Egypt was filled with wonders and glorious deeds, but the cross and resurrection surpasses them all. It is THE awesome, glorious deed. It is the wonder of God. The gods of the nations are still in their graves. Our God not only conquered death but He erased our sin debt in the process and credited us with the righteousness of God. (2Corinthians 5:21; Philippians 3:9) What an awesome glorious deed! We should never forget the wonder of that event! It should always be with us like the journey through the sea was with Israel but more so.

13 "You have led in your steadfast love the people whom you have redeemed; you have guided them by your strength to your holy abode. There is that term again, *hesed.* ESV calls it steadfast love; KJV calls it mercy; NIV uses unfailing love. All are true. It was God's merciful, unfailing love that led them out of captivity, and through the wilderness. That is what led us to salvation and leads us through the wilderness of life. And where are we headed? The Promised Land is God's holy abode. We are going home, to our Father's house. (John 14:2) It is there that we will live forever. The strength of God will see us safely home. He delivered us and He will see us home, all by His steadfast love and His own strength.

You might get battle-worn and wonder if you can make it. Let me assure you that you can't! But the strength of the Lord will! His unfailing mercy will!

The testimony of what God had done put the fear of God in many of the surrounding nations. They knew what God did to Egypt and many times they stood back and let Israel pass by because of that testimony.

Your testimony of deliverance is also a powerful tool to get the attention of the world. (1Peter 3:15) If God can bring you out of the slavery of sin, He can do the same for them. It causes them consider the strength of the Lord and His ability to save.

17 You will bring them in and plant them on your own mountain, the place, O LORD, which you have made for your abode, the sanctuary, O Lord, which your hands have established. Because of the wording of this verse, some have suggested this chapter was inserted later after the Temple was built. The vocabulary and grammar, however, suggest that it is a very old song. Mountain often represents kingdom and the word translated "sanctuary" is simply "holy place". Together you have the Holy Land. The hand of the Lord will plant them in the Holy Land. It need not just mean the

Temple in Jerusalem but the whole land of Israel, which is more fitting to the context. (Psalm 78:54)

Let us take this personally. The hand of the Lord will bring us in and plant us in His holy kingdom. He will see us safely to our heavenly home. It is His doing. The trip is easier if you will cooperate, but He is the One that makes us a part of the final sanctuary of God. The fact that this song points to our ultimate redemption is evident in the fact that the song we will sing in heaven is called the Song of Moses and of the Lamb! (Revelation 15:3)

That was the song! Moses sister, Miriam, turned it into a praise chorus of two lines, tambourine and all. I can't imagine it being sung only once through, can you? They surely repeated it many times. You have Moses' hymn rich in theology and Miriam's praise chorus to sing our joy from the heart. Both are good! Both are beneficial and edifying. Did everyone hear that? Enough said!

Now, after such an amazing time of complete deliverance and celebration, you would think that they would maintain that grateful attitude for months or years to come. Amen? How about three days?

22 Then Moses made Israel set out from the Red Sea, and they went into the wilderness of Shur. They went three days in the wilderness and found no water. We aren't sure what Shur means or where Shur is but we can be sure that Shur is surely in the wilderness, and it's also a spiritual place I'm sure you will visit many times. (Psalm 66:10)

Remember that the cloud is leading them, that great column of cloud that went before and shaded them from the intensity of the sun. For three days it led them until they arrived at the first watering hole. Any water they had would have been carried with them. They were probably about out of water for themselves and their herds.

23 When they came to Marah, they could not drink its water because it was bitter. (That is why the place is called Marah.) They finally arrive and the water is undrinkable. I don't know if it was called Marah before or if something had polluted this spring before they arrived and so they called it Marah.

Many generations later Naomi will change her name to Mara because she is bitter over the death of her husband and sons. (Ruth 1:20) Bitterness can be a condition of the heart or a taste that makes something unpalatable.

The people started to become bitter about the bitter water. They began to complain. After all, they had children and elderly among them. Did they remember that just a few days earlier they had been singing that the Lord was their strength, their song, and their salvation?

Sometimes when we declare something, the Lord will test us to show us that we haven't quite attained to the stature we thought we had. We understand something with our mind, but the first test that comes along reveals our heart is not really at rest, at home, with the truth.

24 And the people grumbled against Moses, saying, "What shall we drink?" Why are they grumbling against Moses? The cloud led them there! Well, some people have the good sense to realize it's not a good idea to complain to God, especially after He has marvelously delivered you. So, instead, they again pick on His servant. "He's an easy target. He's meek. What's he gonna do, call down a lightning bolt? Complain to him! He's the one that came and got us out of comfortable Egypt. There was plenty of water there!"

Realize that they have a legitimate and urgent need. Our complaints are often something very legitimate, but an illegitimate response. What would the right response have been to the circumstance? It would have been to look to the One that they sang was their salvation and their strength. (Psalm 50:15) Why didn't they ask Him for the answer to the situation?

Grumbling against God ordained leadership is deeply entrenched tendency of the flesh. It is one that that generation will never really walk in victory over and it will cause them immense problems, and eventually their death.

Moses did what they should have done. He did what we should do. *25 And he cried to the LORD, and the LORD showed him a log, and he threw it into the water, and the water became sweet.* God miraculously gave him the solution. It sounds like that log somehow absorbed the bitterness of the water or neutralized whatever the problem was. It may have been a supernatural answer with a natural solution or a miracle.

Just think how God had prepared that tree for that very moment to be the solution to the problem and to teach His people. But even greater, is the fact that God prepared the cross, the solution to sin, from before the creation of the world. (Revelation 13:8) We can see a parallel in how the cross takes the bitterness out of life and provides living water to refresh us and enable us to make it through the journey of life. (John 7:37)

There the LORD made for them a statute and a rule, and there he tested them, *26 saying, "If you will diligently listen to the voice of the LORD your God, and do that which is right in his eyes, and give ear to his commandments and keep all his statutes, I will put none of the diseases on you that I put on the Egyptians, for I am the LORD, your healer."* This was the Lord's lesson. Life will present you with all kinds of difficulties. You will be tested over and over again, but if you will listen to the voice of the LORD, and do what is right, obey His commandments, then He will be JHWH Rapha to us – the Lord that heals. The ailments of Egypt won't follow them to the Promised Land.

Affliction is often the way that the Lord gets our attention. (Psalm 119:75) If we will listen and obey, He won't need to get our attention. That is what was happening here. Where would they turn in the difficulty? Would they look to the Lord? Would they listen to His voice?

The greatest affliction of Egypt was a stubborn, unrepentant heart. That is the bitter affliction that God made sweet with a log on Calvary! If we will look to the LORD, He will be the healer of our sin sick souls.

Now remember, Jesus told us that not all affliction was the result of sin. (John 9:2-3) However, it is often the way that God gets us to face our sin. Learn the lesson without the illustration. Listen now. Obey now, and God will be JHWH Rapha to us.

27 Then they came to Elim, where there were twelve springs of water and seventy palm trees, and they encamped there by the water. As soon as the lesson was taught, they got a reprieve, a spring for every tribe and the shade of the palm for each elder. God gives us times of rest.

How quickly we go from celebrating God to complaining about our next situation! Remember, God is guiding us through it all and testing us to see if we believe today what we sang about yesterday. (1Chronicles 16:12) He has lessons for us in it. He is fixing those truths in our hearts so we will react differently next time. This is a statute of God. If we will diligently listen to the voice of the LORD our God, and do what is right in his eyes, and give ear to His commandments and keep His statutes, we won't be afflicted like the world. He will be the LORD our healer until the day we totally healed and sing the Song of Moses and of the Lamb before the throne of God. (Revelation 21:4)

Questions
1 How is the Song of Moses different from the world's songs of victory?
2 How is our song similar to that of Moses'?
3 Why is it necessary for God to be a warrior?
4 What attribute of God leads us through life?
5 What is the song we sing in heaven? Why?
6 How long did their joy last?
7 What was wrong with their complaint?
8 How was the statute related to the test?
9 When does God become JHWH Rapha to us?

God's Provision Exodus 16

Before we get into our passage for today, I want us to see something that is not spelled out in the story. When the people left Egypt, they were a "mixed multitude", Hebrews, Egyptians, slaves of other nations. All the believers in YHWH left together. That is never brought up again. The whole multitude that passed through the sea are now referred to as Israel. So it is with the followers of Yeshua of Nazareth that pass through the waters of baptism. We become one. (Ephesians 4:5) Our chief identity is no longer this nationality, or that race, or that class of people, but children of faith, children of Abraham, sons and daughters of God. (John 1:12) The Gospel invites everyone into a new family, the family of God. (Revelation 21:6)

The Israelites already had their first two big tests. The first was at the waters of the Red Sea when all seemed lost, but God delivered them in an unforgettable miracle. Then after only three days, they found themselves dying of thirst at a watering hole that was undrinkable. God once again showed that He is the answer for every situation in life. We left the Israelites in a place of reprieve, the oasis of Elim, with its 72 palms and 12 springs of water.

God won't leave us in that place of ease for long, because we need to grow. (James 1:2-3; 1Thessalonians 3:3) God is working on our sanctification. (Hebrews 10:14) He has redeemed us and we are bound for heaven, but there is still a lot of work to be done in our minds and hearts. Most of that work is done in the wilderness, not at the oasis. So the cloud moved them on to the wilderness of Sin.

The place, Sin, does not mean sin as we know the word, but they did sin in Sin. It is now about 45 days into their journey. *2 And the whole congregation of the people of Israel grumbled against Moses and Aaron in the wilderness, 3 and the people of Israel said to them, "Would that we had died by the hand of the LORD in the land of Egypt, when we sat by the meat pots and ate bread to the full, for you have brought us out into this wilderness to kill this whole assembly with hunger."* It sounds like they wish they had died by one of the plagues rather than to be hungry. This is one of the weaknesses of man. We need to eat. But food can easily become a god to us, a source of satisfaction that we exalt. (Psalm 78:18) Not until you decide to purposefully go without food will you realize the powerful influence food has on your life. This was one of the gods of Egypt that hadn't yet been addressed. Has it been addressed in your own life?

God could have provided for them from the first day they left, but He was teaching them about their hearts. He is testing them so that they can see where they seek satisfaction, and where they turn in times of struggle. (Exodus 20:20) It's no different today. If you have never fasted I would encourage you to do so. Take a day, or two or three, and drink water or even some juice, and you will be able to relate to this trial the Israelites are going through.

On the other hand, remember that they had flocks and herds. It wasn't that they had nothing to eat. The flocks produced milk. They could be slaughtered for meat, but the flocks were their wealth. They weren't quite as desperate as they made it sound. We usually aren't. (Exodus 34:3)

They were ready to go back. Funny how we remember the "good old days" but forget details, things like taskmasters, and long hours of labor, beatings, lack of freedom etc. All we remember is the one thing we are currently missing. Instead of giving thanks for what we do have, like Eve in the Garden, we focus on the one thing we don't have and wonder why God would be so harsh as to withhold this one thing. (Genesis 3:6) Love withholds it that we might grow spiritually.

The people blamed Moses for their predicament, but really, all our dissatisfaction is ultimately aimed at God. Notice, too, that they say that Moses brought them out of Egypt. Moses will have to address these misconceptions.

4 Then the LORD said to Moses, "Behold, I am about to rain bread from heaven for you, and the people shall go out and gather a day's portion every day, that I may test them, whether they will walk in my law or not. 5 On the sixth day, when they prepare what they bring in, it will be twice as much as they gather daily." God sent the answer. He would provide. He is Jehovah Jireh. (Genesis 22:14) The people needed to see their own heart before God met their need, and that is often the case with us. I would suggest that in every trial we face, we first look at our own attitude. Where did we go first? What or who do we blame? Is there another god in our heart? What is God trying to teach us through the difficulty? And what is His solution to the situation? Can I do what Moses suggested before, *"Stand still and see the salvation of God"*? (Exodus 14:13)

God is teaching them to trust His word and obey Him. We should learn to obey because His commands are for our good. (Deuteronomy 10:13) He gave them very specific commands. Gather so much on these days. Don't gather more except on the day before the Sabbath and then gather twice as much.

6 So Moses and Aaron said to all the people of Israel, "At evening you shall know that it was the LORD who brought you out of the land of Egypt, 7 and in the morning you shall see the glory of the LORD, because he has heard your grumbling against the LORD. For what are we, that you grumble against us?" Why they didn't realize that it was the Lord that delivered them after the plagues, the Red Sea, and Marah is due to human nature. (Psalm 78:11) Israel is revealing the heart of man, just as Pharaoh revealed the heart of man. What does God have to do for us to give Him the credit?

A life size reproduction of the tabernacle is being handed to us right when we get to that passage in Exodus. Some people will think I planned it. The material for Wednesday night Bible study happened to start right where we were last Sunday in Exodus. Some will think it is a coincidence. Some will realize it is God. How many times have we seen God provide the perfect illustration for where we were in a sermon series? Will we give Him the credit due Him and recognize His hand? It is not me! It is the grace of God! What am I? Moses says what are we? We are dust. (Psalm 103:13) Without the breath of life we go back to the dust. Our salvation is of God. Our ministry is of God. The fruit is of God. Recognize it and give God the glory due Him!

8 And Moses said, "When the LORD gives you in the evening meat to eat and in the morning bread to the full, because the LORD has heard your grumbling that you grumble against him— what are we? Your grumbling is not against us but against the LORD." ... 12bThen you shall know that I am the LORD your God.' " That should have put the fear of God into them. The last time God said, *"Then they will know I am the LORD"*, was about the army of Egypt before they drowned. (Exodus 14:18) The difference is that God added a reassuring, *"your God"* on the end of the phrase.

God is patient and gracious. They didn't deserve it, but God dealt with them as children. They are just learning to walk. (Psalm 78:38) Most of us are in the same place, complaining about the one thing we lack when we have been given so much. The Lord meets our need, and hopefully we learn the lesson and know that He is the LORD our God!

13 In the evening quail came up and covered the camp, and in the morning dew lay around the camp. 14 And when the dew had gone up, there was on the face of the wilderness a fine, flake-like thing, fine as frost on the ground. 15a When the people of Israel saw it, they said to one another, "What is it?" For they did not know what it was. There have been numerous practical explanations how this may have been possible. Quail do migrate at night when it is cool and then collapse in the morning after flying so long. The problem with that natural explanation is the quail came in the evening.

The manna has been explained as a secretion of a desert aphid, but does anyone serious think there were that many aphids in the desert? Then the miracle would have been just as glorious, billions of aphids that secrete their nectar five days a week, and double on Friday, but nothing on Saturday. Why do unbelievers have such a hard time accepting the possibility of the God of creation doing something supernatural?

The people had never seen that white stuff before, so the called it "What's it?" in Hebrew, manna. (Actually "man" but through the Greek and Aramaic translations we came to call it manna.) Manna in the morning every day and on this special occasion quail in the evening. (Not to be confused with Numbers 11.)

Each person was to gather about two quarts and four quarts on Friday. It seems that no matter how big or small you were, it was just enough for you. (2Corinthians 8:13-15) In the instructions was an implied test. If you gathered more than you were told, by the next day it would stink and have worms. On Friday you had to believe it wouldn't if you gathered two days worth. Those who disobeyed found that God's word was true. If they went out Saturday morning, there was no manna to be found anywhere.

Because they disobeyed, Moses became angry. Moses had come to the place of complete confidence in the word of the LORD. He didn't have the patience of God that saw them as children in the school of faith. He couldn't understand why they didn't believe God's word.

Sometimes your leaders are impatient as well. "We wonder why you can't discern something is not of God, or how you could dabble in the world, when the Word of God is clear on that subject. We get upset when you do not take God at His word. It's not that we are mad at you, but that we know your obedience to the Word is best for you. We need to have patience. You see, we are all in school. We may be in different classes, but we are all in the school of life nevertheless.

This story so clearly shows us God's attributes of patience and loving- kindness. After all they've seen, they are still maligning God's intentions for bringing them out of Egypt. "…you have brought us out into this wilderness to kill this whole assembly with hunger."

How heartbreaking that must have been for God to hear, and yet, He knows their stage of spiritual growth and is humbling them to teach them that man shall not live by bread alone but by every word that proceeds from the mouth of God. (Deuteronomy 8:3)

The answer to the question, "Why God?", is always the same. Because He loves us! It's because He wants our faith to grow for our eternal good. (Galatians 5:6) He accepts us as we are because of our faith in Jesus' sacrifice, but He won't leave us where we are. That is why He tests us. That is why He leads us to places of thirst and hunger, so that we will hunger and thirst after Him.

27 On the seventh day some of the people went out to gather, but they found none. 28 And the LORD said to Moses, "How long will you refuse to keep my commandments and my laws? 29 See! The LORD has given you the Sabbath; therefore on the sixth day he gives you bread for two days. Remain each of you in his place; let no one go out of his place on the seventh day." 30 So the people rested on the seventh day. The Sabbath is a controversial topic to many today. When we get to the laws given to Moses, we'll discuss it more fully. The Sabbath rest goes all the way back to the creation story. (Genesis 2:2-3) It preceded the laws of Moses. This was another test, just as the order to gather only a certain amount on certain days, so they were to rest on the Sabbath and devote it to the worship of God.

The New Testament clearly shows us that for the early Christians the day of worship became the first day of the week, Sunday. (1 Corinthians 16:2) It was called the Lord's Day as Jesus is our Sabbath rest. (Hebrews 4:9-11) The Apostle Paul tells us a number of times that we are no longer under the law. His most definitive statement on a day of worship is in Romans 14:5 (ESV*) 5 One person esteems one day as better than another, while another esteems all days alike. Each one should be fully convinced in his own mind.*

If you decide to take a day, whether Saturday or Sunday and do nothing but worship, good for you. If you are convinced that every day you should be dedicated to God in your every action, then good for you. We all answer to God for our own convictions and not for another's. (Romans 14:13) Know in your own heart how God is leading you. Don't condemn another believer because they are led differently regarding these debatable issues. (Colossians 2:16-17) Physiologically it is good for you to take a day off. No other culture at the time had this custom. God blessed His people with rest. We need it!

33 And Moses said to Aaron, "Take a jar, and put an omer of manna in it, and place it before the LORD to be kept throughout your generations." There was something about this manna that they were to always remember. It was first placed in the tent of meeting where Moses met with God. After the Ark of the Covenant was built, it was one of the three elements in the Ark. (Hebrews 9:4)

Not only was it a reminder of God's faithful, miraculous provision for the Children of Israel during their 40 years of wandering in the desert, but it was also a sign of God as the Great Provider for all His creation. (Psalm 147:9)

Most importantly, it looked forward to the great provision of God. Humanity has a spiritual hunger that can only be filled by God alone. We try to fill that spiritual emptiness with all kinds of things, food, entertainment, security, power, but nothing fills that great void. (Ephesians 4:19)

During Jesus' earthly ministry, He fed the multitudes with a few small fish and five small loaves of bread. (John 6:11) It reminded the people of Moses and the manna in the wilderness. They asked for Him to feed them again as sign that He was indeed the Messiah. (John 6:30-31)

32 Jesus then said to them, "Truly, truly, I say to you, it was not Moses who gave you the bread from heaven, but my Father gives you the true bread from heaven. 33 For the bread of God is he who comes down from heaven and gives life to the world." John 6:32-33 (ESV) Moses didn't give them manna. God did. Jesus point was this, God is the only One that can really meet our need. The manna was just a shadow of the real bread from heaven. The real bread from heaven is the Man who comes down from heaven and gives His life to the world. Of course, Jesus was speaking of Himself.

He went on to make it clear. *48 I am the bread of life. 49 Your fathers ate the manna in the wilderness, and they died. 50 This is the bread that comes down from heaven, so that one may eat of it and not die. 51 I am the living bread that came down from heaven. If anyone eats of this bread, he will live forever. And the bread that I will give for the life of the world is my flesh."* John 6:48-51 (ESV) God has provided bread that gives not just physical life, but eternal life. It is the very body of Jesus who took our sins upon Himself and died in our place. (Isaiah 53:6) He is the bread of life.

What is it, that white wafer upon the earth that tastes like honey? It's a picture of God sending from heaven the answer to our desperate need. Without Him, we will starve spiritually.

Manna is still falling! Every morning we rise and many of us have a habit of going and collecting enough for our spiritual hunger for that day. Some gather a little and some a lot, but it ends up being just enough. He truly satisfies!

Prayer: Father give us a spiritual hunger for our daily bread. Give us the Word made flesh. Help us to see Him through the enlightened eyes of our heart. Give us a greater revelation of the dimensions of Your love and the life that You give us in your bread from heaven, Jesus. Amen!

Questions
1 Who makes up the family of God?
2 Why isn't the Christian life easier?
3 What was the next test they faced?
4 Why didn't God give them manna from the start?
5 Where is our dissatisfaction ultimately aimed?
6 Why did Moses become angry with the people?
7 What was the origin of the Sabbath?
8 What did the Apostle Paul teach about the Sabbath?
9 Why did God have them keep a jar of manna?
10 How does this relate to Jesus?

Testing God Exodus 17:1-7

The LORD had tested the Israelites at Marah. They expected to replenish their water supplies, only to find the water was bitter. They looked to Moses for the solution. God showed Moses the answer that He had prepared in advance, a log that would make the water sweet.

As we go on through the record of the Exodus, we find that even though they accuse God of bringing them out in the desert to starve them, He didn't really rebuke the people at all. God was humbling them and teaching them that man does not live by bread alone, but by every Word that proceeds from His mouth. If they would listen to God, He would be their healer. Are we living by every word that proceeds from the mouth of God? (Deuteronomy 8:3)

God will discipline them more severely and the reason He does so is related to the tests. God does not give us tests so that HE can learn how we are doing. He gives us tests so that WE can learn how we are doing. When the state of our heart is manifest, we should seriously consider what needs to change and how that change might come about. (James 1:23-25)

My son works for a company that helps those studying for a CPA license by giving them tests. The tests are to show them where they are weak and need more study. The tests aren't to condemn them, but to help them improve and eventually pass the real exam.

God gives us tests. At our Wednesday night Bible study, someone asked what the difference was between test and temptation. A temptation is to lure us into sin and destruction. A test is to reveal our weakness that we might improve. God never tempts us. James tells us that is not in His nature. (James 1:13) Satan tempts. God tests. One is meant to bring you to ruin. The other is meant to open your eyes to your weakness.

Sometimes, as we are being tested, the enemy of our soul will tempt us. (1Peter 5:8) That is what happened in the wilderness of Sin. God was testing them to teach them how little they looked to God for their needs. Satan was tempting them to give up and head back to the secure abundance of the Nile. Satan wanted them to go back to serving Pharaoh instead of God. There was a test and a temptation. They come from different sources and for different reasons.

We all go through tests. In that test there are temptations. The tests are to teach. The temptations are to destroy. Learn from the tests. Reject the temptations. (1Peter 5:9)

After receiving the quail and the daily manna, the cloud led them little by little to Rephidim. 1 All the congregation of the people of Israel moved on from the wilderness of Sin by stages, according to the commandment of the LORD, and camped at Rephidim, but there was no water for the people to drink.

They moved at the commandment of the LORD. The LORD said to follow His Presence in the cloud. When they cloud moved, they were to move. The cloud was a Theophany, a manifestation of God. In a sense, it was Immanuel, God with them. To follow the cloud was to obey the commandment of the LORD. It carries the idea of walking with the LORD, of following Him through life. We might think they were blessed to have something physical to follow, and they were, but remember the cloud has now led them to three places of frightening uncertainty. (Acts 14:22)

It's not so different today. In Christ, we try to follow His word and His will for our life, and yet we face the same type of situations that we feel are disastrous. We can't see the answer or the reason. We begin to doubt whether or not we are following God as we should. We ask ourselves, "Is God mad at us for some reason we aren't aware? Is this illness or that conflict the result of my sin?" (Psalm 119:75)

That is something we should consider. But often it is a test. It reveals how much we really trust the LORD. It shows us where our trust is placed. Yes, there are those times that we will not understand what it is all about, and yet we trust God and wait on His Word. (Psalm 139:23-24)

Now they have come to Rephidim. It means resting places. Some believe this is Wady Fairan. If so, then it is long row palms and tamarisk trees at the base of tall cliffs. It often runs with water. This time it was dry! Didn't God know that? Did He intentionally lead them to another point of desperate need? Yes! He is testing them again.

When we don't learn the material the first time through, we need to be taught again and tested again. Will they now look to the LORD? Will they wait on His word? Will we?

Unfortunately for them, they showed they had not learned from Marah. They repeated the same sinful actions at the wilderness of Sin, by blaming Moses and maligning him. *2 Therefore the people quarreled with Moses and said, "Give us water to drink." And Moses said to them, "Why do you quarrel with me? Why do you test the LORD?"* They were turning the test around and instead of learning from the test, they decided they would test God. (Deuteronomy 33:8)

We would not understand completely what was happening here without verse 7 and other passages that explain it for us. The people hardened their hearts, like Pharaoh did. They asked if God was really among them. They demanded that if He really was, that He perform for them according to His covenant and do so right now! They were putting God to a test. The test was for them, but they flipped it around and said, "No, the test is for God! If He is really with us, then provide water!"

Scripture will look back to this and denounce it as a defiant and rebellious act. (Deuteronomy 9:22) Jesus will quote to Satan, "Do not put the LORD your God to a test." (Matthew 4:7) God doesn't need to be taught anything. He has no blind spots. To test Him is to say He is in error and needs to improve. The Israelites were really saying, "God, you've failed to give us water when we need it. Keep your covenant with us or we'll stone your representative!!"

This is a major lesson for the Israelites and for us. When we demand that God perform for us to prove Himself, we are reversing roles with God. We are taking the place of the Creator as judge and putting God on trial.

Here is an eternal truth that we are reminded of by King Ahaz (Isaiah 7:12), by a psalmist (Psalm 78:41), by Jesus (Luke 4:12), and by the author of Hebrews (Hebrews 3:8-9). Man does not test God! God tests us. Tests are to expose our imperfections and help us grow. We are not to test God by demanding that He serve us at our whim.

"God if you are really there then ..." God is really there whether you get the answer you want or not! Just because God doesn't act the way we think He should does not change the reality of who He is or who we are. He is still all-knowing God (Hebrews 4:13), and we are still limited creatures with imperfect knowledge. (1Corinthians 13:12)

3 But the people thirsted there for water, and the people grumbled against Moses and said, "Why did you bring us up out of Egypt, to kill us and our children and our livestock with thirst?" Here they go again with an accusation we will hear until that generation dies off. They have a real need. The young, the elderly, the animals, all need water. They haven't learned from the last tests that in times of need we are to look to our heavenly Father, present our need, and wait for His word.

I don't know if anything is more hurtful to a godly leader than to have those they serve malign their motives. There is no way to defend oneself, for they have already seen your sacrificial service but chosen to add the motivations they have imagined. Moses could not rip out his heart and show it to them. All he could do was continue to meekly serve them and hope they would one day be willing to be honest with what they observed. Moses is serving the people at God's leading, not his own or theirs.

4 So Moses cried to the LORD, "What shall I do with this people? They are almost ready to stone me." Do you remember how tenaciously Moses tried to get out of accepting this role? (Exodus 4:13) It may have been fear of Pharaoh, but it also may be that he had tried before and had his motives maligned. (Exodus 2:14) Remember, *"Will you kill me as you killed the Egyptian? Who made you a ruler over us?"* After all the miracles and proofs that YHWH is God and Moses is His chosen leader, they are still unchanged.

5 And the LORD said to Moses, "Pass on before the people, taking with you some of the elders of Israel, and take in your hand the staff with which you struck the Nile, and go. When we studied the role of elders in the church last January, we noticed that it went all the way back to the Exodus. God has always used individuals to lead, but these individuals are not above anyone or over one another. Moses is one of them. He is in the lead, but we will see later that the Spirit that is on Him will be on the other elders as well. (Numbers 11:17)

With such a large group, not everyone would see what was about to take place. The event will be very significant, so the elders will be a witness to convey it to the rest of the congregation. In that sense, the church is the same today, only we have the Great Shepherd, Jesus, as the head Shepherd. The elders serve the congregation at His leading. (Hebrews 13:17)

The same rod that brought judgment on the Egyptian gods and turned the Nile water into blood is now about to provide water in the desert. God told Moses, *6 Behold, I will stand before you there on the rock at Horeb, and you shall strike the rock, and water shall come out of it, and the people will drink." And Moses did so, in the sight of the elders of Israel.* It sounds like the cloud went and hovered over the rock at Horeb to show Moses which rock to strike. The LORD was definitely among them! In front of the elders as witnesses, Moses struck that rock and water poured out in sufficient quantity for the Israelites.

An interesting aside is that Rephidim also can also mean "low places". If this was a place of low elevation in the wilderness, the water would have formed a lake which the people and herds could gather around.

The Apostle Paul tells us this was another picture of Christ. (1Corinthians 10:4) The Old Testament refers to God as our rock. (Genesis 49:24) It implies an unchanging place or firm foundation on which to build.

But what does it mean that the rock was struck with that rod of judgment and from it came a river of water? Halfway chronologically between Moses and Jesus came Isaiah, who filled in the picture. He prophesied, *4 Surely he has borne our griefs and carried our sorrows; yet we esteemed him stricken, smitten by God, and afflicted. 5 But he was wounded for our transgressions; he was crushed for our iniquities; upon him was the chastisement that brought us peace, and with his stripes we are healed. 6 All we like sheep have gone astray; we have turned every one to his own way; and the LORD has laid on him the iniquity of us all.* (Isaiah 53:4-6 ESV)

That rock, Christ Jesus, had our iniquities placed upon Him, and because He took our place, He was smitten by God's rod of judgment that we might be saved. The same Hebrew word is used in both texts, *naka*, to smite. The same Hebrew words to strike and smite were used in applying the blood to the doorframe of the Israelites' homes. They were struck and smitten with the blood of the lamb. (Exodus 12:22)

As Moses struck the rock before witnesses that were to convey what happened to others, so Jesus was struck and raised with witnesses that were to proclaim it to others. (Acts 2:32) As water that gave life to the thirsty multitude flowed in abundance from the rock, so the water of life flows from Jesus springing up within the one who places their trust in Him. (John 4:14) He was struck once for us all that we might live and not die. (Hebrews 10:12-14)

As we wander through the wilderness of life, we come to the wilderness of Sin. We expected to find satisfaction in the natural, but it was dry and unsatisfying. We knew we must have a spiritual drink or die of thirst. We may have even complained that God had not met our need. Then along came a witness, someone who saw that the rock was struck for us, to give us the water of life. We come to the water and drink our fill, and there is more than enough. Our spiritual thirst is satisfied. Will we remember next time to look to the Lord? (Isaiah 51:1)

Sometimes we look to the elders. They can share their water with you, but they are not the source. The rock that was smitten is the source. They are just here to point you to the rock, to remind you it is the source.

7 And he called the name of the place Massah and Meribah, because of the quarreling of the people of Israel, and because they tested the LORD by saying, "Is the LORD among us or not?" Testing and Quarreling were the names that would be remembered for this experience. Centuries later the psalmist would remind them of the experience. *8 do not harden your hearts, as at Meribah, as on the day at Massah in the wilderness, 9 when your fathers put me to the test and put me to the proof, though they had seen my work.* Psalm 95:8-9 (ESV)

The author of Hebrews tells us that the application in his day was for the new believers who wanted to return to a religion of works to avoid persecution. (Hebrews 3:11-14) We see the same today. People quarrel with God when they say they can't accept a God who would sacrifice His own Son. They quarrel because they can't grasp the greatness of His love and the eternal nature of His existence. But even more, it's because of the hardness of their heart. They want God to perform on their own terms. They want to quarrel with God and have Him fit their preconceived idea of what He should be like.

Any believer can do the same. We want God to act in certain ways in our time, and we ignore what He is already doing and the way He is doing it. It is a hardening of our heart and another way to test God. Henry Blackaby reminds us that we are to be like Jesus in watching what God is doing and joining Him, not think up a plan and ask God to join us. (John 5:19)

At Marah God gave them a statute and a promise in response to their sin. He invited them to look to Him. Now, a short time later, the test is repeated. Now they get a warning. Don't quarrel with or test God. As we grow, a little more is expected of us. Another test is coming on the heels of this one. God is drilling home the lessons for their good and ours as well. These things happened to them that we might not sin as they did. Paul wrote, *9 We must not put Christ to the test, as some of them did and were destroyed by serpents, 10 nor grumble, as some of them did and were destroyed by the Destroyer. 11 Now these things happened to them as an example, but they were written down for our instruction, on whom the end of the ages has come. 12 Therefore let anyone who thinks that he stands take heed lest he fall.* 1Corinthians 10:9-12 (ESV)

Yes, God is among us. He is our rock. He meets our spiritual thirst. He is our covenant God who bore the judgment we deserve that we might live. Let us never doubt that and test Him. Let us not harden our heart and quarrel with His holy justice. Let us look to Him and drink freely and frequently of the water of life. (John 3:14-15)

Questions

1 What is the difference between a test and a temptation?
2 How are our tests similar to Israel's?
3 Why does God repeat tests?
4 How did the people test God? Do we?
5 How did they threaten God?
6 Why was Moses distraught?
7 Why did God have Moses bring the elders?
8 Who is the Rock of Israel?
9 What is the reality behind the picture?
10 How do people quarrel with God today?
11 Discuss 1Corinthians 10:9-12

It's a War! Exodus 17:8-16

We are at least 45 days into Israel's wandering in the wilderness. We have seen God defeat their enemy in the Red Sea. We've seen several tests, bitter water, hunger, and a repeat of the test of thirst. We've seen God's patience with the people and provision and unfailing love for them. And we've also seen a number of illustrations of Jesus in foreshadowing events that would help future generations understand that God's plan has always been the same. (Isaiah 46:9-10)

God told Moses that there was a reason that they had to go the round about way through the wilderness instead of up the Way of Horus along the Sea. The reason was that they would face war and would become afraid and turn back. (Exodus 13:17) The nation was not battle hardened, and that route would have brought them against some of Egypt's military outposts.

As they journeyed, it was only natural that the weaker people would lag behind. The elderly or families with very young, and herds with numerous baby animals would tend to be toward the rear. Because the weak were in the rear, it was the most vulnerable part of the column. (1Samuel 15:2)

A local people called Amalekites took advantage of this and raided the rear of the camp. Listen to how Moses later described it. Deuteronomy 25:17-18 (ESV) *17 "Remember what Amalek did to you on the way as you came out of Egypt, 18 how he attacked you on the way when you were faint and weary, and cut off your tail, those who were lagging behind you, and he did not fear God.* God had previously told Israel that nations would hear of what He did to Egypt and stand back as Israel passed. (Exodus 15:16) But the passage I just read tells us that the Amalekites did not fear God.

The fear of God is the beginning of wisdom. (Proverbs 1:7) If you think you can get away with something and God won't see it or hold you accountable, you are a fool. The Amalekites were fools. The fool says in his heart, "There is no God!" (Psalm 14:1)

They are descended from Esau and have the same temporal mindset that Esau had. (Genesis 36:12; Numbers 24:20) They thought they could raid the weak part of the camp of Israel and gain a few spoils of war like slaves, herds, and stolen goods. The fool lives for this life only. He or she thinks that if they can gain this world's goods, regardless of how they do it, regardless if it is unethical or evil, they are better off. Their shortsighted perspective is focused on the temporal pleasures of this life and denies any eternal consequence. That was Amalek, and for that reason they are a symbol of the flesh nature of man.

8 Then Amalek came and fought with Israel at Rephidim. 9 So Moses said to Joshua, "Choose for us men, and go out and fight with Amalek. Tomorrow I will stand on the top of the hill with the staff of God in my hand." Given Moses description in Deuteronomy, I think Amalek fought a kind of guerilla warfare. Moses had to send an army after them to engage them head on. Apparently, God had given Moses instructions as to how to deal with these marauders.

I would like for us to consider the sovereignty of God in the matter. They did not go one way to face a more sophisticated and better-equipped army, but they did face these people who were a better match for them. This was a way of teaching battle to the fighting men of Israel. God doesn't give us more than we can handle. (1Corinthians 10:13) Neither does He always expect us to just sit back and watch like He had them do at the Red Sea. (Exodus 14:13) God is training us little by little.

The same is true in the spiritual realm. He gives us those tests that won't overwhelm us but will teach us and help us grow. You can be sure that God will never give you a test that will defeat you if you will look to Him. That is the point of this encounter. It is a different situation with a unique solution, but the answer is the same. Look to God. They had just learned that lesson in this very place as God provided manna and quail. Now, will they look to God and listen to His word as they face an enemy in battle? (Deuteronomy 8:3)

Moses is going to take the rod of God to a hilltop where the soldiers can see him. In his hands is that symbol of the authority of Almighty God, the rod of God. Some have speculated that it may have been ornamented with some shiny objects which would make it more visible, and that is why it is referred to later as a signal pole or banner.

Moses took Aaron his brother and a man named Hur with him. Hur is Hebrew equivalent of "Whitey". It was a common name. Josephus tells us that he was Miriam's husband.

We don't know if the LORD commanded them to come along or if Moses just had the good sense to bring along some assistants. There are some things we should do alone and there are others that wisdom would dictate the need for assistance.

Joshua was to muster an army in one day. This is the first we read of Joshua. He is half the age of Moses and may have already been a natural leader preparing men to protect their family and herds. (Joshua 14:7) The Scripture tells us that they went up from Egypt armed, so they do have weaponry. (Exodus 13:18)

10 So Joshua did as Moses told him, and fought with Amalek, while Moses, Aaron, and Hur went up to the top of the hill. Sword and shield battles were often won or lost dependent on who tired or lost hope first. As soon as someone turned to run, they were exposed to sword and arrow. Once a few fell, others would frighten and turn. Battles were often one-sided massacres depending on who turned to run first.

Moses presence on the hill with the rod of God as an ensign was assurance for the novice warriors of Israel. It would remind them of the defeat of Egypt with that same rod. It would remind them that God fought for them. (Exodus 14:14)

11 Whenever Moses held up his hand, Israel prevailed, and whenever he lowered his hand, Amalek prevailed. Some believed that this was a picture of Moses interceding in prayer and is a lesson in persevering in prayer. Though that is a valid lesson, I don't think that is the main message of this passage.

The lesson here is first and foremost that we look to God to be our strength. Secondly it is that we often need the help of the people of God because of the weakness of the flesh. (Proverbs 24:6) That lesson will be reinforced in the next chapter. We are physical beings that get weary. As Moses arms tired and the rod was lowered, the soldiers below lost sight of the rod and would get discouraged. When it was raised again they encouraged themselves with the memories that rod invoked. If their eyes were not on the sign of God's presence with them, they would have been the first to turn and would have been defeated.

12 But Moses' hands grew weary, so they took a stone and put it under him, and he sat on it, while Aaron and Hur held up his hands, one on one side, and the other on the other side. So his hands were steady until the going down of the sun. Aaron and Hur may not have known why they had come, but it didn't take them long to figure it out. They were there to help Moses do what God had called him to do. (Proverbs 27:10) They were the physical strength behind Moses' obedience. Moses couldn't obey on his own. God and Moses both knew that. That is why Aaron and Hur were called.

Most tasks the Lord assigns us are carried out with an Aaron and Hur The church worship service relies on numerous people, the elders, the worship team, the office administrator, the deaconesses, Children's church teachers, intercessors, and greeters. . I had help from two different couples proofreading my books. The lone ranger jobs are the exception rather than the rule.

When we receive the tabernacle we'll need Aarons and Hurs from every church that are willing to help. Later in the Scriptures, David will declare that all people should share in the reward that comes from the effort, frontline people and those who stay behind. (1Samuel 30:24-25) From the preacher to the technical person at the soundboard, everyone shares the reward because together they make it possible.

God seems to delight in cooperative efforts. That is one reason He has blessed the churches in Sedona. We are more than willing to work together and help one another. Look at the Trinity! The Father gives the plan, the Son carries it out, and the Holy Spirit illuminates what the Son did. God even uses us to share His love with others. God blesses us when we work together for His glory. (Psalm 133:1)

13 And Joshua overwhelmed Amalek and his people with the sword. This means the army under Joshua's command prevailed. "Amalek and his people" sounds like the leader of the enemy was named after his ancestor Amalek. Sometimes a leader's name will be passed down to each successive leader.

14 Then the LORD said to Moses, "Write this as a memorial in a book and recite it in the ears of Joshua, that I will utterly blot out the memory of Amalek from under heaven." Was this a special scroll or just a reminder that when the record was written to be sure to include this? The verse does indicate that Moses knew that Joshua would be his successor. God would see that the Amalekites eventually became extinct. Saul and David did inflict the final blows on the Amalekites almost 400 years later. (1Samuel 30:17)

15 And Moses built an altar and called the name of it, The LORD is my banner, Altars of stone were built to worship the LORD after a significant encounter. We've seen that with Noah (Genesis 8:20) and with Abraham (Genesis 12:7-8), Isaac and Jacob (Genesis 26:25; 35:7).

The translation "banner" is probably incorrect in this verse. It later became used in that manner, but at this time the word was used of a signal pole around which an army would rally for instruction. The rod (*nes*) was something like a flagpole. Since the rod of God represented the authority of God, Moses was saying that the rod represented God. JHWH is my rallying rod. He is the One we Israelites gather around for our war briefing. He is where we go for our battle tactics and instructions.

16 saying, "A hand upon the throne of the LORD! The LORD will have war with Amalek from generation to generation." The translation here is also in question. NIV *"for hands were lifted to the throne of the Lord"* point one to think Moses meant it was his prayers that won the battle. That, however, is not the case. ESV has a better translation here, *"A hand upon the throne of the LORD!"* It can be understood in two different ways. One is that God's hand is on His throne swearing by His throne that He will have war with Amalek for generations to come. Since Moses' hand was mentioned it is more likely that it refers to Moses' hands on the pole that symbolized the throne of God, the authority of God. The latter would point to the sovereignty of God in winning the battle. Moses' hand was on the symbol of the throne, meaning God was right there with them.

The passage has revealed another name of God and therefore something of God we should remember. He is JHWH *Nissi*! Like Israel, we will face battles in life. God allows them. He guides us to them. He plans that we not face too much at one time. He uses them to train us to look to Him.

Here, in another test, they did look to God, to the authority that staff represented. You could say this was one of the great moments of the wilderness wandering, because they followed through on the last lesson. They learned to listen to God and look to Him. They believed that His authority could conquer their enemy.

One of our greatest enemies is the flesh, our old nature! We drag it around with us like a dead corpse, but it is always ready to resurrect itself and take our life over if we will just listen to it for a moment. Like Amelek, it is opportunistic. It takes advantage of our weaknesses. It probes for any opening in which it can come in and rob our soul. It aims to steal our righteousness, our joy, and our peace. It would take us captive, if possible, to serve it again. (Romans 6:4)

All of us have weaknesses. All of us come under attack. It can be anger, or lust, or greed or any number of fleshly weaknesses that he attacks. We need a rally point. We need a place to go where we can look and be encouraged. JHWH is the pole, the banner to which we turn. (Isaiah 51:5)

In another declaration that YHWH and Jesus are the same, Isaiah predicted that banner would be Jesus. Isaiah 11:10 (ESV) *10 In that day the root of Jesse, who shall stand as a signal* (NIV- banner Hebrew - *nes*) *for the peoples—of him shall the nations inquire, and his resting place shall be glorious*. Jesus has become the rallying pole for those who have received His salvation, and isn't His rest glorious. (Hebrews 3:14-15) We run there to inquire of Him exactly how to resist the flesh, and we have found rest for our souls.

And just as Moses clung to the rod that represented the throne of God, brothers and sisters, we cling to another pole, the cross of Calvary. In clinging to the cross we cling to the Throne of God, for it was God's sovereign power and authority that caused Jesus to be the sacrifice for our sins. (Isaiah 53:4) That pole is lifted high and draws us all to Jesus. (John 12:32 ; In John 3:14-15, Jesus referred to Numbers 21:8 that uses the same Hebrew word *nes* to describe the cross.) It is there we see the love that flows from the throne of God. It is there that we know Amalek – the flesh, will be defeated. God is at war with it in every generation.

We know we can't fight the battle alone. If we don't look to the pole, if we don't remind ourselves that He wins His battles and nothing is too hard for Him, if we look at our own ability, the flesh begins to take the upper hand. But then we look back to the cross and we know, no power on earth or in hell can stop Him. I am His chosen child and He is my Almighty God. He will perfect that which concerns me. (Psalm 138:8) He will finish the work He began. (Philippians 1:6) I will stand on the other shore and see Him face to face and the work will be complete. Amalek will be annihilated once and for all. His evil marauding will come to an end. The trumpet will sound and the work will be done! Hallelujah! (1John 3:2)

Remember, we will be at war until that day comes, but God has promised to be at war with Amalek too. And God has promised that Amalek's days will come to an end! So fight on! Stand firm! But most of all, keep your eyes on the rally pole, our banner, the cross that represents God's final sovereign victory. (Hebrews 12:2) When your eyes are fixed there, you will find you are fighting with His strength. You will not give in to fear or forget that His authority is supreme. With that courage, you will not turn and run, but will march on to victory by the grace of God! (1Thessalonians 5:23-24)

Questions
1 Why is Amalek foolish?
2 What was their evil tactic?
3 What were the Israelites learning?
4 Why was sight of the rod important for the soldiers?
5 Why didn't Moses do this alone?
6 What did God promise to do to Amalek?
7 Why did Moses build an altar?
8 What is the new name of God?
9 How can we relate to it?
10 What is our nes?
11 How can we relate to this story?

Saved x 2 Exodus 18

Imagine having been in Moses' sandals those last three months. What an amazing adventure! He'd met the burning bush, tried to get out of the mission but God won't let him. His brother met him and together you encounter Pharaoh. God humiliates the imaginary Egyptian gods, one by one. The nation experienced the first Passover, walked through the sea, and saw their enemy drown. Then they experienced the tests, the thirst, the craving of food, and the last experience was the defeat of the Amalekites where God showed Himself to be JHWH *Nissi*, the Lord our Signal Pole. (Exodus 17:15)

Just as God had promised, Moses has returned to Sinai. Remember that when Moses needed some reassurance, God told him he would know it was all of God when he returned and served God on this mountain. (Exodus 3:12) Well, here he is back at the mountain, only now there is a lake at the base of the mountain and a new nation. The God that meets people at this mountain had proved Himself to be their source of living water. (1Corinthians 10:4)

There was obviously a word of mouth passing of news in Midian. Remember when Jethro's daughters saw Moses the first time, they knew he was Egyptian. (Exodus 2:19) They knew what an Egyptian dressed like, so they must have had periodic encounters with that culture which would naturally result in the exchange of news. Part of this probably came about through trade. Jethro had "heard all that God had done for Moses and Israel".

Moses had gone to seek leave of Jethro after God had given Moses his assignment. (Exodus 4:18) It is very possible that Moses planned to send Zipporah, his wife, and their two sons back to Jethro at the border of Egypt, and arranged for Jethro to meet them at Sinai when he returned.

Some people have argued that Moses had divorced Zipporah because of the phrase in verse 2, "sent her back" *shilluhim*. For every argument to support the idea of divorce there is a counter argument. I do not believe the evidence is strong enough to seriously consider that to be the case. The next verse calls her his wife.

5 Jethro, Moses' father-in-law, came with his sons and his wife to Moses in the wilderness where he was encamped at the mountain of God. The mountain was called the mountain of God when Moses first took Jethro's flocks there. We have archeological evidence that the region worshiped YHWH and also the fact that they descended from Abraham. (Genesis 25:4) Their knowledge of God was limited. It must have been a great encouragement to Jethro to hear the news of Moses' adventure, and to have the confirmation that it had all come to pass as the God of their fathers' had foretold.

Jethro sent word that he was coming and bringing Moses' wife and two sons. *7 Moses went out to meet his father-in-law and bowed down and kissed him. And they asked each other of their welfare and went into the tent.* Does it strike you as strange that after two months of being away from his wife and sons that he would run to greet his father-in-law with a kiss? I can just hear a modern day woman say, "Hey what am I, chopped liver?"

Moses must have been very close to his father-in-law. A great leader would wait in their tent and expect the other party to bow to them, but Moses was a meek man who knew he had little to do with the great things that had occurred. Culturally it is hard for us to relate, but remember Moses has been on a spiritual journey that was probably started by Jethro sending him to the mountain of God. Now Moses has passed up Jethro spiritually and knows that YHWH is more than a tribal deity.

They went into the tent to talk over all that God had done and what Moses had learned about YHWH since they've been apart. It should always be a joy to us when someone we mentor passes us up spiritually and ministers to us. Barnabas and Paul (Acts 13:2) became Paul and Barnabas (Acts 13:43) as the ministry of Paul surpassed that of Barnabas.

Imagine the joy of going over those momentous events, that roller coaster ride of highs and lows. But more than the wonder of any particular miracle was the revelation that YHWH was so great that the Egyptian gods were proved to be worthless. This had little to do with Moses or the people. If anything, Moses may have pointed out his doubts, reluctance to obey, and disappointments in the way God led him. It was all about a gracious and loving God that keeps His promises and has an end in mind that is greater than we could imagine. The increasing revelation of YHWH struck a chord in Jethro's heart. The revelation of God's word through Moses had been confirmed in the plagues and the tests.

10 Jethro said, "Blessed be the LORD, who has delivered you out of the hand of the Egyptians and out of the hand of Pharaoh and has delivered the people from under the hand of the Egyptians. Jethro praised God for all the good He had done for Israel, for their deliverance from captivity and the defeat of Pharaoh. His heart must have been overwhelmed with the assurance that YHWH is indeed Creator God. In fact, the next verses indicate that this is a conversion experience for the priest of Midian, Jethro.

11 Now I know that the LORD is greater than all gods, because in this affair they dealt arrogantly with the people." It sounds as if he was not sure before. Though he probably worshiped YHWH, he had no evidence that the God of that mountain was any greater than the gods of the nations. Now he has more than enough evidence. If he doubted Moses' encounter with YHWH before, he doesn't doubt it now. The impossible has happened. Everything YHWH predicted has come to pass in a greater way than they could possibly have imagined. The arrogant gods of Egypt couldn't stop JHWH.

Do you know that YHWH is greater than all gods, than wealth, than power, than fame, than anything the world has to offer? Is there anything worth pursuing that even comes close to God?

I think that at times we are where Jethro was, wondering if all these promises will really come to pass. We might think Christianity is just another religion. Then God proves Himself to be incomparably great in some way that connects with our heart, and we believe. We realize He is the only thing worth pursuing. The proof is all around us if our eyes are willing to see. (Isaiah 6:3)

Once we believe, we must act on our faith and seal our conviction. *12 And Jethro, Moses' father-in-law, brought a burnt offering and sacrifices to God; and Aaron came with all the elders of Israel to eat bread with Moses' father-in-law before God.* A burnt offering is the complete consummation of an animal by fire. (Leviticus 1:9) It implies the complete dedication of the life with nothing held back. Jethro also brought additional sacrifices, portions of which may have been shared with Moses over the fellowship meal. He was a believer.

It's pretty amazing when a priest can humble himself and receive what his former disciple brings as a more complete revelation. Jethro believes, and he has acted in solemn ceremony sealing that conviction. Sacrificial worship went all the way back to the sons of Adam. (Genesis 4:4) Jethro knew about God but the text leads me to believe that this was when he came to know God personally.

The passage says they ate before God. This might mean they ate before the altar but I think it meant they ate before the pillar of cloud. Jethro had to be moved by that manifest presence of God.

Eating together in the ancient world implied friendship and peace with those at the table. To eat before God implies to be at peace with God. (Exodus 24:11) Though Jethro may not have fully understood it, that sacrifice looked forward to God's provision. That is the only way man can be at peace with God, the sacrifice of Jesus, the Son of God. (Romans 5:1)

What a joyous reunion that was! But the next day it was back to work for Moses. The people were just getting use to being free. As slaves, they really had no rights. Now they were a free people with their own property. They were also a new nation. They had to know how to deal with the many situations that arose among them. Do you have a right to buy back something you sold for the same price? What if someone is watching your animals and one is stolen? Are they liable? What kind of restitution do you deserve if someone knocks out one of your teeth? There were all kinds of questions about actual disputes.

13 The next day Moses sat to judge the people, and the people stood around Moses from morning till evening. The judge sits while the plaintiff and defendant stand, even as it is today. As their leader and prophet, Moses had to ask God for the rules for this new nation. Jethro watched a full day of this and asked Moses why he operated that way.

15 And Moses said to his father-in-law, "Because the people come to me to inquire of God; NIV translates it that they come to seek God's will. Moses was their priest. He heard from God. So Moses explained to Jethro that he had to get the laws for the new nation from God. Each situation required that he find out the rule to establish a standard. Moses was creating the first genuine theocracy. The law of God was to rule and God was the final judge. The laws and the religion were one. The king and the prophet were one.

Some people want a theocracy today. That won't happen until Jesus returns. Jesus said, "My kingdom is not of this world." (John 18:36) We cannot legislate righteousness. In a democracy, we can vote for godly principles; we can even encourage the Christian faith, but we will never be a theocracy. That is the real reason for separation of church and state. We need freedom of religion not freedom from religion. Even Israel will later have a king and a high priest. The man that tried to do both was stricken by God. (2Chronicles 26:19) Any nation that claims to be one is dangerous because man is at the head claiming the authority that belongs to God. This is what Islam would like to force upon the world.

17 Moses' father-in-law said to him, "What you are doing is not good. 18 You and the people with you will certainly wear yourselves out, for the thing is too heavy for you. You are not able to do it alone. After Jethro's conversion and now a day of observation, he had some advice for Moses. "You can't do it alone." One commentator writes that this is the world's wisdom interjected upon the new nation and that it resulted in the Sanhedrin that killed Jesus. At the same time the author claims that Jethro was converted.

Is there room for common sense in the Kingdom of God? Of course there is! But it isn't so common, and the Holy Spirit can at anytime override it with the uncommon. The converted soul will find it more and more common to them. Jethro could see Moses was trying to do too much and it was frustrating for the people.

Sometimes leaders like to be the go to person. They like the attention and the feeling of importance, of being indispensable, but God is the only indispensable One. Had Moses' asked for a solution? If so, perhaps Jethro's advice was the answer. God's will is usually what is best for you and for everyone involved. Moses was working himself to death and the people were tired of waiting. It was too heavy a burden, and he needed help.

19 Now obey my voice; I will give you advice, and God be with you! You shall represent the people before God and bring their cases to God, 20 and you shall warn them about the statutes and the laws, and make them know the way in which they must walk and what they must do. Jethro wasn't asking Moses to deny his calling. He was still to hear from God and warn the people of how they must live to please God. But he didn't need to deal with every single little issue or ones that already had a precedent that they could follow.

21 Moreover, look for able men from all the people, men who fear God, who are trustworthy and hate a bribe, and place such men over the people as chiefs of thousands, of hundreds, of fifties, and of tens. This is a figurative way to say that there needed to be a judicial hierarchy, not literally a judge for every ten people. I imagine in most cases the elders became the judges. They would memorize laws that had been given by God to Moses. They were to be men who had the fear of God and hated bribes. It is the basis for our Western judicial system today! (Deuteronomy 1:15-17)

If the case was appealed or the judge could not make a decision, the case worked its way up the ladder until it reached Moses. He was the Supreme Court. He took the matters to God. He would go to the Tent of Meeting and present the case before the LORD. This is where much of the Levitical Law originated. Some people think it came from Moses meeting God on Sinai. That was true for the Ten Commandments and the instructions for the Tabernacle, but the rest came from Moses inquiring about cases before God.

Wouldn't it be great if today the qualification of a judge was that they feared God and hated a bribe? Many of the original American colonies required political candidates to be a believer in Jesus Christ and the Bible to run for office. We have drifted so very far that is difficult to get a judge on the Supreme Court if they do profess a faith in Jesus as Lord.

Leaders need to share the burden of leading. Authority must be delegated to keep any one individual from burning out. *22 And let them judge the people at all times. Every great matter they shall bring to you, but any small matter they shall decide themselves. So it will be easier for you, and they will bear the burden with you.* Just as Aaron and Hur had held up Moses' arms during the battle with Amalek, godly men need to come alongside Moses to help in judging the cases that arose in Israel.

The next verse shows us that Jethro expected Moses to check his advice with the LORD. After hearing the testimony to date of Moses' experiences with God, Jethro surely had no doubt that Moses would do that. *23 If you do this, God will direct you, you will be able to endure, and all this people also will go to their place in peace."* In other words, "God will direct you! You'll see that it is within God's will to share the burden. You'll see that you weren't meant to do it alone. You'll keep from being overworked and breaking down, and the people will get a timely answer." This is the basis for a speedy or timely trial.

Moses followed the advice of his father-in-law and found it was of God. The people chose the men and Moses appointed them to their positions. (Deuteronomy 1:13-15) These were not inherited positions but were appointed on the basis of their integrity. This is very similar to the selection of elders in the church Jesus established, and for the same reason. One man can't do it all. He would burn out and the people would be frustrated. (Galatians 6:2)

Even a new believer can be inspired with a common sense solution to a problem. Nations have followed the Jethro pattern and found it very helpful. If one judge is out of line, the others higher up will see the mistake and correct it. At the top should be those most qualified. All along the ladder should be judges who seek apply the law that should conform to the will of God. This is where we get a nation of laws. At the top, they look to their constitution (or Torah for the Jews) for clues as to the guidelines for their decisions because of the conviction that the constitution was inspired. The whole system goes back to Moses' father-in-law.

While our secular judges are bound by law and precedent that may or may not be inspired, our elders are to look to Scripture and pray to discern the leading of the Holy Spirit. (1Peter 5:2-3)

What can chapter 18 teach us today? No matter how anointed we are, we need help. (Ecclesiastes 4:9) This is the reason the church descriptions always consist of a unit with many parts. (1Corinthians 12:12) Moses led Jethro to salvation, but then Jethro led Moses to a practical salvation. Overwork is just as detrimental to us as an individual and a family as laziness can be. Are you trying to do too much? Do you need to delegate something to others? Find that balance that God has for you and you'll be more effective. God is concerned about the physical and practical as well as the spiritual. What a gracious God we serve! How can you help others that are overworked?

Let's also consider that the testimony of God at work in our lives can win others to faith. Bring them into your tent and share the story of what God has done! (Mark 5:19) Maybe you, like Jethro knew of God but you need to recognize He is God of all creation, the only God, and give your whole life to Him, as represented in the burnt offering. Nothing else is worth pursuing with your whole heart!

Questions
1 What kind of relationship did Jethro and Moses have?
2 What was the first thing they did?
3 What converted Jethro?
4 How did he express His worship?
5 What did he observe the next day?
6 What was the situation?
7 What was Moses explanation?
8 What was Jethro's solutions?
9 Why might we believe it was of God?
10 How is it applied today?
11 What's missing today?
12 What is your application?

Prepare To Meet God! Exodus 19

Two months into the journey and they have arrived, but what a disappointment! It was no land of milk and honey, rather it was barren desert mountain. And this was the place to which Moses was so excited to return? It was sure an exciting two months, but now this? Gathered around the lake that just formed at the base of Sinai, the people must have been discouraged, and that means Moses would have been tempted to be disheartened.

God knew that it would come to this even before Moses left for Egypt, so *12 He said, "But I will be with you, and this shall be the sign for you, that I have sent you: when you have brought the people out of Egypt, you shall serve God on this mountain."* Exodus 3:12 (ESV) The prediction had come to pass. That sign must have encouraged Moses that he was walking obediently in God's will in spite of the problems he had had with the people. (Exodus 17:4)

But what does it mean to "serve God on this mountain"? Remember, to serve also had the implication of worship. (Matthew 6:24) The people were serving Pharaoh, but now they are freed to serve God. The rest of the book of Exodus will flush out all that entails for the nation of Israel.

Though they are headed to the land promised to the patriarchs, Sinai is their primary destination. The last two months have been a crash course in preparing them to hear and receive the Word of God.

That is true in many of our lives. We had to come to the end of our self and see over and over that we need God. We had to get hungry and thirsty (spiritually) before we were at a place where we were ready to hear and obey. (Matthew 5:6) We had to face an enemy and find God was the only way to win the battle. Then we are ready to listen, and that is the primary destination of everyone! God works in every life to bring them to a place where they can receive His Word.

They were redeemed by the blood of the lamb (Exodus 12:13), delivered from bondage, baptized in the Red Sea, (1Corinthians 10:2) but they still needed to discern His voice and learn His laws for their life. Sound familiar?

Obeying God's Word does not earn us any favor with Him. They were already redeemed. The grace of God preceded the Law of God. But the Scriptures are our instruction manual in how to live a life that is pleasing to Him. One of the first signs that we are redeemed is our desire for the Word, and that is because we have a desire to please our Savior. (Psalm 119:2-3)

The rest of the book of Exodus takes place in this location of Sinai. About one year will pass while they are camped there. Moses will climb this mountain to meet with God seven times.

3 while Moses went up to God. The LORD called to him out of the mountain, saying, "Thus you shall say to the house of Jacob, and tell the people of Israel: 4 You yourselves have seen what I did to the Egyptians, and how I bore you on eagles' wings and brought you to myself. As Moses was going up the mountain, God called out to him. This is the first ascent. It sounds like God gave him the orders before Moses reached his destination.

First, God wanted them to keep in mind what He had done for them. Verse 4 is a summary of chapters 6-19. He had borne them on eagles' wings. Eagles will shove their chicks out of the nest when they get too big. If they left them alone they would just stay there waiting for mom to feed them and eventually starve. She has to push them off the edge of the nest, but then soars after them to catch them if they don't catch the wind. (Proverbs 30:18-19)

God had shoved the Israelites out of the nest. They were definitely floundering. Considering their threats to stone Moses, we might say they were dropping like a rock. (Deuteronomy 32:11) With each fall, God swooped under them and spared them as He patiently taught them that flying meant trusting in Him. (Isaiah 63:9) They indeed caught the wind in the battle with Amalek, but now they need to learn how to thrive. Remember how God has caught you. Remember the flight lessons! (Isaiah 40:31)

And what did God say was the destination? "brought you to myself." It was the presence of the Lord. God delivers us so that He can bring us to Himself. (Matthew 11:28) He does it all because He wants to be with us. That is an incredible thing, especially in the light of the rest of this chapter, as the holiness of God threatens to destroy anyone who would get too close! Keep that dynamic tension in mind.

Next, Moses was to relay their special relationship with God. *5 Now therefore, if you will indeed obey my voice and keep my covenant, you shall be my treasured possession among all peoples, for all the earth is mine*; The question that immediately arises is whether or not the "if" is related to their salvation. In chapter 6 verse 7 God already declared, *7a I will take you to be my people and I will be your God...* In 2:24 God already called them His firstborn son.

Treasured possession must therefore mean a special relationship with God that the redeemed may enter into IF they are obedient and keep the covenant. Obedience isn't part of a two-sided deal; it is the expression of gratitude for what God has done.

God added that if they obey His voice and keep the covenant they also shall be to me a kingdom of priests and a holy nation. The main idea in being a kingdom of priests is their access to King. Yes, they would end up in the Promised Land, which was the crossroads of the world's trade routes. There they would have the Court of the Gentiles, a house of prayer for all nations. (Isaiah 56:7) They could convey the words given to Moses and the prophets to those on the trade routes. Some prophets would even be sent to other nations. But first and foremost, it meant access to the King of the kingdom.

God was about to descend from the mountain and meet with them. To meet with God is the high privilege of all believers. We are a kingdom of priests because of the blood of Jesus that makes us holy. (1Peter 2:9)

Moses was to deliver this threefold message of God. Remember how God brought you to Himself. You must listen and obey, then you'll have the privilege of being His treasured possession, a nation of priests. J. A. Motyer remarks that this pattern is extremely important in understanding the pattern of Scripture and our place as the covenant people of God within it. The sequence is this: the saving acts of the LORD, our response of obedience, and the blessings obedience brings. That is why verse 4 is past tense and 5 and 6 are future tense.

    The telltale characteristics of a child of God are that they keep, listen to, and obey the Word of God. When they do, they are a treasured possession. They have access to the very throne of God. Please don't misunderstand this point. All who place their faith in what Jesus did for them have the righteousness of God in Christ Jesus, but it is when we walk in disobedience that our intimacy with God is broken. (Isaiah 59:2;1Peter 3:7) We may still be in covenant, in other words be in saving grace, but like someone who has stubbornly ignored their spouses sincere requests, we avoid their presence. (Psalm 66:18) It is when we serve each other that we really treasure one another. Would God want you to represent Him when you are walking in disobedience? He treasures you because you are in Jesus, but He doesn't treasure a condition of disobedience.

    Moses hurried down the mountain to relay the Word of God to the people. 8 All the people answered together and said, *"All that the LORD has spoken we will do."* And Moses reported the words of the people to the LORD. Moses got an unequivocal "Yes!" from the people. They declared they would be obedient. They wanted to be God's treasured possession. After all they have seen, the amazing intervention, the miraculous provision, and the defeat of their enemies, who wouldn't want to have access to this God?

    Moses headed back up the mountain to give God the answer. This is trip number two. *9 And the LORD said to Moses, "Behold, I am coming to you in a thick cloud, that the people may hear when I speak with you, and may also believe you forever."* God would appear to the people as a theophany. When they hear God speak the Ten Words they will know Moses truly does "talk with God".

    Clouds throughout the Scripture became a picture of the presence of God. A cloud was God's presence leading them through the wilderness. (Exodus 13:21) Jesus ascended in the clouds and will return with clouds. (Acts 1:9-11) The idea is that God's unveiled glory would be too great for any human being to witness. God must hide the bulk of His glory from being manifest or we would die. (Exodus 33:20)

    Just as we will see a consuming fire to be representative of His glory, the holiness of God will not abide the presence of evil. (Habakkuk 1:13) When the tabernacle will be built, the priest must enter the Holy of Holies in a cloud of incense. It is not that God can't see through it, it is that we need to understand that we are so sinful, that were it not for the grace, mercy, and love of God, His justice and holiness would rightly consume us. We Americans have almost completely lost this fear of God. The Proverbs tell us the fear of God is the beginning of wisdom. (Proverbs 1:7)

God's next instructions to Moses are along this same vein of thought. *10 the LORD said to Moses, "Go to the people and consecrate them today and tomorrow, and let them wash their garments 11 and be ready for the third day. For on the third day the LORD will come down on Mount Sinai in the sight of all the people. 12 And you shall set limits for the people all around, saying, 'Take care not to go up into the mountain or touch the edge of it. Whoever touches the mountain shall be put to death. 13 No hand shall touch him, but he shall be stoned or shot; whether beast or man, he shall not live.' When the trumpet sounds a long blast, they shall come up to the mountain."*

The people had three days to prepare to meet God. They were certainly an unholy people, and no amount of preparation on their part could make them holy, but God wanted the idea to sink in. There would be space even between the veiled glory of God and the people in the most consecrated condition they could muster.

There are limits to what God will put up with. These limits around the holy mountain where God was to come down are also pictures of the boundaries of God's grace. Moses could go up anytime, for he was God's servant. God had already dealt with his heart. But the nation was still entertaining idolatry and unsure if JHWH is the only true God.

God is dangerous! Or as the Chronicles of Narnia so aptly state it, "He's not safe, but He's good!" In fact, He's so good that He obliterates evil. He is like antimatter on evil. It must be dealt with if it is in His holy presence. (Isaiah 6:5)

Moses went down the mountain again and relayed the need for getting ready to meet God. Moses was acting as a priest, preparing the people to meet God. I don't think they understood the vast gulf between their condition and their holy Creator. Most people today do not grasp their true condition. That is why they cannot understand our desperate need for the Great High Priest that Moses pictured, Jesus. (Hebrews 4:14)

Moses added that there should be no sexual intercourse during this time of preparation. We must understand that he is not implying that sex is evil. There was sex in the Garden before the fall of man. (Genesis 1:28) Sex is a wonderful gift of God to be enjoyed in the confines of marriage. (Hebrews 13:4) But remember, marriage is a picture of our relationship with God. (Ephesians 5:23-24) Sexual relations should be a total giving one person to the other. God had them abstain from that total intimacy to focus on a total intimacy of a different nature, intimacy with Him.

16 On the morning of the third day there were thunders and lightnings and a thick cloud on the mountain and a very loud trumpet blast, so that all the people in the camp trembled. The burning bush was the same manifestation of Almighty God, but now the people need a clearer revelation of God's awesome presence, and that reinforced that gulf between their condition and God.

Have you ever been in the middle of powerful thunderstorm? It's frightening but awesome at the same time. When the light and sound come at the same time, you know it's really close. Your heart pounds. You can feel the burst in the air. Your hair will even stand on end with the electrical charge. Imagine experiencing that and the ground shaking, and the whole mountain is smoking and shaking. The trumpet grows louder and louder until your ears can hardly take it. You know the holy God that struck down the firstborn, is coming to meet with you.

You've heard me say it before, but we need the reminder. Every time we pray we should imagine grabbing hold of the ends of two giant downed power lines. We come before Almighty God. If it were not for the blood of Jesus we would be consumed in an instant. (Hebrews 10:31)

God called Moses up the mountain again and God repeated the rules about boundaries and even warned the priests that they too must be sure they are consecrated. The office does not automatically make them holy. The same is obviously true with pastors and elders. We must be sure our lives are sanctified. (Hebrews 12:14)

Moses seemed to think this was unnecessary, but God sees things man doesn't see. God has no desire to destroy life. He is always seeking to transform the wicked. (Ezekiel 18:23) He wants His grace to prevail, but He must be just. It may be that there was a temptation to step into the cloud and try to see more of the glory of God. That would be fatal to someone who wasn't sanctified.

Moses went down the mountain again and made sure the people and the priests understood. The man of God obeys even when he doesn't understand. When all was as God instructed, God came down the mountain and spoke the Ten Words. They are the Ten Words that were to guide the community of Israel. He gave order to creation with ten words and now He is giving order to a nation with ten words.

The holy and awesome God spoke to man. Through His Word He became intimate with man. This is the marriage ceremony of Israel and JHWH.

Do you see the parallel to what Jesus did for us? Mankind needs to be prepared to meet God, to receive His word. Jesus' teaching made it clear that the gulf between us and God is great. (John 3:3) Jesus described the punishment of hell that awaits those who are not prepared to meet God. (Matthew 5:29-30) But then Jesus made a way for us to be holy.

The glory of God was manifest on the cross. Yes, the sky went dark, the ground shook, but the real glory was the man on the cross who was bearing the wrath of a righteous God for your sins and mine. He entered the darkness of the cloud and the wrath of God fell on Him as He bore all our sins. (Matthew 27:45) The veil in the Temple that kept people from the presence of God was torn. (Matthew 27:51) He made it safe for us to enter the cloud by giving us His righteousness, making us holy before a holy God. (Hebrews 7:19)

As a man, Jesus blazed the way for us into the presence of God. (Hebrews 9:11-12) If we will hear His words and obey them, which is only possible because He makes us a new creation, the promise of being a treasured possession, a kingdom of priests, becomes ours. (1John 2:5-6;

1Peter 2:5) We can walk in disobedience and have our prayers hindered, but why would you want to?

The plan has never changed. It is just more fully revealed. God is still as awesome and holy, but through Jesus, God brings us to Himself! (Hebrews 8:6) The tension between God's desire for intimacy and the distance between a holy God and us is done away in Christ Jesus. In Jesus, the boundaries are lifted, and you can enter into the cloud. Are you grabbing a hold of those power lines?

Questions
1 What was the primary destination? Why?
2 What is one of the first signs of conversion?
3 What is the picture of being borne on eagle's wings?
4 …for what purpose?
5 Discuss the dynamic tension in the chapter.
6 What does the "if" and "then" relate to in verse 5?
7 What is "treasured possession"?
8 What is a "nation of priests" imply?
9 What is the pattern in verses 4 and 5?
10 How did God convey the need to fear Him?
11 Why the abstaining from sexual relations?
12 Go over the trips up and down the mountain and their purpose.

Ten Words (part 1) Exodus 20:1-12

Let's remember what has just taken place. Moses has gone up and down the mountain three times already. The people have agreed to abide by the laws that God is about to give. They have been given three days to sanctify themselves. They have been warned not to touch the mountain or try to go into the cloud to see God lest they die. The priests were warned that they too must consecrate themselves. Then, God came down!

What does that mean? Since God is a spirit that is present everywhere, how can He come down? It is for our sake that God manifests Himself in a physical form so that we can relate. God isn't a cloud, or the lightening and thunder, or the shaking of the mountain, or even a voice. All those things are to help us relate to His glory, holiness and power. To "come down" points to God's transcendence and that He graciously stoops down and enters our fallen world. (Psalm 11:4) The manifestations are to help us understand His nature and our relationship to Him. That is especially true of Jesus, the incarnation of God. (John 1:14)

God has come down and will now speak to the people. We know from verse 22 that this is not just God alone with Moses. God will have Moses climb the mountain again and be with Him for 40 days, during which time the commandments etched by God's finger into two stone tablets.

We need to place ourselves there with the trembling Israelites and imagine the sites and sounds to get the full impact. The ground is shaking.

The mountain is smoking. Trumpet blasts fill the air. Suddenly a voice overrides it all and declares, *2 "I am the LORD your God, who brought you out of the land of Egypt, out of the house of slavery. 3 "You shall have no other gods before me.*

The God that showed the Egyptian gods to be worthless, the God that defeated Pharaoh and his armies, the God that parted the sea and led them through the wilderness was the God that was speaking. He communicates with us in words, in comprehensible language. He created languages, and He chose Hebrew to communicate to the world the words of order. It has been said that ten words brought order from chaos at the creation of the world. Now, ten words were being delivered to bring order to a chaotic new nation and all of civilization.

The first four instructions have to do with our relationship to, and worship of, the God that delivered Israel from bondage. The fifth is a transitional command, and the last five are the basis of how we relate to one another. The first group Jesus summed up as loving God with all your heart, soul, and mind, and the second group as loving your neighbor as yourself. (Matthew 22:37-39) Today we'll just be looking at the first five and I'll give you some tips to help you remember them.

Let us first set our thinking right side up. The world teaches us distorted ways of thinking. We commonly see rules to be confining and limiting our freedom. The opposite is true. The Law of God is the truest form of liberty. (John 8:31-32)

Look at the Garden of Eden. God had one rule. You can enjoy everything freely, just don't eat of the tree of the knowledge of good and evil. (Genesis 2:16-17) That was the freest man has ever been, but there was an unbendable law and breaking it was punishable by death. When Satan deceived Eve into thinking she was denied freedom, she yielded to the temptation and lost the freedom she once had. (Genesis 3:1) Sin creates bondage. Sin is not freedom. (John 8:34) Obedience to God's laws is the path to freedom. (Psalm 119:156) Other gods enslave; living without rest enslaves; murder, lying, adultery, and every broken law of God will end in a loss of freedom. So let's first change our mindset about what the Law does for us, as this speaks to the motivation of the Law Giver, which is love. (Psalm 119:64)

The first Word is God is first. Number one is that God is number one. Nothing should come before God! In regards to our modern culture and its gods, John MacArthur wrote the following: Self-expression, moral freedom, materialism, and hedonism are the prevailing gods. Those gods, as clearly pagan as any in the ancient Greek or Roman pantheons, have inevitably spawned the epidemic breakdown of families, illegitimate births, sexual evils of every sort, unequaled growth of drug addiction and crime, and the wanton destruction of unborn babies. In the name of intellectual and scientific progress, godless philosophies have long dominated secular as well as much private education.

These are the gods that enslave most of the world today. We pay tribute to them in our commercials, with our material wealth, and in our daily conversations. They are as worthless as the gods of Egypt, Greece, or Rome. (1Samuel 12:21) They only enslave and destroy. Why would we even consider putting them before God? They do offer a temporary pleasure to the senses, but the price is the destruction of our body and soul, and they eventually destroy our culture. No wonder God demands that they must not take His place.

4 "You shall not make for yourself a carved image, or any likeness of anything that is in heaven above, or that is in the earth beneath, or that is in the water under the earth. God is not prohibiting art as some have taken this to mean. He is prohibiting the worship of any object or shape. He is a spirit. (John 4:24) The things that we fashion are merely a copy of something He created. The Egyptians made amulets in the shape of the animal that represented a god, such as a dung beetle or a cow. They would bow before it. God was commanding them to forsake that practice.

5 You shall not bow down to them or serve them, for I the LORD your God am a jealous God, visiting the iniquity of the fathers on the children to the third and the fourth generation of those who hate me, 6 but showing steadfast love to thousands of those who love me and keep my commandments. Sin has generational effects. The consequences of our sin affect our children. In other passages, God clearly declares that each person suffers for his own sin and not that of his fathers. (Ezekiel 18:20) Is this a contradiction? I believe God is warning us that our actions affect our children's mindset and patterns of behavior. Then they will suffer for their own sin. Notice God does not say He hates them but that their iniquity is visited upon the following generations of those who hate God. It is a well-known fact that the abused often become abusers. The child of a criminal is likely to be incarcerated. You can probably identify good and bad patterns that you developed from watching how your parents dealt with life.

When I do marriage counseling I have the couple do a chart of their parents and the good and bad habits they acquired from them so their spouse will know what they are dealing with. It is my conviction that God is warning those who would hear these commands that obeying them blesses their descendants far down their family line, while disobeying them will create problems for next few generations.

In this verse God declares that the reason for the command is His jealousy. Human jealousy is often selfish envy of something that steals the affection of someone we desire. That is ungodly.

Is God jealous over your worship of a little golden image of a cow? Let's be clear, He is not jealous of the cow, but jealous for your heart. The godly jealousy of our Creator is a burning love that desires us to be absorbed in what is good. He is good. Idolatry is always destructive. God's jealousy is a passion to see you live in a way that is best for you, and that is to be in a love relationship with Him. An idol is anything that comes between you and God. (1John 5:21)

When we think of the first commandments, we should read into it a passionate love. Allow me to say it how I think of it. "I love you so much, I forbid you from destroying your life and that of you children and their children on worthless things that distract you from my love for you."

Here is that wonderful word again, *hesed,* God's steadfast love (mercy – KJV). But notice that it is not the general love that He has for all mankind. It is shown to those who love Him and keep His commands. God is saying that those who choose iniquity hate Him. Those who choose to keep His commands do so because they love Him. (John 14:15) God demonstrates His steadfast love to those who love Him.

God is telling us we have a choice. We can see our sins affect our children, or we can see His steadfast love on their lives. Thousands implies a thousand generations which is the wording in Deuteronomy 7:9. Which have you chosen? It is one or the other!

We can remember the second command is not to bow down to idols by thinking of the number two as someone on their knees bowing before an idol. But don't forget that our idols today are materialism, hedonism, and self-exaltation. Our bowing down can be how much time we spend focused on those pursuits. (2Kings 17:41)

7 "You shall not take the name of the LORD your God in vain, for the LORD will not hold him guiltless who takes his name in vain. Contrary to popular thinking, this is not primarily using God's name as a curse word. That meaning is implied (Leviticus 24:10-16), but this is mainly referring to using God's name as an oath and then not keeping the oath, in other words, in a dishonest way. (19:12; Deuteronomy 5:11) This is why we promise to tell the truth with our hand on the Bible. It reminds us that we are in the presence of God, and aware of His power to judge us. To use His name in vain is to invoke His presence as a witness and then do something that is ungodly.

In one sense we do that quite easily by saying we are a Christian and then doing something ungodly. When someone tells you they will never hire a Christian contractor, it is because they experienced someone taking God's name in vain.

We can remember this is command number three by picturing the number three as a drawing of lips. Our lips should not take His name in vain. If you've said you are a Christian, you better glorify God with your behavior.

8 "Remember the Sabbath day, to keep it holy. We have discussed this one recently when the command was given to not collect manna on the Sabbath. (Exodus 16:29) The early church changed their day of worship to the first day of the week as Christ rose on Sunday and Pentecost took place on Sunday as well. (1Corinthians 16:2) Once again, Romans 14 gives us the New Testament guidelines in regards to sacred days. *5 One person esteems one day as better than another, while another esteems all days alike. Each one should be fully convinced in his own mind.* Romans 14:5 (ESV)

A day to enjoy God and His goodness is not only healthy spiritually but physically and emotionally as well. Sunday is a good day to do that because we worship on Sunday, but for many it is not possible to take the day off. God is not demanding that the letter of the Law be meticulously kept, but rather is looking to see if we want to please Him by keeping the spirit of the law. Jesus is our Sabbath rest. We cease from our own works and find our spiritual rest in His accomplished work. (Hebrews 4:3, 10)

We should note that the passage is not only for the Hebrews but also for everyone, servants, travelers, and even working farm animals. God cares about all His creation. Productivity actually increases when you take regular periods of rest.

We can remember command number four by picturing a four as a person standing with arms straight out and bent upward from the elbows in prayer.

The fifth command is a transitional one. *12 "Honor your father and your mother, that your days may be long in the land that the LORD your God is giving you.* I refer to this command as transitional because the first commands are about our relationship with God and the last about our relationship with one another. This is about our relations with others, but it also speaks to our relationship with God. Jesus calls God our heavenly Father. (Matthew 6:9) Our earthly parents are supposed to be an example of the heavenly Father. We honor them because God placed them in authority over us. (Titus 3:1) They gave us life. They nurture and care for us. All those things are true of God. Jesus and Paul both referred to the importance of this command (Mark 7:10; Ephesians 6:1-3; 1 Timothy 5:4)

This is the only commandment that comes with a promise attached. If you want to live a long life, you'll obey this one! We can remember commandment five as being in the center and related to God the Father and our earthly father and mother as authority in the center of our life.

We can show honor not only by obedience, but also by respecting them, looking for the good qualities they possess, and caring for them in their old age. Remember, we will all be in their shoes one day, and we should do unto others as we would have others do to us. (Luke 6:31)

Some parents are poor examples of our heavenly father. Their children struggle with the idea of God as a heavenly father. Nevertheless, we honor them because we honor authority. All authority is in place by God's permissive will. (1Peter 2:13-14)

Our culture once respected authority and honored those that served in government. In the 1960s, our culture rebelled against authority. There are always those that abuse the authority that is given them, from police to pastors, but the office they represent should still be respected. Respecting authority is respecting God who allowed the authority to be in place. Without authority, there would be no order. One thing worse than bad authority is no authority.

The popular opinion today is to judge each situation without any universal truth but rather how it feels to you at the moment. It's referred to as situational ethics.

The commands of God however, teach us that there is no such thing. What is in accord with the character and nature of God is truth in all cultures and at all times. All people in every age should recognize that there is only one true God. They should worship Him alone. They should never dishonor His name or take it lightly. They should set aside time to worship Him and to rest because He set that example of a day of rest for us. They are invited to enter His rest. They should honor their parents. These truths are always valid. Take any of them out of life, a home, or a culture and you will see the iniquities of the fathers that hate God visited upon their children.

Can you see it in our culture? I've watched the change in my lifetime. There has been a steady erosion of these principles. Those of you that are older have witnessed even more of a change. However, we are only responsible for our own decisions. We can choose to show our love for God by obedience to His commands. We can have the promise of His love affecting a thousand generations after us. We can walk in the blessing of being His treasured possession, a nation of priests. (Exodus 19:5-6) Regardless of where our nation goes, we can see God's blessing on our own life and the lives of our children.

Some would ask if these laws are still applicable. Didn't Jesus do away with the Law by nailing it to the cross? (Colossians 2:14) As we get into the Laws that governed the nation, we'll see that many of the laws were related to ritual worship, health, and societal rules for the nation. They were rules that separated Israel from the world as God's unique people. The Ten Words, however, are moral principles that are forever valid for all people.

Jesus did fulfill the Law in our place, and the Laws that separate Jew and Gentile were done away with by Jesus that we might be one. (Ephesians 2:14-15) The moral principles, however, remain forever because they are a reflection of the nature of our unchanging God. In fact, Jeremiah predicted that when the new covenant came, God would write them on our hearts. (Jeremiah 31:33)

We don't keep these principles to earn favor with God. As we'll see next week, that is not possible. We have all broken them consistently. We strive to keep them, with the help of the Holy Spirit, because we are grateful for the forgiveness that has brought us salvation through the cross of Jesus. These commands are guidelines for those who love God. That is why we should remember them, meditate on them, and strive to let them guide our life each day. (Psalm 119:97)

Let's see if you can remember the first five from the pictures we've associated with each. 1 – God is to be number one in our life. 2 – You should never bow to an idol (an idol is anything that comes between you and God) 3 – Do not take God's name in vain. Use it with respect and dignity it deserves. 4 – remember the Sabbath. Take time to rest and worship. 5 – In the center comes honor for our parents. We honor the authority that God has placed in our lives. He is the ultimate authority. These were the words that thundered from the mountain when God spoke to man.

These are words that bring freedom and order to our life. They set us on the right path, a path in line with God's very nature that we and our children may be blessed. Will you take the time to memorize and meditate on these eternal truths?

Questions

1 What is the setting for this chapter?
2 What is the first Word?
3 What are our idols today?
4 What is the second Word?
5 What are its curses and blessings?
6 What is the motivation for this Word? Explain.
7 What is the third Word and its application?
8 What is the fourth Word? How does Apostle Paul redefine?
9 What is the fifth Word? Why is it transitional?
10 What is the promise it carries?
11 What is the basis for eternal truth?
12 Why are these laws still applicable today?
13 What motivates us to live these Words?

Ten Words part 2 Exodus 20:13-21

How do you know if you are in a liberal church? You know when they call the Ten Commandments the Ten Suggestions!Deuteronomy 6:4-5 (ESV*) 4 "Hear, O Israel: The LORD our God, the LORD is one. 5 You shall love the LORD your God with all your heart and with all your soul and with all your might.* God elaborated on what that meant in the first five commands. Do you remember them?

One: God is number one!
Two: Don't make idols or bow to them.
Three: Don't take God's name in vain.
Four: Remember the Sabbath.
Five: Honor your father and mother.

It is our jealous husband asking to be first in our lives, not because He is selfish but because He wants what is best for us. He doesn't want us thinking less of Him than He truly is. He wants us to reverence and respect Him by honoring His name. He wants us to set aside time for Him. He wants us to honor the His authority in our lives. God wants what any husband would desire of his bride.

Now we move to what Jesus said was like the first great command, loving our neighbor as ourselves. (Romans 13:9) If we honor Him, then we honor those made in His image. We will see the dignity and potential in every human life. That does not mean that everyone reflects the glory of God or expresses His image, but that we all have that potential. (Genesis 9:6)

Here are our guidelines of action toward one another: Command number six spoken in an audible voice to the people declared. *13 "You shall not murder."* The word for murder in Hebrew includes causing the death of another through carelessness or negligence. This does not cover warfare or capital punishment as both are allowed in other passages. (Exodus 21:13; Numbers 21:2-3)

We might assume that we have no problem with this one, but Jesus elaborated on it in a way that includes us all. Matthew 5:21-22 (ESV) 21 *"You have heard that it was said to those of old, 'You shall not murder; and whoever murders will be liable to judgment.' 22 But I say to you that everyone who is angry with his brother will be liable to judgment; whoever insults his brother will be liable to the council; and whoever says, 'You fool!' will be liable to the hell of fire.* Anger with your brother was declared to deserve the same punishment as murder! To express that anger in words was something for which you should be tried in court. To call someone a fool is to balance on the rim of hell!

Why is Jesus so severe? He sees as God sees. He sees the anger in the heart is making selfish demands while forgetting our own need for forgiveness. (Matthew 6:15) He sees what we would do if it were not for the fear of consequences.

When the insult is spoken, it means the thought has gone from the heart to the lips. Action has been taken, and it sets in motion a series of events that leave lifelong scars, and sometimes actually ends in a death. (1John 3:15)

To call someone a fool in Jesus' day was to say that they were godless, without morals, a degenerate. (Psalm 14:1) Jesus said that was dancing with the devil. Satan slanders and accuses. It is the opposite of the of the New Testament command to love one another, to encourage, and build one another up. (Romans 13:10)

Righteous anger is another matter. It is not out of selfish demands but rather from the heart of God that detests evil. Jesus expressed righteous anger several times. (Mark 3:5; John 2:15-17) It had nothing to do with not having His way and everything to do with His opposition to man's stubbornness toward God.

Like the laws regarding our relationship with God, the laws regarding our relationship with man are based on the character of God. Murder is wrong, because God is the life giver. The time of one's passing is God's prerogative, not ours.

You can remember number 6 if you picture a bomb with a fuse. Number six is, "Do not murder".

14 "You shall not commit adultery. The meaning is quite clear, and yet our culture has chosen to ignore this one. Have you noticed how the breaking of these commands is glorified by the film industry? It is the sign of the decline of a civilization. When hedonism becomes the god of choice the end of that society is not far behind.

The Biblical definition of adultery is for a man to have relations with a married woman. Both parties were considered guilty of adultery. Once again, the law is based on God's character. Adultery is wrong because God is faithful. He keeps His word. He keeps His promises. (Numbers 23:19) An adulteress has broken her promise to her husband and the man involved has helped.

Jesus expanded this command as well, and He did so in way that causes most men to shudder. Matthew 5:27-28 (ESV) *27 "You have heard that it was said, 'You shall not commit adultery.' 28 But I say to you that everyone who looks at a woman with lustful intent has already committed adultery with her in his heart.* If you are a man with red blood and testosterone, you have more than likely broken this command. Does that excuse us? No! It does tell us that man is fallen and selfish. (Isaiah 56:11)

I've heard all kinds of excuses for this one. "God doesn't mind if we enjoy the beauty of His creation." No, He doesn't. But when you look on another person and think of how you could use them to satisfy yourself without regards to the consequences in their life or the life of those around you, you are considering the height of selfishness. (Proverbs 18:1) You are entertaining being of a very different spirit than God who is faithful and true to His word.

Physical attraction is natural, but what you do with that attraction in your mind and heart is where sin enters. "She is lovely!" can quickly change into other thoughts. As children of God we are to capture our thoughts and make them obedient to Christ. (2Corinthians 10:5) The concept implies that we cannot always keep out a passing thought or impulse, but we can decide whether or not we will reject it or contemplate it.

Pornography is an increasing scourge on the world made even more prevalent by the internet. It objectifies women and turns shape and form into idolatry. It is addictive and destructive. Anyone who thinks one can take that fire into their mind and not be burned, is fooling them self. (Proverbs 6:27)

This thought world, where our battles are won and lost, is a key component of all these commands. The way we treat our thoughts depends on where our heart is set. If your heart is set on things above, you will capture your thoughts and make them serve your Lord Jesus Christ. (Colossians 3:2) If your heart is set on this world, you will contemplate those destructive thoughts that are not of God. Thought patterns turn into action. Actions turn into a lifestyle whether for good or evil.

If you let anger control your thought life, it will be expressed in things you say. (James 1:19-20) If you let lust control your thoughts it will turn your eyes and lead you further and further down the road to actions. For the born-again follower of Jesus, the contemplation of evil brings conviction, guilt, and shame. That is God's protective hand. It is the Spirit of God within you that is disgusted with the contemplation of evil. We repent, and are cleansed, and the next time the evil thought tries to invade, we take it to the cross. (1John 1:9) You may have to do it a million times. Every time you do, you are walking in victory. Don't think the enemy of your soul is just going to give up and leave you alone.

To remember number 7, picture a heart with crack in it in the shape of a seven. Number seven is, "Do not commit adultery".

15 "You shall not steal. Theft is taking something God has put in another's care. It is really saying that God made a mistake in giving it to them. It is rebelliously declaring, "I should be the custodian." It is the same selfishness as adultery. It is saying, "That person should be mine and not their spouse's. God made a mistake in allowing them to marry. He or she should belong to me." Whether an object or a person or even ideas, to take what belongs to another is really selfishly rebelling against God's providence. As with the other commands, we can see that the contemplation of the heart is just as important as the action itself.

An easy way to remember this is to picture a burglar's mask. It is the shape of an eight. Number eight is, "Do not steal".

16 "You shall not bear false witness against your neighbor. Since Jesus expanded the meaning of neighbor to anyone we should happen to meet, this command is telling us to not lie – period! (Luke 10:36) The language of the command implies a courtroom situation but can be applied to any situation in which you speak of someone else. Leviticus 19:11 tells us not to deceive anyone. That broadens it even further.

In other words, we are to be truthful. Why? Because God is true and in Him is no lie. (1John 2:21) It is not in His nature to deceive. (Titus 1:2)

Some have argued that a lie could serve a good purpose such as saving a life. Should Germans have told the truth if they were hiding Jews in their attic during Nazi Germany? How many of us really face that kind of situation? You can complicate the simple command by imagining scenarios, but the thrust of the command is like that of all the commands. Are you operating from a heart of love or selfishness? The letter kills but the Spirit gives life. (2Corinthians 3:6) If you are standing before a just and holy God, what would He have you do?

We know the difference between justifying our actions to get what we want, and struggling to do what is right before God, even when it may cost us dearly. Don't fool yourself.

When wrestling against temptation, we can usually see what is of God and what is not by examining whether or not we truly want God's will or our own way. If we use clichés like, "God wants me to be happy!" or "God just put this in front of me so it must be His will!", we'd better watch out! The honest heart can tell when it is seeking God first without regard to our own inclinations or desires.

You can remember command number nine is "Do not lie" by thinking of a 9 lying down.

Finally, the last of the ten is the clincher. *17 "You shall not covet your neighbor's house; you shall not covet your neighbor's wife, or his male servant, or his female servant, or his ox, or his donkey, or anything that is your neighbor's."* Covet means to intensely desire something for your own. God looks upon the heart. This why Jesus said that even to look on a woman to lust after her is adultery. This is the root of thievery, a heart craving after something that belongs to another.

God desires for us to find our contentment in Him. When our hearts are satisfied in Him, when the first commands are truly kept from the heart, we don't have the need to see things in this life as a source of satisfaction. (1Timothy 6:6) If we are satisfied with God, we don't make idols out of His creation. We take time to be with Him. We won't be lusting after another's wife or stealing to obtain things or lying to advance our self over others. (Hebrews 13:5)

When the rich young ruler came to Jesus and asked the way to eternal life, Jesus told him to keep the commands. Matthew 19:18-20 (ESV)18 He said to him, "Which ones?" And Jesus said, "You shall not murder, You shall not commit adultery, You shall not steal, You shall not bear false witness, 19 Honor your father and mother, and, You shall love your neighbor as yourself." 20 The young man said to him, "All these I have kept. What do I still lack?"

Did you notice Jesus quoted all the relational commands except for the last one? The young ruler was outwardly perfect, but inwardly his heart craved the security of wealth. Jesus answer was to give his wealth away to break the covetousness in his heart. If greed is your vice, kill it by finding the joy in giving... "and come follow me." (Luke 12:15)

You can remember command number ten is not to covet by thinking of the number one as a door cracked open with two eyes staring through at a big diamond ring that is the zero.

Coveting things is trying to fill the void in our hearts that only God can fill. You can't keep the commands unless your heart is filled with God. The Law is our schoolmaster to bring us to Christ. (Galatians 3:24) It shows us the basic level of goodness/Godness to reveal how lost we are. Then we know we need a Savior.

Some of you saw the Way of the Master program that was the inspiration for the numbers as pictures to memorize the commands. Ray Comfort approaches people and asks them if they are going to heaven. He goes through a few of the commands with them and as they confess that they have broken them, he explains that they are lying, murdering, adulterers. Then he shares the way of salvation. I wouldn't recommend that method on everyone. My conviction is that we need the leading of the Holy Spirit rather than a formula, but Ray's point is valid. People aren't likely to come to Christ unless they see how desperately they need Him.

18 Now when all the people saw the thunder and the flashes of lightning and the sound of the trumpet and the mountain smoking, the people were afraid and trembled, and they stood far off 19 and said to Moses, "You speak to us, and we will listen; but do not let God speak to us, lest we die." We have casually gone through this sermon and for most of us its just another Sunday. But remember, they were hearing the voice of God. The ground was shaking, the mountain was smoking, and God's voice thundered.

Their response was to ask Moses to be their priest. "You go meet with God and tell us what He says. It's just too frightening for us!" In one sense, that is what God wanted. (Deuteronomy 5:28) He wanted them to trust Moses was hearing God. He wanted us to see in Moses the need for our Great High Priest, Jesus. He is the one that would make the intimacy God desired with mankind possible, through His death for our sins. Now we can truly become a kingdom of priests. (1Peter 2:9-10)

20 Moses said to the people, "Do not fear, for God has come to test you, that the fear of him may be before you, that you may not sin." Don't fear but do fear. Don't fear that God is an angry, judgmental, destroyer of life. He's not your enemy. He has come to teach you to fear His justice upon sin. It is His love for you that wants you to live in the freedom of His laws. It is His love that desires that your life be free from the consequences of sin. Fear His justice, but don't fear His intentions toward you. He longs for you to find life in Him. (2Peter 3:9) He longs to be first in your life. He desires to make you His treasure and that you have access to Him at all times. (Matthew 11:28-30)

While the people stood back from the mountain, trembling in fear, Moses went into the thick darkness of the cloud and received the words of the covenant. Later, He will go up to receive the tablets carved with the finger of God and receive instructions for the building of the Tabernacle.

The very next instructions are about worship. Through sacrifice the people would look forward to the One who would give them access to God without the fear of judgment. Sacrifice pointed to the need of judgment and the severity of sin. The stones of the altar of worship were not to be chiseled, but natural stone. It pointed to the salvation having nothing to do with man's work. It would all be of God who would provide the perfect lamb that would take away the sins of the world. (John 1:29)

We could never keep these ten rules. Jesus kept them in our place, and then took the judgment we deserve for breaking God's basic rules. In accepting what He did for us, we find we have been made right with God. We have access to His throne without fear. We strive to keep the commands because our hearts have been changed. Will you memorize them? Will you meditate upon them?

Questions
1 Go over the first five words from memory.
2 How did Jesus sum up the last five?
3 How did Jesus expand on the sixth?
4 On what are these laws based?
5 What is the technical definition of 7? Jesus definition?
6 How do we resist temptation?
7 What is in the heart of someone who breaks the eighth command?
8 What is the technical meaning of 9? The broad meaning?
9 What causes us to break the tenth?
10 How can we recall each command?
11 What purpose does the Law serve?
12 Explain fear in verse 20.

Book of the Covenant Exodus 21-23:9

After God spoke from the cloud to the nation, they pleaded with Moses to be the go-between. They wanted him to hear God's voice and tell them what He said. It was too frightening and overwhelming to hear it personally. So Moses entered the cloud and received the Book of the Covenant. It is recorded in chapters 21 through 23 as written down by Moses. "It is an application of the Decalogue (Ten Commandments) specifically for the social context of Israel as a nation." (John D. Currid, *A Study Commentary on Exodus,* 2:57)Though laws in different cultures and nations may vary, they should be based on the moral absolutes of the Ten Commandments.

Many of these applications were in use in other nations in the East, but there are some major differences. The fact that similar laws have been discovered does not negate the inspiration; rather, it confirms that God was inspiring other nations to seek fairness and equity. (Acts 17:26-27)

The greatest difference, of course, is that this is not a covenant with a king and his conquered masses but with the King of the Universe and His chosen people. Obedience to the law is not merely submission to a conquering lord, but is, in fact, righteous living. (John 14:23)

Some of the uniqueness of the laws of God included protection for the weak. Foreigners, women, and orphans had special provisions to keep the strong from taking advantage of them. God warns that He is the protector of the weak. (Exodus 22:22-24) Other cultures simply saw the weak as having little or no rights.

As you read through these laws, you might be tempted to think, as I did, that they are tedious rules for long ago. But as we look at these laws in their cultural setting, we can see that the background principles from the Ten Commandments are those that the most advanced societies adhere to today. The applications brought obedience to God and living a spiritual life into the everyday practical situations. We still struggle with some of these issues today.

The Book of the Covenant actually begins in chapter 20 verse 22 with laws about the altar. The people had just asked Moses to meet with God on their behalf. God's first set of instructions were how to have the people meet with God in a way that was not quite as intimidating as their encounter at Sinai. They were to meet Him at the altar. Instead of trembling before His manifest presence, they came with a sacrifice. The sacrifice pointed to a substitution that would take the punishment they deserved. It reminded them of the Passover Lamb through which they were saved from the final judgment on sin, which is death.

Of course, it was only a picture pointing to the Lamb of God, Jesus, the ultimate sacrifice. (John 1:29) Right at the beginning of the rules for living, God was pointing to the work He would do to make it possible for them to meet with Him without fear. It was to be at the altar of the cross where the justice of God was satisfied. (Romans 5:8-9)

The next set of laws deals with slavery, or what would be better called indentured servitude. When someone could not pay their penalty in court, or if they were unable to pay their debts, they could get a no interest loan or sell six years of service to a fellow Israelite. A six-year contract would be made at half the price of hiring a person each day for the same amount of time. (Deuteronomy 15:18) They would receive the money in advance to pay their debt or fine and would receive room and board. When they finished their six years of service their master was required to set them up with enough provision to restart their life. It was kind of like a do over.

(Deuteronomy 15:12-15) It was a win-win situation. The eventual goal was a prosperous master and a free and independent worker with new skills and a fresh start.

Many people, and I include myself, have thought that the Bible authorized slavery in that culture and at that time. However, that just shows our ignorance of Scripture and culture. You see, in this same set of laws, the person that steals another human and sells them faces the death penalty. (Exodus 21:16) That means that every Israelite was serving according to their free will. You can't condone what we would call slavery on Biblical grounds. As a matter of fact, it was when slaves in Europe were allowed to take communion that slavery began to come under attack as inhumane and was soon outlawed.

Servants also retained certain rights while the served. If their master killed them, he forfeited his own life. If in the process of punishing the person for not fulfilling their duties the servant was injured in some permanent way, they were free from fulfilling the rest of the time they owed their master. If they came with their wife and/or children they left with them when their time was up. No other legal system in the world at that time gave servants these kind of rights.

The modern application would be to respect the rights of workers and see that they are paid in a way that is both fair to the employer and the laborer. The employer should help the worker learn new skills to advance them. Employers should not take advantage of employees. Workers should have the right to human dignity. Severance should ideally be on agreeable terms with both parties.

Perhaps the most difficult part of these laws for us to relate to is the fact that women were treated differently. If a servant woman was given to another servant in marriage, she would not leave with him but had to remain with her master. Some would point to this as the Bible endorsing chauvinism, but that is not the case. The culture of the day must be understood. Being a servant ensured the woman of support and security. To leave with a man who had previously failed in business and might fail again was not a happy proposition. If the man who had married her was successful, he could redeem her. This ensured that he could actually make a living so that the woman's basic needs could be met.

Some people found serving a household so beneficial or grew so attached to the family that they gave themselves in service to that home for life. We'll talk more about that at the end of the message.

Consider the benefits of this system. Each person could retain their dignity by paying their debts and not being forced to beg or sell their family property. While working for your master, you would learn better business practices and possibly new skills. When you left that home, you left with your dignity and ready to start again. Welfare in the form of charity was for those who were unable to work, not for able-bodied people. Charitable giving to those who were incapacitated was and still is considered by Jews to be one of the most righteous acts honored by God. (Psalm 112:9)

The applications to today are obvious. Today, many have found that they have to take a job at half of what they were making just to get by. This what the Old Testament servant was doing. Better to retain your dignity by working at any job than to start taking handouts. If you are able, you can and should work. Whatever it takes to pay what you owe must be done, even if it is humbling.

In our effort to be helpful we give too many outs for those who would avoid their commitments. Judges order a fine and the offended party never collects. Credit is extended and paid back at a fraction of the cost. People refuse to take a lower paying job and the government gives them a paycheck. Charity to those who have no other option is God's way but handouts for the irresponsible is not!

I realize this is a very political statement in our time, but we have come to this passage at this time by God's design. Sometimes I'm asked to preach on a person's favorite political issue. Here at Wayside Bible Chapel, we go through the Scriptures one book at a time, verse by verse to see what God has to say to us today. When we get to a particular passage, I'll tell you what it says and you can decide if my application is faithful to the Word or not. Our goal is to faithfully interpret the passage in its original setting, then draw an honest application to our day whether we like what is says or not. (Hebrews 4:12)

The next section is on capital crimes. The first is execution for those who commit murder. The two words (murder and execution) are different in Hebrew. God requires capital punishment for those who carry out a planned homicide. Where does the Bible stand on capital punishment? It demands it! Now you might have a question about the legal process or the humane way to execute the guilty, but there is no question as to whether or not God demands capital punishment (Genesis 9:5b-6) when two witnesses' testimony agrees. (Deuteronomy 17:6-7)

In the case of unintentional homicide, or what we would call involuntary homicide, God provided for an escape. The family of the person that died would try to avenge the death of their loved one. The person who accidentally killed the person could flee to one of the cities of refuge that were scattered throughout the land and find protection, or he could flee to the altar in the tabernacle. (Numbers 35:6) However, if it was proven by a trial to be intentional, he was to be dragged out and executed.

The next capital crime must be seen in light of the language and culture. Anyone who curses or strikes father or mother is to be executed. I want to do a sermon series soon on Biblical authority. This is hard for us to accept because we don't understand that to dishonor those God has placed over us is to dishonor God. First, we need to understand that the word in Hebrew for "strike" is a violent attack such as attempted murder. It is completely the opposite of the fifth command to honor your parents. (Exodus 20:12)

Cursing your parents was also a much more serious matter than we see it today. It meant to disown them. It was usually in the case of when a person refused to care for their parents in their old age. To destroy the family was to destroy the nation. Jesus referred to this crime in Matthew 15:3-6. It was selfishly denying parental support, letting them starve.

The third case requiring capital punishment is kidnapping and selling the person as a slave. This shows how adamantly God was opposed to what we call slavery. It is reminiscent of what Joseph's brothers did to him, and what Egypt did to the nation of Israel. (Genesis 37:26-27)

The next crimes covered involve personal injury. We won't go through all the laws and what was equitable but some of the cases are like reading headlines of a modern newspaper. Remember the dog attack in San Francisco that killed a man? The people who owned the dog were not charged until it was discovered that the dog had injured someone before. That's covered in the Book of the Covenant. If you injure someone, do you also have to pay for their loss of income? It's covered. Is the one that caused the injury liable for hospital bills? It's covered! What if you injure a pregnant woman and her baby dies. It's covered.

The law of God imposed strict penalties on anyone who harmed an unborn child. It treated the injury of an unborn child the same way it treated the injury of any other human being. (Page: 138
-Preaching the Word – Exodus: Saved for God's Glory.) Where that leaves us with today's abortion issue is obvious. I didn't write it, God did through Moses. And regardless of our inclinations or preferences, our standard should be the unchanging Word of God. His justice is the only true justice.

The laws and their sentences imply that when we are out of control, we are responsible. We can't get out of it by saying it was an accident. We chose to lose control through rage or drugs and therefore we are responsible for the outcome. That is God's sense of justice.

These things could be taken right out of our headlines. The really sad part of this study is that it is no longer politically correct to refer to the Bible when making laws or enforcing sentences. It has become more popular to refer to European or UN guidelines. There are forces at work in America that are working to erase our Christian heritage. There was a day when Senators and Justices quoted the Bible to back their opinion. We now ignore the wisdom of Scripture to our own peril. (Psalm 119:105)

Finally, let me address briefly the eye for an eye saying. We've all heard the "eye for an eye and tooth for tooth Scripture. Again, if we don't understand the context and application it can sound barbaric. The purpose of the expression was to limit the amount of retribution to that of the crime. It was a way of saying the punishment should fit the crime. It should not be more, but neither should it be less. They did not take the expression literally, as is seen throughout these laws, but interpreted it as justice needing to be served. To slap a person on the hand for theft is too lenient. To cut off the hand for the same crime is too harsh.

I'd like to close by returning to the issue of servants. In some cases, a person who sold them self as a slave decided that at the end of their six years of service that they did not want to go free. It really isn't that hard to imagine. If you struggled to make it on your own but thrived under the direction of a master, you might want to stay as a part of his household.

In some cases, the servant actually fell in love with the family he served and did not want to leave. He may have married another slave and not be confident that he could make it on his own to redeem her. He would then ask his master if he could serve him for life. The master would then call for the elders of the village to come to his home and pierce the ear of the servant with an awl on the doorpost of the home. (Deuteronomy 15:16-17)

The act was rich with symbolism. It meant the man's ear was now to be attentive to the master of the home to serving his commands. (Exodus 29:20) The servant's own desires would have to come second. He now had a home and provision for life. It was a form of security, but it was also a lifetime of service.

The author of Hebrews says that this was true of Jesus' relationship with the Father. (Hebrews 10:5) Jesus' ear was opened to the Father above His own desires. He served for life. The Father's will always came first. When the Apostle Paul and other Apostles called themselves bondservants, they were saying it was true of them too.

Now, let me ask you, how is it going trying to make it out there on your own? Do you love your Master? Maybe your spouse is His servant and you realize that will never change. How would you like the security of being in the family of God? Think about that for a moment.

It comes with one major demand. Your ear must belong to your Master. You have to place your desires second. But oh what a loving and generous Master Jesus is! And what security! Do you really want to go out there and try to make it on your own? Wouldn't you be much better off as servant of the Living God?

There is one thing you have to confess: *"I love my Master and I do not want to go free."* He is not hard to love. In fact, His love begets love in us. (1John 4:19) And as far as freedom goes, what you thought was freedom, well, lets just say it's highly overrated, if not an outright lie. You shall know the truth and the truth shall make you free. (John 8:32) What do you say? Shall we call the elders?

If that is true of you this morning, let us take this commitment as seriously as life and death. Take hold of your right earlobe Place it on the gate of heaven. Are you ready for the awl? Let's say it together. "I love my Master Jesus, and I do not want to go free. I choose to be a bondservant of the Lord Jesus Christ."

Questions
1 What is the Book of the Covenant and its purpose?
2 What were these laws based on?
3 What is the difference with other laws of that time?
4 To what does the first set of laws pertain? Why is it first?
5 Does the Bible condone slavery?
6 Why are men and women treated differently?
7 What are the benefits of the system?
8 What crimes required capital punishment?
9 Explain capital punishment of a child.

10 What kind of crimes are covered in the next set of laws?
11 Are you a bondservant?
12 Explain the responsibilities and benefits.

Draw Near Exodus 24
Ratifying the Covenant

We begin with Moses still on the mountain in the cloud of glory hearing God's instructions for the Book of the Covenant. God is telling Moses to go down, and bring others back up, but not all the way up. He was to bring Aaron and two of his sons, and the 70 elders (the basis for the Sanhedrin).

They are to come up and worship from afar, and yet the description sounds like God comes to meet them half way. Then, Moses alone goes all the way up to commune with God and receives the tablets of stone. God had spoken Ten Commandments to the entire nation, (Exodus 20:18) but at the time they were not yet written down.

3 Moses came and told the people all the words of the LORD and all the rules. And all the people answered with one voice and said, "All the words that the LORD has spoken we will do." God must have burned those three chapters into Moses' mind, because he relayed it all by memory. Science has shown that we are devolving at a fairly rapid rate. I don't think it was as much an effort for the mind of man 3500 years ago to remember all that material. We've seen the amazing feats of memory that were possible in the first century.

Moses conveyed rules for the nation and all the people agreed to abide by them. Remember how different this is from the nations around them. In those nations the king would tell the people what they must do. They obeyed or they suffered the consequences. In the case of God with Israel, He is asking His chosen people if they will abide by these rules for daily life, including worship guidelines, cycles of feasts and rest, and all of it for their good. (Deuteronomy 10:12-13) One is a conqueror to his vassals to tell them what he will tolerate. The other is from a holy God telling the people He loves the way of righteousness. There is a vast difference. The nation responded that they would accept The Book of the Covenant as a way of life.

Now the agreement must be ratified or sealed. In that day, covenants were sealed with blood. Blood is life. (Leviticus 17:11)
4 And Moses wrote down all the words of the LORD. He rose early in the morning and built an altar at the foot of the mountain, and twelve pillars, according to the twelve tribes of Israel. The Israelites had plenty of experience at cutting stone, but the altar is of uncut stone. (Exodus 20:25) Only the pillars would be cut. The remains of a large altar and the round

sections of pillars are still visible at the base of one of the potential sights of Sinai, Jabel al Laws.

Then Moses had the young men offer burnt offerings and peace offerings of oxen on the altar. Some pictographs on the altar at Jabel al Laws are of oxen.

7 Then he took the Book of the Covenant and read it in the hearing of the people. And they said, "All that the LORD has spoken we will do, and we will be obedient." Again, the people committed themselves to obeying God's instruction. Moses took the blood of the oxen and sprinkled it on the sides of the altar. He took the rest and sprinkled the people. Just as the death of those animals was irreversible, so the covenant was an irreversible act. This was an agreement between God and His people. It was sealed with the blood of the animals. This makes their later acts of rebellion and words about returning to Egypt a serious breach of the agreement. (Exodus 32:1)

Last week we read about the covenant of the bondservant sealed with his own blood on his master's doorpost. Did you take that as seriously? Would you have taken it a more seriously if we actually took an awl and shed a little blood from your earlobe? You can see how blood makes an issue of greater importance. We can only guess the difference in the human blood shed from so many lives if Israel had actually kept these laws throughout their history.

Greater still is the eternal difference that our lives can make if we take seriously our commitment to the shed blood of Jesus! Amen? It is a covenant not based on what we do, but what He has done for us on the cross. (Hebrews 9:14) Like the covenant on Sinai, it does come with some instruction for living. *"If anyone loves me he will keep my commands. My command is this, that you love one another."* (John 13:34; 14:23)

Drawing Near to God

9 Then Moses and Aaron, Nadab, and Abihu, and seventy of the elders of Israel went up, 10 and they saw the God of Israel. There was under his feet as it were a pavement of sapphire stone, like the very heaven for clearness. Here is a great mystery that the people of the Old Testament did not understand. There is what appears to be a contradiction running throughout the Old Testament Scriptures. Jacob was stunned that he did not die after seeing the face of God with whom he wrestled. (Genesis 32:30) Samson's parents expressed the same. (Judges 13:22) Isaiah saw God on his throne. (Isaiah 6:1,5) Yet, the Old and New Testament tell us that no one has ever seen God, and that no one can see him and live. He is a transcendent Spirit. To "see" then is to fully experience His presence. Jesus said He is the only one to have ever seen the Father. (John 6:46) The holiness of God eradicates evil! Jesus alone can "see" God because He alone is holy.

So just what did these people see? How is it that they survived the encounter? Jewish scholars have seen this same problem and decided to call this visible manifestation of the invisible God, the Prince of the Countenance. He is called the LORD and fully represents the LORD, yet he is different from the LORD. But this creates another problem. How can God share His name? His name is the sum of His character. If a being has the name of the LORD and the authority of the LORD how is he different from the LORD?

That is why the Apostle Paul said that Jesus is the manifestation of the invisible God. (Colossians 1:15) He shares God's name and God's attributes. The major difference is one is seen and the other unseen. One is called the Father and the other the Son and yet they are one. Jesus said to Thomas, *"If you have seen me, you have seen the Father."* John 14:9

John the Beloved, who recorded that expression, had a revelation of the glorified Jesus on the island of Patmos. Listen to his description in Revelation 1:12-18 *12 Then I turned to see the voice that was speaking to me, and on turning I saw seven golden lampstands, 13 and in the midst of the lampstands one like a son of man, clothed with a long robe and with a golden sash around his chest. 14 The hairs of his head were white like wool, as white as snow. His eyes were like a flame of fire, 15 his feet were like burnished bronze, refined in a furnace, and his voice was like the roar of many waters. 16 In his right hand he held seven stars, from his mouth came a sharp two-edged sword, and his face was like the sun shining in full strength. 17 When I saw him, I fell at his feet as though dead. But he laid his right hand on me, saying, "Fear not, I am the first and the last, 18 and the living one. I died, and behold I am alive forevermore, and I have the keys of Death and Hades.* That is the New Testament vision of Jesus after He ascended into heaven.

Now lets compare that with what Ezekiel saw five hundred years earlier in Ezekiel 1:26-28 (ESV) *26 And above the expanse over their heads there was the likeness of a throne, in appearance like sapphire; and seated above the likeness of a throne was a likeness with a human appearance. 27 And upward from what had the appearance of his waist I saw as it were gleaming metal, like the appearance of fire enclosed all around. And downward from what had the appearance of his waist I saw as it were the appearance of fire, and there was brightness around him. 28 Like the appearance of the bow that is in the cloud on the day of rain, so was the appearance of the brightness all around. Such was the appearance of the likeness of the glory of the LORD. And when I saw it, I fell on my face, and I heard the voice of one speaking.*

Why are they so similar? Did John copy Ezekiel or are they both seeing the same eternal glorified Jesus who before His ascension prayed in John 17:5 *5 And now, Father, glorify me in your own presence with the glory that I had with you before the world existed.*

They were all seeing the same being because the glorified Son of God has always been the same except for the short span of His earthly ministry in which He emptied Himself of His glory to walk among us. (Philippians 2:7-8) This is the same One that the elders, Aaron and sons, and Moses and Joshua were seeing. Jesus veils His glory so that so that we are able to look upon Him and live. The fully unveiled glory of the Father OR the Son cannot be seen by mortal man.

Listen to the words of the Apostle Paul (Rabbi Shaul) describing Jesus in 1 Timothy 6:16 (ESV). *16 who alone has immortality, who dwells in unapproachable light, whom no one has ever seen or can see. To him be honor and eternal dominion. Amen.* Yet, Paul had seen Him on the Damascus road. The vision blinded Him, but He said He saw the resurrected Jesus. (Acts 22:14) You can get a glimpse of His veiled glory, but you could not withstand a full revelation of it! This is somewhat understandable, and yet a great mystery as there is so much yet for us to know.

The elders of Israel were seeing the veiled glory of Jesus. They saw the same sapphire like throne before Ezekiel saw it. 11 And he did not lay his hand on the chief men of the people of Israel; they beheld God, and ate and drank. To eat and drink before God was to be at peace with Him. (Exodus 18:12) The covenant was confirmed and all was well. God and the people of Israel had come to an agreement on how life should be lived.

Every time we celebrate communion we are doing the same. We eat and drink in His presence. We have peace with God because of His gift of His only Son. The covenant is confirmed. We come to an agreement on how life should be lived, by faith in Jesus the Son. (Galatians 2:20)

We should notice a pattern that we will see in the Tabernacle of the coming chapters. The people were not allowed in. The priests and elders came only so far. Now Moses alone will go all the way in.

There are three depths of relationship. There is the outer court with the altar and laver. Everyone can come to the sacrifice. All are invited to partake of Jesus, but only a few will wash (Titus 3:5) and come into the Holy place and be illuminated by the light of the Holy Spirit and feast on the bread of life. Only a few will offer prayers at the altar of incense, and fewer still will enter to be in God's presence and commune with Him. (Revelation 3:20)

12 The LORD said to Moses, "Come up to me on the mountain and wait there, that I may give you the tablets of stone, with the law and the commandment, which I have written for their instruction." Moses went all the way in. Before he did, he left Aaron and Hur in charge. If people needed decisions, they could go to them. Apparently, Moses sensed this would take some time. He told the elders to wait and took Joshua a little further up with him.

Moses waited for six days on the mountainside with Joshua until on the seventh day the LORD invited him into the cloud of glory. It appeared to the people below as a devouring fire. Even though God called him up, he had to wait for God's timing to come in.

18 Moses entered the cloud and went up on the mountain. And Moses was on the mountain forty days and forty nights. The next seven chapters are God's instructions to Moses while he was on the mountain during those 40 days. God etched into stone the two copies of the Ten Commandments. When covenants were made, each party received a copy of the agreement. We often see pictures of five commands on one stone and five on another. It's not that God couldn't find a big enough stone and had to have a page two. He made a copy for Him and for them but both would go in the Ark of the Covenant because He was coming down to live with them.

Moses also received the detailed instructions as to how the Tabernacle was to be built. God even chose the craftsmen. (Exodus 31:2-3) He showed Moses the whole, like a three-dimensional blueprint that was to be copied. (Hebrews 8:5) Our next two weeks will be on the details that God ordained to be filled with meaning. It has been said that the Tabernacle is the greatest visual aid to help us understand the things of God.

I would like to end the message this morning by having you consider where you are in your walk with Jesus. Are you at the base of the mountain where the altar is? Are you in the outer court? That is where we first meet God. We come to the sacrifice, recognizing we are sinners and God is holy. Without a sacrifice, never the twain shall meet. Then we recognize that the sacrifice was the only acceptable one, Jesus, the Lamb of God.

That is a great place to be! If you have come there this morning, won't you enter into the covenant? Let the seriousness of the blood of God's Lamb shed for you draw you in to a lasting relationship based on that loving, sacrificial act.

Are you at the laver, being sanctified to go up to the mountain itself. John told us that if we confess our sins, God is faithful and just to forgive us our sins and to cleanse us from ALL unrighteousness. (1John 1:9) He helps us clean up our act, and we must, if we are to go up the mountain and eat in His presence.

Have you put your foot on the mountain, gone into the Holy Place and let His Word and His Spirit enlighten your mind. Do you eat His word as you would your daily bread? Are you nourished by it? Are you communing with Him in prayer? Are you in awe of His presence? Have you begun to see Him? Are you amazed that you are still alive? Don't forget it is only possible because of the blood of the new covenant.

Where is all this headed? Is it a devouring fire or a cloud of glory? It depends on your point of view. If you are still at the base of the mountain, it's a devouring fire to all that must be removed from your life. If you are half way up the mountain, it's a cloud of glory.

Will you enter in? When you do, you lose all sense of time because He is timeless. (Hebrews 13:8) You'll commune with Almighty God and realize how little but how special you really are. You'll find your value is in the fact that God loves you. It's there that you receive the plans He has for your life. It's there that we find the instructions for how He would have us worship. It always seems like you are alone with Him. That is how it seems to everyone. There is intimacy. We don't want to leave, but we know we must. We have to carry out the plans He has given, and we are delighted to do so. That's because our delight is to please Him and do His will. (Hebrews 10:7)

What is your next step in the journey? You don't have to rush it, but you do need to be willing. (John 10:9) Will you remain at the altar with the masses? Or will you be satisfied to sit on the side of the mountain and wait with the elders? Or maybe nothing short of standing at the edge of the cloud with Joshua will do? Or do you have a hunger to go in and hear His voice? (John 10:3) I hope you won't be satisfied until you enter in!

Questions
1 What is the setting for this chapter?
2 Why were covenants ratified with blood?
3 How was the New Covenant sealed? Implications?
4 Give examples of seeing God in Scripture?
5 How are we to understand the mystery?
6 What two descriptions bear remarkable similarity?
7 What is the implication of eating before God? And for us?
8 What are the three depths of relationship on Sinai?
9 What has been called God's greatest visual aid to us?
10 Where are you on the mountain/tabernacle?
11 How strong is your desire to go to the next level?

From the Inside Out Exodus 25-27

The elders and Aaron and sons, along with Moses and Joshua, ate in the presence of the LORD. Moses and Joshua were called up the mountain and, after waiting six days, Moses was called into God's presence. The Israelites saw the presence of God as a devouring fire, but Moses saw it as a cloud of glory. Thus began Moses 40 days with God. We can read about it in the next seven chapters, but obviously a lot more took place those 40 days than what was recorded. What was recorded were the essential instructions that God gave to Moses, and those instructions dealt mostly with the Tabernacle.

It begins with God inviting the people to make a contribution for God. *1 The LORD said to Moses, 2 "Speak to the people of Israel, that they take for me a contribution. From every man whose heart moves him you shall receive the contribution for me.* Does that strike you as strange? How can we contribute anything for God? (Acts 17:24-25) It is really giving back to God the things that He has given into our care. Everything we have is really God's anyway. It seems to me that it is grace that calls it a contribution. Who was it that convinced the Egyptians to give them all these treasures? It was all God. God gave it all to them not that many days earlier. He knew what materials He would ask for and that is what the Egyptians gave to the Hebrews as they left Egypt.

Notice how graciously God puts it, From every man whose heart moves him you shall receive the contribution for me. He doesn't demand what is His, but asks for people to give according to their heart. That is the same wording the Apostle Paul uses for his collection for the impoverished saints in Jerusalem. (2Corinthians 9:6) Give according to how God moves your heart. We get to make a contribution for God! That is incredible grace.

It is God's way of allowing us to participate in what He is doing, (Ephesians 2:10) and yet it all comes from Him.

We'll find out seven chapters later that there had to be some serious discipline (Exodus 32:33-35) before they are given this opportunity, but when they are (Exodus 35:4-5), the response is overwhelming. (Exodus 36:5-7) They had to be restrained from giving. They had generous hearts and they responded to the stirring of God within them. May that ever be true of God's people when it comes to contributing for the things of God!

8 And let them make me a sanctuary, that I may dwell in their midst. That is the whole purpose of the collection and the following instructions. God desired to give them a portable Sinai experience. He would manifest His presence consistently in this tent they were to build. "Let them make me a *mishkan*" – a holy place, a place set apart for the holy God to be with His people. "A place that He can *shakan*" – live among them. That is where we get the term Shakina glory, the dwelling glory, to describe that ball of light that hovered under the wings of the cherubim over the atonement cover.

This is all about God being with man again. You can think of atonement as "at one meant". That intimacy of walking with God was lost in the Garden of Eden. Through Abraham there was a glimpse of the restoration of that relationship. (Genesis 48:15; James 2:23) Now in Abraham's descendent, leading the people to the land God promised to Abraham, there is plan of restoration. Build the tent and make it a holy place (sanctuary) and God will be manifest among you. He is everywhere, but He will be uniquely present in this tent.

God in a tent! There is another amazing thought. But then again, isn't that what every believer in Jesus becomes. It is how Jesus described Himself, *"The Word became flesh and tabernacled among us."* John 1:14

9 Exactly as I show you concerning the pattern of the tabernacle, and of all its furniture, so you shall make it. As we go through the furniture in the Tabernacle, we'll see that a lot of the details are missing. We really have to guess at what certain things looked like and how they functioned. This instruction filled in the details for Moses. God showed him the details. A picture is worth a thousand words, well, Moses was sure to understand after God showed him.

I think we should keep in mind that there is 25 times as much information on how to build a tabernacle for God than there is on how God made a universe for man. There must be some profound significance in every detail. We'll just touch the surface, but when we get to heaven, I think the intricacies of spiritual reality embedded in the design will blow our mind.

God begins His descriptions from the inside, where He will dwell. He begins with the Ark of the Covenant in the small innermost room called the Holy of Holies. This box was made of acacia wood, a tree still common in the region. It is a very dense wood and resists decay. The wood was covered inside and out with hammered, or plate, gold. Gold represents the holiness and purity of God as well as His kingly authority.

On top of the box is the lid called the Atonement Cover (a better translation than Mercy Seat). Each end of the cover had an angel called a cherub, the plural is cherubim. Their wings met over the top of the cover. Under their wings was the *shekina* glory. (2Kings 19:15)

You will recall that when Adam and Eve were cast out of the Garden, two cherubim with flaming swords kept them out from re-entering the Garden. (Genesis 3:24) It could be said that Cherubim protect the holiness of God. They are not little baby angels or women with lovely hair, but massive warring angels that scare the beegeebees out anyone that encounters them. There were also embroidered images of the cherubim on the curtains that entered the Tabernacle and the one that divided off the Holy of Holies.

Within the box are the tablets written with the finger of God. (Exodus 31:18) In that part of the world, covenants were made in duplicate so that each party had a copy. We often see pictures of commands one through five on one side and six through ten on the other. It is much more likely that the entire set was on both stones. They were both in the box for God was living with His people. The Israelites guarded their copy by leaving it in the safest place possible, the Ark of the Covenant. God kept His copy there as well. Next week we'll address the other items in the Ark.

The poles that were used to carry the Ark were also of acacia wood covered in gold and were to always remain in the rings attached to the ark. Unlike our model and many pictures, the poles were on the sides, behind the cherubim. We know this because 1Kings 8:8 tells us the poles stuck out into the Holy Place. They had long poles so that a large number of Levites could carry the weight of the gold involved in the Ark. When it was moved it was covered with waterproof hides so that it was not visible.

Over and over we see this conflict of a holy God with sinful people. Again, we get the picture of God being like anti-matter on evil. He annihilates it! So this dwelling place is among the people and yet separated from them by multiple tents, the smoke of the incense, and permission for only one person a year to enter in after numerous cleansing rituals. There is great desire by God to be with us and yet without glossing over the horror of our sinful condition.

The next piece of furniture described is the Table of Presence/Showbread. It too was of acacia wood and covered with gold and was in the outer room called the Holy Place. The table held two stacks of bread six high, twelve in all. They represented the tribes. Each week they were to be replaced with fresh bread and the priests were to eat it.

In other religions of the East, people would bring food as an offering to their gods. The showbread was about God being the Great Provider for His people.

The table was also the place the golden bowls, pitchers, and plates were kept. The pitchers were for drink offerings, the bowls for the blood of the sacrifice, and the plates for incense.

In the same room on the opposite side was the Lampstand, the menorah. Hammered out of 75 pounds of pure gold and made to look like almond branches with leaves and buds, the seven wicks at the end of each branch. Some believe they were to always stay lit and others that they were only lit at night with the exception of the innermost flame that always stayed lit. The specially prepared olive oil for fuel was added daily and the wicks were trimmed each morning.

The idea was that just as the tents of Israel had evening lamps, so God's house had an evening lamp. The difference was that He never sleeps, so unlike the lamps in the tents of Israel that were put out before sleeping, His lamp stayed lit throughout the night. (Psalm 121:3-4)

There was one more piece of furniture in the Holy Place, the Altar of Incense. We have to skip over to chapter 30 to get a description of it. I do not know why the description was set aside until the final details were given. If you have an idea please share it with me.

It was also of acacia wood and covered with gold. It was much smaller than the other pieces but carried in the same way with gold covered acacia poles. Only sacred incense according to God's formula was to be used in this altar, nothing else. Once a year on the Day of Atonement the priest anointed the horns of the altar with the blood of the sacrifice.

It is commonly believed that the incense represented prayer going up for God's people. (Psalm 141:2) It was to be tended each morning when the priests cared for the Lampstand so that incense was always kept burning upon it.

The tent that covered these two rooms was hung over acacia frames (panels) covered in gold and set on silver bases. Silver came from the redemption money of the firstborn males. (Exodus 13:15) Since they were spared the last plague in Egypt, and since the firstborn males were the Lord's, they paid a five silver coin fee to redeem them so that they could enter another form of work. (Numbers 18:16) Since the Levites serve in the Temple they were not required to pay this. We could say then that the tabernacle rests on a basis of redemption. The foundation of God's presence among them was redemption. He desires to redeem fallen man so that relationship can be restored, so that the distance and barriers are no longer required.

Now back to chapter 27, and in the outer court where the common person was allowed, there was the great brazen altar. This was the largest of all pieces seven-and-a-half-foot square and over 4 foot high. It was made of acacia wood but covered with bronze. Bronze was a symbol of strength, but also of judgment. It was seven and a half feet square and a height of four and a half feet.

A screen is described but we don't know if it was on one side to allow the ashes to pour out or in the inside to hold the sacrifice above the flames. The inside was hollow, but many believe it was filled with uncut stones as described in chapter 20. (Exodus 20:25) The tools that were to be used were also to be of bronze.

A ramp of earth was made for the priest to ascend when offering a sacrifice. (Exodus 20:26) There were not to be steps so that the nakedness of the priest was not exposed. That may sound strange, but when we understand that the priests of Baal often sacrificed while they were nude and their worship included lewd acts, we can see why God made a distinct difference in the way sacrifice was carried out.

The outside perimeter was of linen which hung on seven-and-a-half-foot high bronze poles set in bronze bases. Bronze was the strongest metal of that time before the iron age. The stakes that anchored the posts and tent were also bronze. But again, remember that bronze represents judgment. Everything in the outer court reminds the people that justice must be served. The altar is about justice, not about feeding god as in other religions.

Finally, we have the laver or bronze basin. Made from the bronze mirrors the women brought out of Egypt, (Exodus 38:8) it was a water container that was for the priests to wash hands and feet before entering the holy place or after preparing animals for sacrifice.

The bronze basin stood between the bronze altar and the tent. The tent became known as the Tent of Meeting, for Moses would go within and talk with God. We suppose he stood at the inner most curtain and God spoke from over the Mercy Seat through the curtain.

This is how God described His tent home. The people lived in tents, so God too would live among them in a tent. There are times in Scripture when the text uses the common Hebrew word for tent *(ohel)* to describe the Tabernacle.

This is how God comes to meet us, how He deals with our sinful condition. Just like at Sinai, He puts a boundary around Himself and warns us that if we break into His presence it will mean justice and the penalty for sin is death. So He keeps His distance and separates Himself from us. He is everywhere and all knowing, but mercy puts a barrier between Himself and us that we dare not breach. That was represented in the Atonement Cover on the Ark. God was above it and the Law below Him, yet in between is the atonement cover. The blood of the sacrificial goat on the Day of Atonement would be sprinkled first on that cover symbolizing the sacrifice that would one day atone for the sins of the world.

Think of the presumption of sinful man breaking through that mercy barrier into the presence of a holy God. That is what killed Uzzah. The priests weren't even to touch the ark and that is why the poles always remained in place.

It wasn't simply that Uzzah broke the rules, but that he thought he was protecting God from dirt! What is filthier than sin? The dirt isn't vile in God's sight, man is! Dirt has no will of its own to rebel, only men and fallen angels have such audacity. Uzzah's sinful nature came uncovered into the presence of the holiness that annihilates evil. (2Samuel 6:6-7)

First is the inaccessible inner tent with cherubim on the entrance curtain and over the ark like a warning to any who would enter. Yet, just outside that curtain is the altar of incense, prayer going up to Him. Prayer is closer to Him than anything else in the tabernacle. Through prayer He becomes the light that illumines our darkness. Through prayer we find that He meets our need and gives us our daily bread. His grace brings Him out from behind the curtain into the Holy Place touching the lives of the sanctified ones. But until He goes all the way to the altar there can be no sanctified ones to enjoy His light and provision. (1Samuel 2:2; Leviticus 20:8)

In Jesus, He went all the way out to the outer court in the veil of a human body. He came into our world and yet He was still separate from the outer world like the outer tent set off this area from the rest of the camp. (John 9:5) He came out to be the sacrifice, the perfect once and for all sacrifice. (Hebrews 9:26) He tabernacled among us. (John 1:14)

Once He has met us there at the altar, He then washes us at the brass basin. Some think we must wash first and then come to the altar, but no, we will not be washed until we go first to the altar. (Titus 3:5) Once washed we can go back in with Him and experience why He came out, so that fellowship with Him might be restored.

He came out to bring us in. This is the "from the inside out" message of the Tabernacle. God came to us. (John 16:8) He left the glory of heaven, the Holy of Holies, and tabernacled among men to end the tension of the holiness of God and the sin of man by making a way for our sins to be removed. He is the light of the world and the bread of life. He came all the way out to the altar of the cross and meets us there where our sin meets the justice we deserve. He came from the highest of heights heaven to the lowest of depths of this world to remove the distance between us. There He washes us clean and invites us in to fellowship with Him forever.

Don't stop at the altar. That is only the beginning of why He has come all the way out. Be washed. Be enlightened. Partake of the bread of the presence. Let your prayers rise with the incense and enter through the torn veil of His flesh and meet Him within. (Hebrews 10:19-22)

Questions
1 How can we contribute anything to God?
2 What two Hebrew words describe the purpose of the offering?
3 What does it mean to be a *Mishkan*?
4 Where does God begin the description and why?
5 What was on top of the Ark of the Covenant? Symbolize?
6 Why were there so many barriers between man and God?
7 What is the other two pieces in the Holy Place? Significance?
8 What is the other piece in the Holy Place and its symbolism?
9 What was the furniture in the outer court? Why Bronze?
10 Why did Uzzah die?
11 Why and how did God come out?

Jesus in the Tabernacle Exodus 25-27

Last week we went over the descriptions of the tabernacle that God not only spoke but also showed to Moses on Mount Sinai. There are so many details in such a large portion of Scripture that we can be sure that God has filled it with spiritual truth to be discovered. We have already seen how it showed us the steps to intimacy with God. I pray that we will continue to make an honest assessment of how far we have entered in and what we need to do to go all the way in and then obey what we hear. We have seen how God came out to bring us in. (Hebrews 10:19-22)

Today I would like to take you through the tabernacle to show you how it points to Jesus. (Luke 24:27) When Jesus rose from the dead, He told His disciples, Luke 24:44 (ESV) ... *"These are my words that I spoke to you while I was still with you, that everything written about me in the Law of Moses and the Prophets and the Psalms must be fulfilled."*

The Apostle Paul tried to convince the Jews that Jesus was Messiah using the Law and the Prophets. (Acts 17:2) If Jesus is truly one with the Father and has forever been the plan of God to redeem the world as the Scriptures declare (Revelation 13:8) then we would expect God to prepare us to recognize Him by foretelling details of His ministry.

In most seminaries today, there is a trend to interpret the Old Testament as non-Messianic. In other words, these more recent professors are claiming that the original people that heard the text did not interpret it as referring to a coming Messiah. That simply ignores rabbinical writing, and Jewish history, but most of all Jesus' own words. (Luke 4:21)

When John the Baptist was imprisoned, he sent messengers to Jesus to ask if He was indeed the Messiah. Jesus answered by referring to things the prophet Isaiah said would be a part of the Messiah's ministry that were taking place right before the eyes of the messengers. (Luke 11:4-6) Jesus was saying, "How can you doubt it when you see the predictions about the ministry of Messiah taking place right before your very eyes?" Well, somehow, modern professors have educated themselves into stupidity. What is clear to any unbiased reader of the text has become obscure to them. (Jeremiah 5:21)

In the 17th century, the idea of symbolism was taken to an extreme. Every word and object somehow said something spiritual. Because of that extreme, the church backed away from seeing metaphors or pictures of spiritual things that were not clearly stated to be such. In other words, the church swung back in the other direction. Today we are still affected by the move to correct the extreme of seeing some spiritual thing in everything in that we avoid even some of the more obvious pictures God painted for us. I give you that background as an introduction to warn you that some of the message today is what I have personally seen. I think it is a reasonable conclusion but for those pictures not clearly described in other passages as such, you must discern for yourself. I can't imagine that God the Father would not fill the Tabernacle with pictures of Jesus, the Son.

The author of Hebrews tells us that the earthly tabernacle was a copy of true things, heavenly things. (Hebrews 9:23-24) He calls the tabernacle and its rituals a shadow of the good things to come. (Hebrews 10:1) The good things are Jesus and His ministry.

Isn't it interesting that John used the word associated with the tabernacle to describe Jesus' physical existence! The Word became flesh and tabernacle among us. (John 1:14)

Jesus referred to Himself as the Temple that was modeled after the tabernacle. John 2:19-21 (ESV)*19 Jesus answered them, "Destroy this temple, and in three days I will raise it up." 20 The Jews then said, "It has taken forty-six years to build this temple, and will you raise it up in three days?" 21 But he was speaking about the temple of his body.* When it comes to seeing Jesus in the tabernacle, we can be sure we are seeing the same truth that Jesus saw and taught.

Let us begin looking at the tabernacle from the place God begins, the Ark of the Covenant. The ark itself was made, like most of the furniture, of acacia wood. Only this piece was covered within and without with hammered gold. Acacia wood grew in the wilderness and is common even today. It is a tough tight grained wood, but it is just wood. Our Savior came in a human body just like yours and mine, flesh and bone. The great difference is what was on the inside and outside. He was golden on the inside and so His every word and action (the outside) was golden. (John 5:19)

Gold represents holiness and glory. The word for glory in Hebrew *(kabod)* also means heavy or weighty. Jesus is glorious within and without. He declared that His only motivation was to please the Father. (John 8:29) He said His every action was at the direction of the Father. He was the only one that could ever ask if anyone could find any fault in Him and have silence as the response. (John 8:46) His was the only human body golden within and without.

Inside the box were three items, the tablets of the Ten Commandments, Aaron's rod, and a golden jar of manna. John the Beloved wrote that Jesus is the Word made flesh. (John 1:14) He is the incarnation of those commandments. Not only did He live in accordance with them in every way, but in a mysterious way, He is God's word. The Word was with God and the Word was God. (John 1:1)

The jar of manna is a wonderful picture as well. It is a golden vessel like the Ark but it contained God's miraculous provision that had begun to fall each day a short time before the building of the tabernacle. Jesus interpreted this one for us. John 6:32-33 (ESV) *32 Jesus then said to them, "Truly, truly, I say to you, it was not Moses who gave you the bread from heaven, but my Father gives you the true bread from heaven. 33 For the bread of God is he who comes down from heaven and gives life to the world."* Jesus was explaining that the manna was a physical picture of Him. The use of the word "true" points to a Greek idea of things in this world being a shadow of a spiritual reality (the true thing). The Hebrews saw things in the same light, that is, physical pictures pointed to spiritual realities.

The other object in that box was Aaron's staff. When the tribal leaders had argued about God's choice of Aaron as the High Priest, God had them put their tribal staff before the veil. (Numbers 17:2-4) Each staff would be very unique with the clan name carved into it. The next morning, Aaron's staff had sprouted and put forth buds and produced blossoms, and it bore ripe almonds. Numbers 17:8b

This was the proof that God had selected Aaron's tribe, the tribe of Levi, to be the priests. A staff that was dead and dry for generations had come to life and was fruitful. The author of Hebrews tells us that Jesus has become our Great High Priest (Hebrews 4:14) after another order, not the passing order of Aaron, but an eternal priesthood, that of Melchizedek. (Hebrews 5:5-6) And what was the proof of God's choice for our Great High Priest but life out of death. Jesus rose after three days in the grave and that verified God's acceptance of His sacrifice. (Acts 17:31)

In fact, the author of Hebrews goes on to say that Jesus entered the Holy of Holies in heaven and sprinkled His own blood there on the atonement cover on our behalf. (Hebrews 9:11-12) His blood came between the presence of God over that atonement cover and the Law that condemns us underneath it. And you better say, "Thank you Jesus!" that it did.

The next item as we move out from the Ark is the veil. It was a four-inch thick curtain of red, blue and purple linen. It was so heavy that 100 Levites were assigned to carry it when the tabernacle moved. Josephus, the historian, had written that horses couldn't pull it apart.

Again, we turn to the author of Hebrews to find out that the veil represented Jesus' body. (Hebrews 10:19-20) Like the veil, Jesus body was torn that we might enter into the very presence of God. I suppose that when Moses went into the tabernacle to ask God questions about how to resolve issues that he knelt in front of that curtain. The voice of God thundered from the *Shekina* and instructed Moses. The voice came through the veil. The voice came to us through Jesus Christ. (Hebrews 1:2)

When Jesus died, the veil was torn from top to bottom. (Mark 15:38) The temple Herod remodeled had a 60-foot high veil. Through the forgiveness offered to us in the blood of Christ Jesus, we can come boldly to the throne of grace. (Hebrews 4:16)

It is interesting that the New Testament changes the name of the Ark of the Covenant to call it a Throne of Grace. Once the work of atonement was accomplished, there no longer needed to be the separation between a holy God and man, for Jesus made a way for man to be holy. Clothed in Christ Jesus we can boldly go in without fear and ask for help in time of need. (Romans13:14)

The next item of furniture was in the Holy Place. It is the Altar of Incense. The incense was always to be kept burning as a picture of prayers always going up to God. Hebrews 7:25 (ESV) *25... he is able to save to the uttermost those who draw near to God through him, since he always lives to make intercession for them.* Here is a wonderful thought. The author was telling us that the priests had a limited life span and so priest after priest served. But Jesus lives forever to intercede for us. I see this as Jesus always before the Throne of Grace bearing the marks that purchased my freedom. The penalty has been paid. My sins are no longer on the record. (Psalm 103:12) Is there a more comforting thought? Jesus is there right now interceding for you and for me.

Then we move to the lampstand that lit the tabernacle. It was made of pure gold, symbolizing complete holiness (Exodus 28:36), and was the only light in the tabernacle. Jesus answers this one for us. John 8:12 (ESV) *12 Again Jesus spoke to them, saying, "I am the light of the world. Whoever follows me will not walk in darkness, but will have the light of life."* John 12:46 (ESV) *46 I have come into the world as light, so that whoever believes in me may not remain in darkness.* Just as we saw with the true manna, so Jesus is called the true light by John the Beloved, one of Jesus' closest disciples. (John 1:9) That means the light in the tabernacle was only a shadow that pointed to the reality of Jesus.

It has been suggested that each flame represents an attribute of God, holiness, justice, righteousness, loving kindness, faithfulness, mercy, and grace. Jesus' life was ablaze with those attributes. They were never seen so clearly as in His life. (Colossians 1:19)

Then there is the Table of Showbread. It tells us that God is the great provider. The Apostle Paul helps us with this one when He tells us that all our need is supplied in Jesus. (Philippians 4:19) He is the loaf for the spiritual hunger of every tribe. By saying He is the true food and drink, Jesus was saying that He is the reality behind the loaves and drink offerings. (John 6:54-55) He tells us in John 6 that we must eat and drink of Him. We must take Him in to meet our spiritual need. John 6:35 (ESV) *35 Jesus said to them, "I am the bread of life; whoever comes to me shall not hunger, and whoever believes in me shall never thirst.*

Stepping out of the tabernacle and into the courtyard we see everything of bronze where judgment is meted out. If justice were not served, God would not be holy. The largest of all the furniture in the tabernacle was the brazen altar. The blood of the lambs was sprinkled there. Their lives were consumed here as substitutes. But God was never pleased with the blood of bulls and goats. (Psalm 40:6) They just told us of the seriousness of sin.

When you realize that all pain and suffering in our world is the result of sin, if you've traveled the third world and seen any of it, or visited a prison or hospital, you've barely begun to see the high cost of sin. Consider also the wonderful fellowship with God that was lost when Adam sinned! What can cover it? What is justice for all that pain? Is a financial payment enough? Is a life of service enough? Nothing short of life would be equitable justice, and our life is in our blood. (Leviticus 17:11) God wanted us to understand the severity of sin and the real price necessary to atone for it.

Upon seeing Jesus, John the Baptist declared, "Behold, the Lamb of God that takes away the sins of the world." (John 1:29) Jesus' blood was poured out like that of all the lambs that pointed to Him. He was both the scapegoat that was taken outside the camp bearing our sin (Hebrew 13:12-13), and the sacrificial one, whose blood was sprinkled on the atonement cover. It took two goats to represent what our Savior would do for us.

Then we come to the bronze basin, or laver. After we accept the work of Jesus' atonement, He washes us with the regeneration of the Holy Spirit. (Titus 3:5) We can look into that reflection and see a new creation. (2Corinthians 5:17) That's when we realize Jesus has made us priests unto God. (1Peter 2:5) We enter into the Holy Place and find Him to be a light in our darkness. (John 3:21) He illumines our path. We eat His word and drink of His Spirit. We rely on His intercession for us and go through the torn veil and fellowship with God. What the high priest could only do once a year, we have the privilege of doing many times every day. Do we grasp the magnitude of that blessing? (Romans 11:33) We begin to see Him in everything, His hand in the orchestration of our days. (Psalm 139:16) We offer up sacrifices of praise and live to serve Him. (Romans 12:1)

Yes, when God gave the details of the tabernacle to Moses, He had His Son in mind. That's because the heart of God has always been to resolve the distance between His holy being and our sinful nature. There was only one way. Jesus! No one comes through the gates into the presence of the Father in the Holy of Holies but through Him. (John 14:6)

Questions
1 Why should we look for Jesus in the Tabernacle?
2 Why should we see Old Testament texts as Messianic?
3 Why did interpreters pull back from seeing symbolism?
4 How can we see Jesus in the Ark? It's contents?
5 What are the implications of a "true" object in Greek and Hebrew?
6 Of which objects is Jesus called the true reality?
7 How is Jesus pictured in the Holy Place?
8 What is the Ark called in the New Testament? Why?
9 How is Jesus the veil?
10 How do we see Jesus in the bronze altar? 11 How does He fulfill both goats of the Day of Atonement?

Priestly Robes Exodus 28

In the chapter for today the clothing of the priest is described. It is important that we see what God was conveying in the imagery of the priest's garments. Next week we'll see his ordination and daily duties. The very first verse of the chapter sets the tone for what the chapter will describe. "Bring near" is technical term that means to consecrate. To consecrate something is to set it apart for holy use. The clothing that the priests will wear is a part of that "setting apart". They were just like any other men. We'll see in a few weeks that Aaron was probably in the midst of making an idol while God was giving the instructions for his glorious garments. If Aaron was perfect, he wouldn't need to be consecrated.

The consecration begins with special clothing. For the High Priest, Aaron, the most important article of clothing was the ephod. It was similar to an apron. It was to be woven of linen that was blue, purple, scarlet and interlaced with threads of gold. The priest matched the material of the Tabernacle, which visibly showed that this was his place, his sacred duty.

The ephod was sleeveless and made in two parts. There was a front piece and the back. The two pieces met at the shoulder with an onyx stone on each shoulder where the halves joined. On each of the stones were written the names of the tribes of Israel, six on one and six on the other. The idea was that he carried the burden of the people on his shoulders. He carried them before the God of Israel when he went into the Tabernacle. Exodus 28:12 (ESV) *12 And you shall set the two stones on the shoulder pieces of the ephod, as stones of remembrance for the sons of Israel. And Aaron shall bear their names before the LORD on his two shoulders for remembrance.* It is not that God would forget that Aaron represented the nation, but that Aaron needed to be reminded that that was his ministry.

On the front of the ephod hung the breastplate. That translation sounds like armor but it was made of the same material and of the same color as the ephod. It was actually a big pocket about 9 inches square. On the front of the pocket were four rows of three stones. The precious and semi-precious stone colors were the same colors as the ensigns of the tribe they represented. Each stone had the name of a tribe inscribed on it.

The breast piece was attached to the ephod and onyx stone with a golden braid above so that it always stayed over the heart of priest. The bottom portion was attached with a blue cord to the ephod and the sash or band that went around the waist of the priest.

The breastplate was sometimes called the breast piece of judgment, or decision. Exodus 28:30 (ESV) 30 And in the breast piece of judgment you shall put the Urim and the Thummim, and they shall be on Aaron's heart, when he goes in before the LORD. Thus Aaron shall bear the judgment of the people of Israel on his heart before the LORD regularly.

Inside the breast piece were the Urim and Thumim. Literally the Hebrew words meant "lights" and "perfections". We can only speculate from Biblical passages as to what they were and how they were used. There are three main suggestions about them. One is that they were two stones identical in size and shape, but one was white and the other black. When important decisions for the nation had to be decided the leader would come to the priest and ask a yes or no question. This may be the way in which the scapegoat was chosen on the Day of Atonement. The priest would go before the Lord in the Tabernacle and reach in and pull out a stone. The white stone would mean "yes" and the black one would mean "no". Because the names are plural, some suggest there were a number of stones and the majority color would decide. Others think that because one of the stones is named "lights" the answer could be seen by which stone glowed. I think the New Age would be excited about that suggestion.

Still others believe that the words don't stand for stones at all, but rather that the sacred names of God were written on a parchment and kept in the breast piece. When the priest sought an answer from the Lord in the Holy Place, they believe God would stir the air and the lights of the lampstand would cause the letters on the stones on the front of the breast piece to light up, spelling out the instruction from the Lord, showing a trust in God's involvement in every detail of the natural world. Their reasoning comes from the Hebrew letters beginning the words Urim and Thummim. They are the first and last letters of the Hebrew alphabet.

However it worked, we do know that even up to the time of the restoration, the Urim and Thummim helped the people make decisions of national importance. (Ezra 2:63) Hosea predicted that the time was coming when they would not have the ephod to consult. He prophesied the day was coming when they would seek the Lord their God and David their king in the latter days. We are still looking forward to the day when Jews realize the Son of David is their king and Messiah. (Hosea 2:5)

Under the ephod, the priest had a blue robe. On the bottom edge were alternating bells of gold and pomegranates made of blue and red yarn. Exodus 28:35 (ESV) *35 And it shall be on Aaron when he ministers, and its sound shall be heard when he goes into the Holy Place before the LORD, and when he comes out, so that he does not die.*

During the Tabernacle tours we told of how the priest would have a rope around his ankle to extract him in case he died in the Lord's presence. The holy presence of God was dangerous to those who came in without being fully prepared. It wasn't something one did lightly. But why do the bells prevent him from dying? Some would say it warns God that it is the priest coming in so that He veils His glory enough for the priest to survive. Others believe that it is for the priest to be reminded that he dare not make the encounter without being fully prepared according to God's requirements.

Under the blue robe was a checker pattern linen tunic, like the one Aaron's sons would wear. Under that was a pair of breeches, like underwear from the belly to the thighs.

He also wore a turban with a golden band that declared, "holiness to the Lord". All of these articles of clothing were things that consecrated him for his ministry. They set him apart as the one man who goes in before God and represents the people to God. The passage says these clothes are for holiness, glory and beauty. To approach God, these three elements were a necessity.

As we saw in the Tabernacle that everything points to Jesus, so we will see in the clothing of the priest. The problem with the priesthood was that every descendant of Aaron, and Aaron himself, were imperfect people who could never really fully represent their people before God. They had their own sins. God may have overlooked their sin for the time because of their obedience to His Word in how they were to come before Him, but they needed something to atone for their sins as well. The bull that they slew for their ordination was good enough for the ritual, but it was not the reality that would save them. (Hebrews 10:4) Though they represented holiness, glory and beauty, in actuality, they were a far cry from the real thing.

The real thing is Jesus. Let's consider each of the articles of clothing and how it could point to none other than our Savior. The onyx stones on the shoulder of the priest represented carrying the burdens of the tribes before the Lord.

I confess, I get overwhelmed with the burdens of the people. My shoulders simply are not big enough. The more I care, the fewer number of situations I'm able to really carry. There is only one way that I can take on the situations in your lives. That is to know that I can put it on Jesus' shoulders. His shoulders are big enough for the burdens of all mankind! Jesus and Jesus alone has the shoulders to take the burdens of mankind before God. (Hebrews 4:15a) I try to help carry some for a while, but eventually I have to give them to Jesus.

Scripture actually invites us to cast our burden on Him. (1Peter 5:7) Even your own burdens and those of your family are often more than you can bear, but they're never too much for Jesus' broad shoulders. He brings them to remembrance before the Father and you will either receive the grace you need or the change for which you've been praying. (1Corinthians 12:9)

Then there is the breastplate. The book of Isaiah tells us we are engraved on the Lord's hand (Isaiah 49:16), but the breastplate tells us we are engraved over His heart. He is never unaware of what you are facing. He is never out of touch with your pain. His children are close to His heart. (Song 8:6a) The names on the stones were there because they were in covenant with God. You can be sure your name is on His heart if you have entered the New Covenant. (1Corinthians 11:25) Exodus began with God remembering the covenant He made with their father, Abraham. (Exodus 2:24)

And consider how He represents you, as a jewel, a treasure, a precious stone. Each was unique from all the others, valued, and desired. When Jesus intercedes for you before the Father, there upon His heart is your name and mine. (John 10:3) And what the Son asks for, the Father gives. (John 13:3) Praise God!

The blue robe represents the fact that Jesus is from heaven while the linen tells us that He is also one of us. The priests ministered in their bare feet. That means the scars on Jesus' feet always testify to God that He paid the price for our redemption. (Hebrews 6:19-20)

The whole of the priest's wardrobe was to consecrate him and present him glorious, holy, and beautiful. That is what was required to approach God. Can anyone honestly say that there was anyone more glorious than Jesus? Glory is the breaking forth of the attributes of God. We never saw those attributes expressed more clearly than in Jesus. (Hebrews 1:3)

Jesus' righteous anger drove the money changers from the Temple, yet He ministered mercy to the "sinners". The prostitute is told her sins, though many, are forgiven, and the self-righteous Pharisees are called a brood of vipers. The widow's son was raised to life, the Gentiles servant healed, but the legalism that would keep healing from the needy on the Sabbath was condemned. (Matthew 12:12) He was glorious in every word and deed, glorious in the way He lived and died, and glorious in the way He rose from the dead!

None was holy like Jesus. Though many accused Him being of an evil source, none could condemn a single action. (John 8:46) When they condemned His words it was a distortion of what He actually said or refusal to recognize the truth. His holiness was verified in resurrection.

And He is all beautiful. Holiness is beautiful. (1 Chronicles 16:29) David longed to linger in the courts of the Lord and behold the beauty of the

LORD. (Psalm 27:4) Righteousness is beautiful. Truth is beautiful. If there was ever a beautiful life, it was that of Jesus'.

The priest's robes represented all these things, but Jesus was all those things in heart and action. The priest needed a gold plate on his forehead that declared holiness to the Lord. Jesus' mind was holy. Priest after priest failed to be all that God called them to be, but not our High Priest, Jesus. He fulfilled all that was required of the letter and Spirit of the law and remains our High Priest forever. (Hebrews 7:28)

Do you realize that if you are in Christ, the Father sees in you that same righteousness? (2Corinthians 5:21; Isaiah 54:17) That is why the Apostle Paul says to *put on the Lord Jesus Christ*. (Romans 13:14) That is like donning those priestly robes. It is the reality of what they represent. If you are in Christ, the Father sees you as glorious, holy and beautiful. You are consecrated. You have the privilege to approach God!

I know some of you have struggled with the assurance of your salvation. You are afraid your life isn't perfect enough or you haven't had the right experience. Grab hold of this! If you are in Jesus, trusting in what He did for you, you are in those robes! You are accepted!

Now, hear what the author of Hebrews says about Jesus. Hebrews 7:26-28 (ESV) *26 For it was indeed fitting that we should have such a high priest, holy, innocent, unstained, separated from sinners, and exalted above the heavens. 27 He has no need, like those high priests, to offer sacrifices daily, first for his own sins and then for those of the people, since he did this once for all when he offered up himself. 28 For the law appoints men in their weakness as high priests, but the word of the oath, which came later than the law, appoints a Son who has been made perfect forever.* With a priest like that, we are surely blessed!

Finally, there is the Urim and Thummim. It is the breastplate of decision Jesus wears so well. Many of us would like a little pair of magic rocks in our front pocket to tell us what to do. Come to think of it, I saw a lady in the store the other day using a rock to decide which product to buy. Jesus is our "go to" person for decisions. We get a lot more than "yes or no" answers too. He did away with sacred rocks because we have the revelation of His Word. We have a personal relationship with Him.

Imagine if you only said "yes" or "no" to your spouse. I know, some of you think that is true of your husband, but we men communicate in a lot more than words, and so does Jesus. When we focus our life on Jesus and His Word, our desires become His. We have a sense in our heart of what would please Him and what would not. The presence of His Holy Spirit within nudges us in the right direction and sometimes slams doors shut or swings it open through circumstance. It's so much better than a stony "yes" or "no" answer.

I think that many times, I've been too determined to hear a voice within. I'm not denying that there is a still small voice, but it often comes in expressions other than words. Are you open to all the ways that He would speak to you? The supreme way is His word. That is the main source by which we get to know Him. Look at how He's spoken to us in the clothing of the High Priest.

I'm so thankful I live in a day where the answer isn't in stones in my front pocket, but living in my heart. Hebrews 8:1-2 (ESV) *1 Now the point in what we are saying is this: we have such a high priest, one who is seated at the right hand of the throne of the Majesty in heaven, 2 a minister in the holy places, in the true tent that the Lord set up, not man.*

Thank God for sending us the Great High Priest, glorious, holy, beautiful! He brings us near to God, consecrates us with His presence in us and is the sacrifice for us. He makes us what He intended for the nation of Israel, a kingdom of priests that draw near to God. (1Peter 2:9; Hebrews 10:22)

Questions
1 What does the phrase "bring near" mean?
2 Why were the sacred vestments necessary? What about today?
3 Describe the ephod and the breastpiece?
4 How were the Umim and Thummim used?
5 How did God describe the function of the clothes?
6 In what way does Jesus fulfill the pictures in the priest's clothing?
7 Are you wearing those clothes?
8 How does Jesus fulfill the function of the clothes?
9 Why don't we need the Urim and Thummim?
10 Where is Jesus now? Implications?

Consecration Exodus 29

The chapter we are studying today is about the consecration of the priests and the altar along with a brief description of the daily sacrifices. It begins by telling us that the priests must be consecrated to serve the Lord. Consecrated, holy, sanctified are all words derived from the Hebrew word *qadash*. The sanctuary is called *mikdash*. If they are going to serve a holy of God in the holy place, they had to be holy. If they are going to serve in the *mikdash* they have to be *qadash*. The same is true for us. If we wish to serve a holy God, we must be holy. (Revelation 1:5-6)

To consecrate an object or a person is to have them move from one sphere to another, from the common to the sacred, from the profane to the holy. The tabernacle was sacred space. The instruments of the sacrifice and tabernacle were consecrated. The two worlds were not to mix. If someone touched something that was holy it could be defiled and need to be reconsecrated. But as we shall see later, certain things that were called "most holy" actually sanctified that which touched it. It was one way or the other; the two worlds were not to mingle. (Leviticus 10:10)

The chapter shows three rituals that are a picture of what must take place to set a priest apart from the common realm for God's sacred duties in the realm of the holy. The three offerings of ordination include the bull as a sin offering, a ram as a whole burnt offering, and a ram as a fellowship (peace) offering.

It began with Aaron and his sons being washed, probably at the bronze basin. Exodus 29:4 (ESV)*4 You shall bring Aaron and his sons to the entrance of the tent of meeting and wash them with water.* It was a picture of separating oneself from the moral pollution of the world. The New Testament tells us we are washed by the water of the Word. (Ephesians 5:26; Titus 3:5)

Then they donned their sacred robes. That is where consecration begins with us as well. We must be washed by the word of God and regenerated as pictured in baptism. (1Peter 3:21) Then we put on the Lord Jesus Christ, making no provision for the old nature to fulfill its desires. We step into Christ and out of our old nature that is of this fallen world. (Galatians 3:27)

The passage gives us a brief summary of the two robes, that of the High Priest, and that of his sons. We studied them last Sunday. (Priestly Robes) Aaron was then anointed with oil. (Exodus 30:22-33) Exodus 29:7 (ESV) *7 You shall take the anointing oil and pour it on his head and anoint him.* Anointing was a picture of the outpouring of the Holy Spirit over the person and their ministry. Only the tabernacle and its objects, the priests, and the King were anointed with oil. We are blessed to live in the time since Pentecost when the anointing is for all who will believe. (1John 2:27)

Aaron's sons dressed in a linen tunic with a sash and headband. This was not unusual dress though the pattern was special. All of the sacrifices were rituals that the common Israelite could offer. Still, they had to be the first to offer them before they could assist others in their offerings. The week long process had a few unique elements we will see in the last sacrifice.

The first sacrifice was the sin offering. A bull was brought before the tent of meeting, the tabernacle containing the Holy Place and the Holy of Holies. In front of that tent is where the brazen altar stood. (Exodus 30:18) Aaron and his sons placed their hands on the head of the bull. It was a picture of substitution. Instead of dying for their own sins, they were looking forward to a substitute. The bull was slaughtered. It's blood was put on the horns of the altar, and the rest was poured out at the base of the altar.

We have talked about our aversion to blood in previous sermons. We don't like to be reminded of the high price of sin. We don't think sin is such a serious issue. We justify it, excuse it, assign blame to others or conditions, but the bottom line is sin is deadly, costly, horrifically ugly and utterly selfish. It is so serious that nothing short of blood can picture the justice sin deserves. (Hebrews 9:22)

The fat of the inner parts was burned on the altar. The rest of the bull was taken outside the camp and burned. The author of Hebrews tells us this is a picture of Jesus' sacrifice for us. He is our sin offering. He was taken outside the city also to be placed upon wood and die for our sins. (Leviticus 4:12) Hebrews 13:11-12(NIV) *11 The high priest carries the blood of animals into the Most Holy Place as a sin offering, but the bodies are burned outside the camp. 12 And so Jesus also suffered outside the city gate to make the people holy through his own blood.* Jesus is the ultimate sin offering that consecrates us to God.

The second offering was a ram. This is a whole burnt offering. Again, Aaron and his sons lay their hands on the head of the ram. The ram is slaughtered. The blood is sprinkled on the sides of the altar. The entire ram is consumed on the altar.

The whole burnt offering symbolizes complete dedication to God. The whole of the priests' life is to be dedicated to God. Nothing is to be kept back. The priests were to be living sacrifices on the altar of God's service. Paul picked up on this theme in Romans 12:1 (NIV) *1 Therefore, I urge you, brothers, in view of God's mercy, to offer your bodies as living sacrifices, holy and pleasing to God--this is your spiritual act of worship.* Notice how Paul uses the "pleasing" aspect of the sacrifice of the whole burnt offering. In reference to the aroma pleasing God, he wrote that we should imitate Jesus who *lived a life of love and was a sacrifice of sweet aroma to God.* (Ephesians 5:1-2)

The final offering is the fellowship offering. Once again Aaron and sons lay their hands on the head of the ram is a symbolic act of transferring their sins to it. (Leviticus 16:21) It is slain, but before the blood is sprinkled on the sides of the altar, the blood is used to anoint the right ear lobe, thumb and big toe of the priests. The blood looks forward to the atoning blood of Jesus. It is only His blood that can take away sins and consecrate us for service to God. (Hebrews 9:23-24)

This is the part of the ceremony that was unique to ordination. I believe that the earlobe was symbolic of all the senses but first and foremost of hearing, while the thumb and the big toe symbolize what a person does and the way one's life is lived. The blood of the fellowship offering pictured consecration of those areas of the priests' life. All of his life was now dedicated to God alone. The reality is that blood of Jesus should be applied to all those areas of our life too. (Romans 6:13)

That does not mean that we can intentionally disobey God without consequence. Rather, we are even more liable to punishment should we willfully sin. (Luke 12:48) These same sons will die when they disobey a fundamental principle of God. It did, however, for the sake of their service, set them apart as holy to serve a holy God.

Have you applied the blood of Jesus to your senses, especially your hearing His word, to your actions, and your walk through life? Then you are almost ready to serve a holy God. There is still more to the fellowship offering.

Moses was then to take the blood and the anointing oil and sprinkle them and their clothing with it, consecrating those linen robes to God's service. Every part of life was to be infused with the reality of the substitution that had taken their sins (only really fulfilled in Jesus) and with the Holy Spirit's power and direction.

I would love to take the blood and oil and sprinkle all of us this morning, to infuse us with the reality of the blood substitution and the oil of the Holy Spirit. It would be pretty messy. Life in the service to God is messy, but it speaks volumes of what God wants to do in our life. Every random area of our life should be touched by the sacrifice of Jesus and the anointing of the Holy Spirit. We tend to isolate it to certain areas, but it should cover your senses, your actions, and your direction in life. Is that true of you this morning? Where do you need a fresh sprinkling, not of the shadow that we are reading about, but of the reality? (Ephesians 5:18)

Finally, the end of the fellowship offering is for the sharing of a meal. They were to take the unleavened bread and part of the ram and wave it before the Lord, and then burn it upon the altar. Then they were to take the breast of the ram and more unleavened bread and wave it before the Lord and eat it. It was a meal of peace. (Revelation 3:20)

I believe the heave offering of the thigh of the ram was an up and down motion, which was symbolically saying, "It comes from You; I give it back; You return it to me; I give it back." This is the pattern of a life that is at peace with God. What He has is mine and what I have is His. (1Corinthians 3:23-25; Revelation 4:10)

When two parties were at peace with one another, they would share a meal. God was saying that through all this ritual, they were looking forward to how man could have peace with God. 1

Let's briefly go through the steps of the consecration of Aaron and his sons again. Washed by water, sin atoned for through the sin offering that was burned outside the camp, complete dedication as seen in the whole burnt offering, and then the marking of life with the blood of the offering of fellowship on the main areas of life as well as the sprinkling the blood and anointing oil over the garments. Finally, there was a meal of peace, communion with God. What a picture of the path we take to serve our holy God!

Then we have the consecration of the altar. Exodus 29:36-37 (NIV) *Purify the altar by making atonement for it, and anoint it to consecrate it. 37 For seven days make atonement for the altar and consecrate it. Then the altar will be most holy, and whatever touches it will be holy.* The altar was also to be ritually purified. This was one of the most holy items in the tabernacle. Anything that touched it was considered holy, set apart for God's purposes. (Matthew 23:19)

The reality of this shadow is the holiness of Jesus. When He touched the unclean, such as lepers or the woman with the issue of blood, or the dead, it did not result in His defilement, rather it caused the unclean to be whole. The leper is healed as well as the woman with the issue of blood. (Mark 1:41; Luke 8:44) Even the widow's dead son came to life at the touch of Jesus. (Luke 7:14-15) These were proofs that Jesus is most holy.

Next, the chapter moves to the brief description of the daily sacrifice, in the morning and at twilight. A yearling lamb would be offered on the altar along with two quarts of fine flower, a quart of olive oil, and a quart of wine. They were burnt offerings, meaning the entire animal was consumed. It has been said that the last remnant of the morning sacrifice was being consumed when the twilight sacrifice began which burned until the morning sacrifice. In other words, there was always to be the smoke of the offering of a yearling lamb rising to the Lord.

This is a picture of the eternal work of our Savior. He is our lamb without blemish whose sacrifice is always before the Lord so that we are not consumed. (1Peter 1:18-19) The holy must never mix with the common, and so Jesus' sacrifice ever shows that our sins have been atoned. That is why when John sees Jesus before the throne of God in Revelation chapter 5, He still bears the wounds that caused His death. (Revelation 5:6)

Think of the thousands of lambs throughout Israel's history, the many and varied sacrifices that all point to what Jesus would do for us. One picture could not portray the fullness of it, and so in the different types of offerings we have the pieces of the puzzle that make up the coming Messiah and our life in Him.

Exodus 29:42-43 (NIV*) 42 "For the generations to come this burnt offering is to be made regularly at the entrance to the Tent of Meeting before the LORD. there I will meet you and speak to you; 43 there also I will meet with the Israelites, and the place will be consecrated by my glory.* Where does God meet with us? It is the tabernacle of Jesus' body. (John 1:14) It is there that He has spoken to us. (Hebrews 1:1-2) That was the place that was consecrated for God's glory. In the words of Jesus and the phrases we see in John's gospel and the letter to the Hebrews, we see this was all pointing to Jesus.

God was never happy with all the sacrifice and blood, but it painted a true picture of what was needed. It showed how justice would someday be served and yet grace and mercy would prevail. Substitution! He died in our place. (Leviticus 17:11)

Exodus 29:46 (NIV*) 46 They will know that I am the LORD their God, who brought them out of Egypt so that I might dwell among them. I am the LORD their God.* If you know the tabernacle of the body of Jesus, the One consecrated by the glory of God, then you know it was Jesus that redeemed you from this evil world. You know that He lives among us. His Holy Spirit consecrates us and we know that He and the Father are One. (John 10:30)

He is the reality to which all that these sacrifices pointed. He is our Great High Priest. "The book of Hebrews calls him "a merciful and faithful high priest in service to God" (2:17); "the high priest whom we confess" (3:1); "a great high priest" (4:14); "a high priest forever" (6:20); the "high priest of the good things that are already here" (9:11); "a great priest over the house of God" (10:21). As our great High Priest, Jesus presents our prayers to God, interceding on our behalf. He also stands before God in perfect righteousness, so that we can be accepted in God's sight. (From Preaching the Word - Exodus: Saved for God's Glory.)

He did all this to set you apart as a nation of priests that are at peace with God. (1Peter 2:9) You are consecrated to serve God as you do whatever God has called you to do for His glory. Just as the priests had different ministries, don't be put on a guilt trip that you must do what someone else does. You have your own calling. Find it and do it under God's anointing, bringing Him glory!

Some say that the church has failed, that there are so few that show Jesus to the world. I would say that the fact that we are a work in progress shows we are the church. Jesus does not fail. He is the One completing what He started. (Philippians 1:5) He never fails. Organizations fail. Individuals fail. But the true church continues to be priests to the world, examples of life at peace with God, sharing the path to consecration – Jesus, through their varied gifts and callings. The living martyrs some of us heard yesterday testify to the fact that Jesus is succeeding. His plan goes on around the world unhindered by the failures of man. He truly dwells in our midst, the Lord our God!

If you are here this morning and don't know the wonder of God calling you to the highest calling of all, you are invited to do what Aaron and his sons did. Lay your hands on Jesus' head. Let Him take your sins upon Himself. He wants to do that for you. Be washed in the waters of baptism. Be anointed with the Holy Spirit of God. Be consecrated to a life of serving your Creator.

Questions
1 What does it meant to consecrate something?
2 What was the first act of ordination? Relate to today.
3 What did the putting on of the robes mean to them? To us?
4 Who was the anointing for then? Now?
5 What was the first sacrifice? How was it fulfilled?
6 What was the second? Significance?
7 The third? And how can we relate?
8 How do we see the "Most Holy" principle in the life of Jesus?
9 Describe the daily sacrifices?
10 Go over the descriptions of Jesus from the letter to the Hebrews.

Rebels Without A Cause Exodus 32

To understand what is happening in this chapter we need to remember the setting. Mount Sinai was smoking and trembling when God came down and spoke the Ten Commandments. The Hebrews heard His voice. The people all agreed to live according to God's commands. (Exodus 24:3) They entered into a blood covenant with God. The elders went up the mountain and ate in God's presence. Out of fear, the people refused to meet with God and asked that Moses go represent them. (Exodus 20:19) Moses went on up the mountain leaving Aaron and Hur in charge. Joshua stayed at the edge of the cloud of God's glory waiting for Moses to return.

Every morning the people received the manna as their food provision. Every day they and their herds drank from the water that miraculously flowed from the rock. The cloud that led them covered them from the heat of the sun each day and lit up the night sky as a pillar of fire. (Numbers 9:16)

They wait. They wait some more. Two weeks go by, and then three, four, five, and finally they get tired of waiting. They began to wonder if Moses survived the encounter with God. When would they get going to the Promised Land? They decided to take matters into their own hands, so they took their grievance to the associate pastor with a plan of action. *1 When the people saw that Moses delayed to come down from the mountain, the people gathered themselves together to Aaron and said to him, "Up, make us gods who shall go before us. As for this Moses, the man who brought us up out of the land of Egypt, we do not know what has become of him."*

I wonder if Peter had this passage in mind when he wrote about the delay of Jesus' return? 2 Peter 3:3-4 (ESV) *3 knowing this first of all, that scoffers will come in the last days with scoffing, following their own sinful desires. 4 They will say, "Where is the promise of his coming? For ever since the fathers fell asleep, all things are continuing as they were from the beginning of creation."* It is the sinful desires of man that prompt the denial of a day of accountability. It is denying the obvious, that God intervenes in the affairs of man. We see it all the time. We can read about it in history. We have seen it in our church. Yet, our sinful nature would prefer to make our own god, one that we can manage, one with little or no morality, one created after our own evil imagination.

Moses will come down the mountain and the people will be held accountable for their betrayal of the covenant. Jesus will return, and we will all give an account of our actions before a holy God. (Romans 14:12)

I don't know what happened to Hur, but Aaron must have been the one they knew they could manipulate. Aaron did not confront them. He didn't remind them of Moses order to wait. He didn't ask them to recall the wonders of their deliverance from Egypt, the faithfulness of Moses, the agreement to have no other gods, but instead decided to be a people pleaser. (Galatians 1:10) He took the golden earrings from the people and cast it into the shape of a calf. (Psalm 106:19-22) This was the syncretism of YHWH and Egypt's gods. It was a direct violation of the first and second commandments. It was a graven image and another god. (Exodus 20:3-4) They were to resist the temptation to make any physical object that represented the invisible God.

While in Egypt, they had seen a lot of different kinds of cow worship. The ultimate in bull worship was probably the Apis bull, considered to [be] the manifestation of Ptah, the creator god worshipped at Memphis in lower Egypt. The bull lived in palatial quarters in the precincts of the temple; only the higher echelons of society were allowed to view it from special windows; its death was treated on a par with the death of pharaoh; and the remains were mummified. Images of calves or bulls were associated with the strength and power of the deity, and the idols as well as certain live animals came to be regarded as embodiments of the god. (from John L. Madkay, Exodus p 529)

As soon as their god was made, they began to worship it. The worship of false gods usually degenerates into debauchery, which is the reason they made the god in the first place, justification for their sin. We don't create images today. We create ideologies to justify our actions. It's for the same purpose of doing what we desire, whether elevation of self or just self-gratification. It's an imaginative way to believe we won't be accountable. The whole New Age philosophy is a way to be "spiritual" and yet indulge in your desires without fear of judgment. It's a way to ignore the fact that Jesus will return and judge the earth. (John 5:22)

The Apostle Paul tells us that this passage is specifically for the New Testament church. 1 Corinthians 10:6-7 (ESV) 6 Now these things took place as examples for us, that we might not desire evil as they did. 7 Do not be idolaters as some of them were; as it is written, "The people sat down to eat and drink and rose up to play." The New Testament world had idols that were associated with pagan temple prostitution. The images today go straight to immoral desire by turning the human body into an idol. That is the power of pornography. You can't bow down to it for long before you end up going down the same road as the Israelites.

The problem is in the heart. They must have associated some sense of satisfaction with the cow worship in Egypt. That is the root of idolatry, desiring satisfaction in something outside the will of God. God is to be the One that satisfies our soul. Everything else is a substitute. That does not mean we cannot enjoy His creation, on the contrary, we enjoy it within His will and give thanks to Him for His goodness. Outside of His will is either destructive excess or eventual addiction that is also destructive. The only way to be free is to identify the evil in our hearts and realize it is a poor substitution for God. Then, put it to death by accepting the Lordship of Jesus! (Romans 8:13) Egypt was still thriving in the hearts of the Israelites.

The irony of the situation is that God was giving Moses a way to picture His presence in the Tabernacle while the people were creating their own way. The two ways couldn't be any more different. (1) The people seek to create what God has already provided; (2) they, rather than God, take the initiative; (3) offerings are demanded rather than willingly presented; (4) the elaborate preparations are missing altogether; (5) the painstaking length of time needed for building becomes an overnight rush job; (6) the careful provision for guarding the presence of the Holy One turns into an open-air object of immediate accessibility; (7) the invisible, intangible God becomes a visible, tangible image; and (8) the personal, active God becomes an impersonal object that cannot see or speak or act. The ironic effect is that the people forfeit the very divine presence they had hoped to bind more closely to themselves. (from Donald Fretheim, Exodus, pp 280-281)

This is human nature on display. I want to be spiritual, but I want to be spiritual my way. I want a god I can control, that lets me indulge in my pride, or my lusts, or whatever it is I want to retain. (Psalm 135:18)

7 And the LORD said to Moses, "Go down, for your people, whom you brought up out of the land of Egypt, have corrupted themselves. 8a They have turned aside quickly out of the way that I commanded them. While

Moses was listening to God's plans, the people were making their own. They corrupted themselves. It is a Hebrew term implying depraved moral conduct which is offensive to God. That is a fascinating description of corporate sin. One suggestion for an action can infect a multitude and cause them to corrupt themselves. The New Testament refers to it as leaven. (Galatians 5:9) "Turning aside" is another description. They were on the path the Lord commanded them but they decided to go their own direction, a flesh detour. (Deuteronomy 11:16) The surprise is how quickly they would go this direction while surrounded by the miraculous provision of God. But don't be too surprised, we see it all too often in believers' lives.

Exodus 32:9-10 (ESV) *9 And the LORD said to Moses, "I have seen this people, and behold, it is a stiff-necked people. 10 Now therefore let me alone, that my wrath may burn hot against them and I may consume them, in order that I may make a great nation of you."* Stiff-necked! Have you ever had one; I mean the medical condition. When someone behind you calls to you, you can't really turn your head to face them unless you turn your whole body. That is kind of the idea behind the word. It's a refusal to heed God. It's not that we don't hear, we just refuse to turn, so we continue on our own way. It's the "I'm the captain of my ship and lord of my fate" attitude. "No one is going to tell me what to do, including God!" (Deuteronomy 31:27) It's the animal that will not lower its head to accept the yoke.

This is a dangerous position for anyone to be in. Stiff-necked people always think they're right and never admit they're wrong. They refuse to listen to good spiritual counsel. They say, "I'm sorry; that's just the way I am," and then they expect everyone else to deal with it. They ask for advice, but they don't follow it. They go ahead and do what they were planning to do anyway. And when they get into trouble, they are unwilling to be corrected. "Yes," they say, "but my situation is different," and then they offer some kind of excuse. When they go through suffering, they complain about it, but they never seem to learn anything from it. They never change. They never grow. And the saddest thing of all is that they don't even know it. Since they never bow in true submission to God, they don't realize how stiff-necked they are.

Don't be stiff-necked! Assume that you might be wrong; and when you are wrong, admit it. If you ask for counsel from someone in spiritual authority, try to follow it. Listen when people correct you, especially if what they're saying makes you angry. This is almost always a sign that there's some truth to what they're saying. Learn from God through suffering. Pursue spiritual transformation by spending time in prayer and the Word. Wear the yoke of Christ with glad submission. (from Preaching the Word – Exodus: Saved for God's Glory.)

The Lord appears ready to annihilate them, but we know that He knows the end from the beginning. (1Samuel 15:29) The Lord is giving Moses a chance to exhibit more Christ like qualities.

In our passage today Moses is a type of Messiah more clearly than any other recorded about Him. He is the one that speaks to God face to face. He is the one that comes down from the presence of God to deal with sin. He intercedes for the people and averts the wrath of God that the people deserve. He is the one that is willing to give himself that the people might be saved. He is angry with sin and yet compassionately desires to see the people receive mercy. He is a mortal man but his access to God and obedience to Him saves his people. His faith and character make the covenant possible. What a picture of Jesus! (Deuteronomy 18:15)

By asking Moses to leave him alone, God is leaving the door open for Moses to intercede for his people. In other words, "If you don't intercede then this is what I'll do." It seems God may have been testing Moses by offering to make a nation from him, Children of Moses instead of Children of Abraham. Moses showed his godly character in choosing the good of the people rather than his own pride. (Matthew 22:39-40)

The people were certainly an ungrateful lot, so ready to dump Moses after all the sacrifices he had made for them, but Moses graciously pleaded for them. He reminded God of the promises to Abraham. He spoke of God's reputation in the world. Deuteronomy 9:25 tells us that Moses prayed for 40 days and nights.

14 And the LORD relented from the disaster that he had spoken of bringing on his people. Did God change His plan, or did He prompt Moses to do what He intended for him to do all along? God is righteous, but He is also merciful. (Exodus 34:6-7)

Moses headed back down the mountain with the two tablets engraved by God on front and back. Joshua was waiting half way down the mountain. It sounds to me like Joshua was trying to downplay what was happening. War would be better than rebellion against God. Moses wasn't fooled. He knew what was happening. God had already told him. But when he actually witnessed what was going on, he lost it. He broke the tablets, ground the calf to powder put it in the water and made the people drink it.

Then he confronted Aaron. Exodus 32:21 (ESV) *21 And Moses said to Aaron, "What did this people do to you that you have brought such a great sin upon them?"* Did they forced him? Then Aaron did what is so common, he came up with lying excuse that was so bad it is almost comical. Exodus 32:24 (ESV) *24 So I said to them, 'Let any who have gold take it off.' So they gave it to me, and I threw it into the fire, and out came this calf."* It's a miracle! When we are disobedient, we often make pathetic excuses to justify our actions. He should have just confessed and pled for mercy.

25 And when Moses saw that the people had broken loose (for Aaron had let them break loose, to the derision of their enemies), Here is another interesting phrase, "broken loose". It is the casting aside of restraint. It is letting the flesh do whatever it desires ignoring the consequences and God's commands. (Romans 1:22-24) Sin is breaking loose from God's constraints.

Notice that Aaron had let them do this. As their spiritual leader he was responsible to discipline them. (1Peter 5:2) A great deal of the blame fell on him. The Bible does not record how he suffered for this. You would expect him to receive the fiercest discipline from God. But he is the one that will wear the priestly robes, a sinner covered with Christ. He'll be the perfect example of the grace of God. He is every minister, a failed human leader, but by the grace of God clothed in Jesus (1Corinthians 15:9-10) and anointed for his task.

Moses cried out, "Who is on the Lord's side?" Only the sons of Levi came to him. The people called the idol the "LORD" (YHWH), but once they broke one command, they let go of restraint and all concern for God and His will. They were freed from slavery only to enter another kind of slavery, that of the flesh. (John 8:34)

What follows seems harsh, but compared to what they deserved, (Romans 6:23) it was light. The 3000 that died by the sword were only a small percentage of the total population and were probably the most stubbornly defiant.

The day of Pentecost is the day that Israel celebrates Moses bringing the Law down from Sinai (Simchat Torah). When the Law came down 3000 died. When the Spirit was poured out some 1500 years later at the same time of the year, 3000 were born again. (Acts 2:41) *The letter kills but the Spirit gives life.* (2Corinthians 3:6)

The deaths were a harsh lesson and the judgment was not over. A plague followed. God had clearly shown the people that He would not tolerate such rebellion, and yet He was merciful and did not destroy them all. He heard Moses' intercession and spared them. Still, most of them would die in the wilderness, but they would raise a generation that would go in to the Promised Land.

The message has been about impatience with God, taking things into our own hands and going our own way. As we cast off restraints, the rebellion only increases until God deals with us. Don't let it begin. Submit to God. Wait patiently on Him. (Psalm 130:5) Don't turn from His way. (Deuteronomy 5:32)

Like Moses in this account, Jesus calls out to us today, "Who is on the Lord's side?" To come to Him you have to leave the debauchery of the world, the pride trips, lust, compromises to be accepted, and stand unashamedly on His side. Will you follow the Levites' example and leave the crowd of self-indulgence, bow your head and accept Jesus' yoke, and stand with Him?

Questions
1 Describe the chapter setting?
2 Why did the people rebel?
3 Why a golden calf?
4 How do we justify our actions today?
5 What does the New Testament say about this?
6 How can we be free from idolatry?
7 Contrast their way and God's way.
8 What is "stiffnecked"?
9 How is Moses like Jesus?
10 Contrast this with Pentecost?

Divine Presence Exodus 33:1-16

The highlight of receiving the law ended in tragedy as 3000 were killed and a plague devastated the camp. The Israelites could not even keep the most important commands of God for 40 days. The tablets from God were in pieces at the foot of the mountain. The wailing for the dead pierced the air. But our chapter today hits the lowest of lows.

God will keep His promises. He will give them the land He promised to Abraham. He will even send an angel to make sure it all comes to pass. But it is not THE angel of God (14:19) as He fears the result of dwelling among them. The main purpose of the Exodus is set aside. There will be no need for a tabernacle, no space for God. Their lack of reverence for His word, and stubborn insistence on their own ways has caused God to withdraw His presence for their sake. His holy and just presence would require judgment should they turn to their own ways again. (Exodus 20:5)

3 Go up to a land flowing with milk and honey; but I will not go up among you, lest I consume you on the way, for you are a stiff-necked people." Last week we learned that stiff-necked was an expression for an animal that would resist the yoke of the owner by holding its head up high. It is a refusal to submit. Pride is the refusal to yield to any other than one's own will. The people had just been set free from slavery. You would think they would humbly listen to the God that set them free and be careful to keep the covenant they made with Him. Instead they fell captive to a new master, pride. "We know best! We don't have to obey God. We have a better idea." Like Eve in the Garden, they question what God has said. (Genesis 3:6) A holy God in the midst of a stubborn and rebellious people will mean many more will be judged. So God graciously commits to withdrawing His presence.

4 When the people heard this disastrous word, they mourned, and no one put on his ornaments. It really is a "disastrous word". There is no more disastrous expression than "the presence of God will not be with you." Cain heard something similar. (Genesis 4:14) King Saul will hear it. (1Samuel 16:14) Israel will hear it. (2Kings 17:18) It should send shivers down our spine.

When God is with us, life has meaning and purpose. You can count on the suffering of life resulting in some good purpose. You have a place to turn when the burdens of life become too much for you to bear. There is hope. (Psalm 130:7)

There is nothing more frightening than to be left to our own devises. Our own heart deceives us. (Jeremiah 17:9) And there is a foreboding sense of certain, impending judgment. Our neck is stretched out and our nose is high. We won't accept the yoke, but our heart is trembling. Eventually we convince ourselves that we are the master of our fate and our heart stops trembling. It grows harder and more determined to justify itself in every issue regardless of the facts. It is so hardened that we redefine reality to fit our deception.

Was Moses wrong to intercede for them? After all, they will die in the desert as God was warning. (Numbers 14:22-23) No, Moses did the right thing. He will be commended in Scripture for his intercessory prayer power. (Jeremiah 15:1) There is always hope for redemption until the last breath is drawn. Better to have the presence of God deal with us and suffer the consequences than to not have His presence at all. (Psalm 51:11)

The Israelites had enough of a sense of what God was saying to mourn the very idea of God's presence leaving. Believers know exactly what this is talking about. Our prayers don't seem to be answered. We don't even have a sense that God is listening. It feels as if the heavens are brass. That communion we felt with God is just not there. The joy is gone. (Psalm 51:12) It is an effort to smile. The fruit of the Spirit becomes a thing we must force rather than something flowing spontaneously from us. Why? Our stiff-necked attitude of refusing to take God's yoke is a sign of our stepping away from Him. He does not leave us. It is we who refuse to go with Him. He can say, "I won't go with you" because we aren't going where He is going. (John 12:26)

Verses 7 through 11 look back at how God had been meeting with Moses. The tabernacle will become the official Tent of Meeting, but before it was built Moses had a prayer tent outside the camp. Anyone could go there to pray. When Moses would go out to commune with God, the cloud would descend in front of the entrance of the tent. Everyone in the camp of Israel would stand before the door of their tents and watch as God spoke with Moses.

"Face to face" is an expression of intimacy. Moses did not see a manifestation of a face, for we will see next week that he requests to see some type of manifestation. "Face to face" means that there is no intermediary. At times, God does use an intermediary even with Moses, (Acts 7:38) but Moses was special in that God spoke directly to him. What the people heard, when God came down Mount Sinai, Moses heard on a regular basis.

I believe the reason we have this description of Moses hearing from God at this point in the passage is to emphasize the consequences of God not going with them. That would be the end of divine counsel. When there are disputes, there will be nowhere to turn but the wisdom of man. When the voice of God is rejected, we are left with nothing but men competing for control. Instead of meeting with God in the pillar of cloud, we meet with men in a smoke-filled room.

If we only realized the consequences of our stiff-necked attitude, we would quickly bow our necks. (Zechariah 7:12) We would be mourning and take off our jewelry and fast and pray for God to have mercy and go with us. Even if He destroys us, it's better than going our own way!

I love the little addendum to verse 11, When Moses turned again into the camp, his assistant Joshua the son of Nun, a young man, would not depart from the tent. Joshua reminds me of Peter on the Mount of Transfiguration. "Lord, do you want us to build three little shelters for You, Moses, and Elijah?" (Matthew 17:4) He wanted to hang out there.

When the glory of God is manifest, we savor the sensation, the purity, and the joy of the encounter. But Moses knew life isn't about hanging out in the tent. You go to the tent to get your instructions. Sure, you savor the encounter, but then we must take that encounter into the word and live what we heard.

12 Moses said to the LORD, "See, you say to me, 'Bring up this people,' but you have not let me know whom you will send with me. Yet you have said, 'I know you by name, and you have also found favor in my sight.' 13 Now therefore, if I have found favor in your sight, please show me now your ways, that I may know you in order to find favor in your sight. Moses reminded God of His word. It's not that God had forgotten, but that Moses based His request on what God had already said. This is a great example of how to intercede. Remember what God has said. Remember His word.

Next, Moses brought up His relationship with God. Not everyone can pray with this kind of authority. Remember that in the book of James we are told that the fervent prayer of a righteous man is powerful. (James 5:16) Our walk with God affects our prayer life.

Notice what Moses is asking. He doesn't begin by asking that God renounce what was just declared. He'll get there, but first Moses asks to be shown the ways of God. How does God go about things? What are His ways? Moses knew that if he walked in the ways of God, he would find even more favor with God, and he would therefore pray according to God's will. (1John 5:14) The ways of God are perfect. If we understand the ways of God then we understand what is just and righteous. (Genesis 18:19) The way of the Lord is a stronghold to the blameless. (Proverbs 10:29)

Not knowing the way of the Lord is equated to not accepting God's yoke in Jeremiah 5:5. Moses was asking God to keep him from being stiff-necked by accepting God's yoke. To walk in God's ways is to accept the yoke of righteousness and justice. If our prayers are to be effectual, we must walk in the ways of God. No one is perfect. Perfection is not required for God to hear your prayers. But when you live in the ways of God, your prayers are in line with God's will. You have expectant faith to make your request.

Moses continued his intercession. Consider too that this nation is your people. God had said, *"Go down, for your people, whom you brought up out of the land of Egypt, have corrupted themselves."* 32:7 God called them "your people". Sometimes I hear one parent say to another, "Your child is misbehaving!" Suddenly the child belongs only to one parent. Moses doesn't want to claim ownership. He is reminding God that they are His nation of people. Since they are God's, it is up to God to care for them and direct them. How can they be His nation if He doesn't go with them?

14 And he said, "My presence will go with you, and I will give you rest." We started the message on the lowest note possible, but now we have hit the highest, the promise of presence and rest. God accepted Moses' intercession. Did God change His mind? He knows the end from the beginning. (Isaiah 46:10) He was prompting Moses to intercede for Israel, but He was also giving the people a warning. It can be dangerous to have a holy God present among you. (Proverbs 19:23) But if you walk in His ways of righteousness and justice, His presence gives us rest. (Matthew 11:28)

The author of Hebrews points out that the Psalms declare they did not enter the rest of God. (Psalm 95:11) The rest of God is not found in possessions, but it is experiencing the presence of God. The presence of God is experienced when we walk in the ways of God. He was explaining that Israel never really fully lived in the ways of God. (Hebrews 3:19) They did not know righteousness. True rest is only experienced in Jesus who is the Lord our righteousness. (Jeremiah 23:6)

When we enter into Jesus, we know the rest that only He can give. We no longer strive to please God to gain acceptance. We walk in His ways because we are accepted. And so He writes, *"For we who believe have entered that rest."* Hebrews 4:3a We have righteousness that is not our own. We trust in what He did on our behalf. The way of God is Jesus who declared Himself to be the only way. (John 14:6)

Moses replied, "If your presence will not go with me, do not bring us up from here." If you aren't going, I'm not going. Though Moses knew that God was with him in Egypt, he still had the idea that God was the God of Sinai. If God wouldn't go with them to the Promised Land, Moses was saying they were going to stay where God is at Sinai. In other words, "We're not leaving You!"

Even though the Promised Land had homes, fields, and pastureland waiting for them, Moses would rather live in the desert with God than to be in the Promised Land without Him. I wonder if we could say the same. When it comes to a choice of between abundance or presence, which would we choose? Moses had no problem choosing. He was 80 years old and he had made his choice 40 years ago. He wasn't going to change it now.

Jory and Mac have made that choice over the past year. They have given up abundance to obey God's calling. I'm looking forward to seeing the transformation in Jory when he returns. Would you remember in prayer those who have left all to follow God, to go where He is leading to remain in His presence?

Moses continued praying, *16 For how shall it be known that I have found favor in your sight, I and your people? Is it not in your going with us, so that we are distinct, I and your people, from every other people on the face of the earth?"* What makes a difference between the people of God and everyone else? It is His presence! And how do people see that difference? It is the fruit of the Spirit in our lives. (Galatians 5:22-23; Psalm 139:7)

Remember, walking in His ways is consistent with being righteous, that is, expressing the attributes of God. The fruits of the Spirit are the visible difference. The presence is seen in the love, joy, peace, patience, kindness, and goodness of each child of God. That is how people can see God has favored us. That is how they can become hungry for righteousness. (Matthew 5:6) That is the power behind our witness, the very presence of God.

17 And the LORD said to Moses, "This very thing that you have spoken I will do, for you have found favor in my sight, and I know you by name." Moses had a relationship with God. God initiated it. God developed it, but we can also say that Moses cooperated with it.

In the account we have looked at today, God challenged Moses to become even more intimate with Him. He wanted others to be spared through Moses' intercession, and teach Moses what it meant to stand in the gap. (Ezekiel 22:30)

We often stand at a crossroad. We can walk away from God and still have the blessings we seek, or we can value His presence above all else. Will you say with Moses, "If Your presence does not go with me, I will not leave this place"? Do you want the presence of God so strongly that nothing else compares? Are you desperate to know the ways of God because you desire to know Him and please Him? Do people see the presence of God in your life in the fruits of the Spirit?

What is the priority in your life? I hope you can say you just want God's presence whatever it takes and wherever He leads!

Find time to get alone with God and linger like Joshua did in the tent of meeting. Maybe you have been away from His presence and you want to return to His ways, no better day than today, and no better time than now. (Matthew 6:6)

Questions
1 Why didn't God want to go with them?
2 Who in the Bible has heard the disastrous word?
3 Who leaves whom?
4 What are the consequences?
5 What was the tent of meeting?
6 How did Moses intercede?
7 How do you experience His presence?
8 What choice was Moses willing to make to stay with God? Relate.
9 What is the difference between believer and unbeliever?
10 Is the presence of God your highest priority?

Glory Revealed Exodus 33:17-34:35

The Bible is a series of historical accounts of God's interaction with mankind. The purpose of the record is to teach us about human nature, but more than that, to reveal the nature of God. In our passage today, perhaps more than any other in our Old Testament, God declares to us the essence of His nature.

Moses has just pled with God to forgive the nation for their idolatry and "breaking loose" (Exodus 32:25) and to go with them to the Promised Land. His plea was based on his relationship with God and the promises God had given to Abraham. It also addressed concern for the way the world would interpret what God was threatening to do.

17 And the LORD said to Moses, "This very thing that you have spoken I will do, for you have found favor in my sight, and I know you by name." God granted the request because of His relationship with Moses. The people were saved because God was pleased with their mediator. It is the same reason we are saved today, because God was well pleased with Jesus. (Matthew 3:17) The people didn't honor Moses by obeying his request to wait for him. They were ready to forget him and choose a new leader. (Exodus 32:1) But God honored Moses.

Whose honor do you desire? This is a test every child of God will face. God allows situations in which we must choose between the honor of men and the honor that comes from God alone. (Galatians 1:10; John 12:43) It is an inevitable step in our spiritual growth.

Since Moses had just heard an affirmation of God's relationship with him, he went out on a limb and made another request.

18 Moses said, "Please show me your glory." Moses had seen the burning bush (Exodus 3:3), met with God numerous times on the mountain, ate with the elders in God's presence (Exodus 24:9-10), and spent 40 days in the cloud of glory (Exodus 24:15-18), but he knew that he had only experienced a tiny fraction of the glory of God. Now Moses is asking for as much as he can handle. He had already asked to have a revelation of the ways of God so he could please God (verse 13), but now he is asking to have a visible revelation of His glory.

The word "glory" *(kabod)* is derived from a word *(kabad)* that means heavy, substantial, and so it implies the real substance of something in a good sense. It is the splendor of a thing. The definition of glory that I have found most helpful for my understanding is this: the visible essence of a good thing. There is a glory of earthly things and another of heavenly things. (1Corinthians 15:40) The glory of God is the visible expression of his nature. When we say, "Give glory to God", we are saying we should declare His nature accurately whether in words or in action.

The glory of God was manifest in the life of Jesus. (John 1:14; 17:4) We see the very nature of God in all that He said and did. The Gospels declare the glory of God. Nature, to a lesser extent, declares the glory of God. (Romans 1:20) Moses wanted to see the splendor of the essence of God. That is quite a request! We ask for the same thing when we ask for a greater revelation of Jesus and all that He means to us. (John 14:9)

19 And he said, "I will make all my goodness pass before you and will proclaim before you my name 'The LORD.' Because the LORD is good, and there is no evil in Him (1John 1:5), the essence of His being is goodness. His glory is goodness. In other words, the LORD is saying He will do what Moses asked. The goodness, or glory of God, will pass before Moses.

Then, the LORD repeated it in another way. He said He will proclaim His name. The Hebrew idea of one's name was the essence of who they were and their destiny. The Hebrew portion of Scripture uses this method of clarification quite frequently. It is called parallelism, which is to say something one way and then to say it again in different words so as to add richness to the expression. Glory, goodness, and "name" are all the same idea.

And I will be gracious to whom I will be gracious, and will show mercy on whom I will show mercy. This is a preview of the description of the glory of God. The very fact that God would bother to reveal His nature to rebellious and stubborn man is gracious. God has just had mercy on the Israelites by receiving Moses' intercession for them. He is merciful in having a relationship with a man who was a murderer, Moses. (Exodus 2:12) He is graciously about to renew the covenant after the people broke the first two commands about a month after promising to obey. The first and foremost revelation of the nature of God is mercy and grace.

I frequently hear that the God of the Old Testament is a brutal despot so unlike the God of the New Testament. Those who make that statement don't realize what judgment mankind deserves or they would see these attributes of grace and mercy are a dominant theme of the Old Testament.

Just think about our own situation. Was there any reason Jesus should have been incarnated, lived as an example to us, and died an excruciating death for our salvation? None, but the love in His heart for us prompted Him to extend grace and mercy to rebels such as us. (Romans 5:8)

20 But," he said, "you cannot see my face, for man shall not see me and live." God does not have a face or hands or feet, and yet the expressions of the human body are used for us so that we can relate. To see His face is to see the fullness of his glory, the whole essence of His nature. (1Corinthians 13:12) That includes justice and wrath towards all evil. No human has yet been perfected. Just as we saw that the touch of Jesus made the unclean whole, so the gaze of God obliterates evil. If God granted Moses' request, Moses would have died.

The only man that ever saw the face of God is Jesus (John 1:18), because there is nothing in Jesus that needs judgment. God is gracious toward us in keeping us from facing His justice until His work in us is complete. (1John 3:2-3) Not one of us is ready for a full revelation of God. That is why we need Jesus. Even then, His life in us is getting us ready to live in His presence. We have been made holy but we are being sanctified. (Hebrews 10:14) We are holy because of the blood of Jesus shed for us, but we are still working out what that means in our life. (Philippians 2:12) That is the process of sanctification.

God had Moses stand in a cleft in the rock and covered the opening. As the glory of God passed by, God allowed Moses to see the "back" of God, not the face. The implication is that the penetrating eyes of God's justice would not be toward Moses. Neither would Moses see the fullness of God's glory, but only as much as he was able to handle.

1 The LORD said to Moses, "Cut for yourself two tablets of stone like the first, and I will write on the tablets the words that were on the first tablets, which you broke. Moses punishment for breaking the tablets is getting to cut and haul two more tablets of stone back up the mountain. Remember, Moses is 80 years old! He was one tough guy! An unguarded moment of anger will usually cost us.

God is about to enter into a do-over with Moses and Israel. Moses will go up and spend another 40 days on the mountain. If the people were in a hurry before and couldn't wait, now they get another chance to sit and wait and see if they can do it right this time.

Does that sound familiar? I can sure relate. I'm so grateful for God's do-overs. Sometimes I don't get a second chance, but many times when I fail I get a repeat situation to try again to yield to my Master.

6 The LORD passed before him and proclaimed, "The LORD, the LORD, a God merciful and gracious, slow to anger, and abounding in steadfast love and faithfulness, YHWY, YHWY, (the eternal One!) merciful and gracious! Just as we saw in the preview, the description begins with mercy and grace. The only reason we get a description is mercy and grace. If it weren't for mercy and grace, man would never have survived the Garden of Eden, the flood, Babel, and the numerous wars throughout our history. If it weren't for God's mercy and grace we wouldn't be here this morning (Nehemiah 9:31), there would be no Bible, no salvation, no life and death of Jesus, and we would be hopeless wretches preying on one another instead of loving one another.

But God is gracious, and that's why we just celebrated Thanksgiving. We should be most grateful for these central attributes of grace and mercy. Soon we will celebrate Christmas, the greatest of all acts of grace and mercy, when God became a man to save wretches like us. (1Timothy 1:15)

If God were simply gracious and merciful it would be enough, but He is *7 keeping steadfast love for thousands, forgiving iniquity and transgression and sin,* There is the word I value most, (*hesed*) steadfast love. It is an unshakable love. If it were just for the Son I would understand. If it were just for Enoch and Moses and Elijah I wouldn't be that surprised, but it is for thousands. It is for all those who come to Jesus. (John 14:23) It is even for people like you and me. *"Amazing love, oh what sacrifice, the Son of God, given for me. My debt He paid; my death He died, that I might live!"* (from the song Amazing Love.) *Greater love has no man than this that a man lay down his life for his friends* (John 15:13); and that is exactly what Jesus did for you and for me. *"Love so amazing so divine, demands my soul, my life, my all!"* Love took Jesus to the cross so that our iniquity, transgressions, and sins could be forgiven.

But that does not mean God lets evil go unpunished. God is holy. Justice must be met. ... *who will by no means clear the guilty, visiting the iniquity of the fathers on the children and the children's children, to the third and the fourth generation."* We have seen how the sins of the father or mother can affect the generations that follow. Sinful ways of dealing with life are learned from parents. Harmful ways of dealing with stress are taught by example. God doesn't step in and save us from the consequences of our sin. He lets us deal with it to learn the lesson. Those who do not know Him are driven to Him by the consequences of their actions and sometimes those consequences affect the following generations.

What has God just declared? He has told Moses that He is gracious and merciful. His steadfast love is for many, as well as His forgiveness. Yet, He is holy and just and will not let sin go unpunished. This is God's self-description!

8 And Moses quickly bowed his head toward the earth and worshiped. And when we realize what this means, we ought to do the same. What a mighty God we serve! The revelation of glory came not so much in sight as it did in the words describing God's nature.

9 And he said, "If now I have found favor in your sight, O Lord, please let the Lord go in the midst of us, for it is a stiff-necked people, and pardon our iniquity and our sin, and take us for your inheritance." This is an interesting compromise between God and Moses. God has said that He doesn't want to go with them as He might have to wipe them out because of their many sins. Moses acknowledged that they were stiff-necked, but then went right to the attributes that God had described and asked that God go with them, forgive as sins arise, and keep them as the chosen people.

Isn't that the case with us? We often refuse to bend our neck and accept the yoke and yet we want Jesus to live in us. (Galatians 5:24) We know we won't be perfect and deserve judgment, and yet we rely on the grace and mercy we received at the cross. We depend on forgiveness. We desire to remain God's children and know it is only grace and mercy that makes that possible. (Job 42:5-6)

The parallel is so strong. Perhaps God's answer to them is the same for us as well, since we are also recipients of steadfast love. *10 And he said, "Behold, I am making a covenant. Before all your people I will do marvels, such as have not been created in all the earth or in any nation. And all the people among whom you are shall see the work of the LORD, for it is an awesome thing that I will do with you.* God renewed the covenant. We have a better covenant made with better blood. (Hebrews 12:24) He has done marvels in Jesus and the Apostles and through the ages since. People of the world witness the transformed lives of those who know Jesus as their Master and realize He has done an awesome thing in us.

Then God went over the promises and points of the covenant that He had given them before. They get another chance. I imagine this time they listened more intently. They had seen the consequences of taking it lightly. Sometimes we need to fail and pay the price so that we can get serious. Though most of verses 11 through 26 have been stated earlier, verse 14 reveals a name of God we have not yet encountered. *14 (for you shall worship no other god, for the LORD, whose name is Jealous, is a jealous God)*, When we looked at chapter 20 verse 5 we discussed this nature of God. He is all good and is jealous of anything that would draw us away from His goodness to destructive evil. His is a holy jealousy. I'm glad He is jealous for me.

29 When Moses came down from Mount Sinai, with the two tablets of the testimony in his hand as he came down from the mountain, Moses did not know that the skin of his face shone because he had been talking with God. Moses had seen the glory of God, at least to some extent. The glory shined from Moses' face as if some of it had rubbed off on him. Actually, the Apostle Paul tells us that this is what happens to believers as we linger in the presence of the Lord. Last week we talked about the importance of being in God's presence.

18 And we all, with unveiled face, beholding the glory of the Lord, are being transformed into the same image from one degree of glory to another. For this comes from the Lord who is the Spirit. 2Corinthians 3:18 (ESV) Paul is telling us that it isn't that glory rubs off on us, but rather that it transforms us. This is that process of sanctification. He is telling us that our countenance is changed by being in God's presence just as Moses' countenance was changed. (Ecclesiastes 8:1) You may not get the same kind of radioactive glow, but faces are changed! Sometimes I can tell just by looking at someone that they love the LORD. The brightest faces are those that spend time in God's presence. They are those who come to know the grace and mercy of God and how it is manifested in steadfast love and forgiveness of sin.

What a gracious and loving God, whose desire is to transform us into His wonderful image! (Philippians 3:21) Will you linger in His presence until your face begins to shine?

Questions
1 Why did God grant Moses' request? Relate that to Jesus.
2 What is glory?
3 Discuss Hebrews 10:14.
4 Why did Moses only see the "back" of God?
5 How did God reveal Himself?
6 What was Moses next request? Relate.
7 How does God's answer relate to us?
8 What new name of God is revealed? Explain.
9 How does Moses' shining face relate to us?
10 Are you being transformed?

Stirred Hearts Exodus 35:20 - 36:7

Now that Moses heard the Lord's promise to go with them and give them rest (33:14), the plans to build the Tabernacle could go forward. They could build that space that God had designed for His residence among them. It began with Moses telling the people that the Lord was requesting contributions of all the necessary material and labor from those with *"a generous heart"*. (35:5 ESV) Later on, mandatory minimum amounts would be required from the people to maintain the tabernacle, its functions, and the priests (Numbers 18:21), but the initial space was built from the generosity of the givers. Again, we must remember that it all came from God in the first place. God had told them plunder the Egyptians and made their neighbors favorably disposed to give them all the things they are about to give to God. (Exodus 12:36)

Sometimes we forget that it all comes from God and we begin to get attached to things. Then when the Lord prompts us to give back what He has given us, we start to calculate whether we can afford it. We get the mindset that this is all we will ever receive, as if God is stingy. There is a time to store up in prudent wisdom for times of needs such as Joseph directed the Egyptians to do. (Genesis 41:35-36) There is a time to give the very last of your resources as the Zerapheth widow did with Elijah. (1Kings 17:12-14) Only the Spirit of God can direct us as to which is appropriate at the moment. At the time of the passage we are studying, it was a time to give for the tabernacle of God. It was an honor to have given to such a high and holy mission, the residence of God in their midst.

That is how I feel about some of the missions we have given to, the radio tower in Guinea Bissau, Hope Cottage in Flagstaff, finishing up the mission expansion in India among others. What an honor to be a part of reaching so many lives for our Savior. I'm grateful for the careful way we use our resources for the advancement of God's kingdom that He might dwell in the hearts of many.

When we see the tabernacle, and later the temple, as a picture of the body of Christ (1Corinthians 6:19), with Jesus in our midst, it fits perfectly that the materials came from generous hearts. We are the material for the temple, the living stones (1Peter 2:5), and only those with generous hearts give themselves as material for the dwelling place of God. Of course it is the work of the Holy Spirit that turns us from selfishness to submission. We wouldn't naturally give up our own desires and selfish use of our time and possessions unless we cooperated with the Lord working in our hearts. (Philippians 2:13)

We need to see the blessing in the invitation to contribute to what God is doing. The world paints it as something religious people must endure. It emphasizes the abuse of power and finances because the generosity of Christians embarrasses them. They would use abuse of power as a reason not to give.

What happens when you give in response to the Holy Spirit? I'm not talking about guilt giving or giving to get to get something in return. When you respond to the Holy Spirit and sacrifice, you accept God's invitation to be a part of what He is doing. He could do it all by Himself, but He graciously includes us. Then He records it and promises to repay you one hundred times. I'm not speaking of the prosperity gospel, but of the promise of Jesus. (Matthew 19:29) The reward may be spiritual or physical, in this life or the next. If you believe the Scriptures, you'll prefer the reward in eternity.

That isn't the motivation for our giving, but it is a reality of obedience to the Holy Spirit. Of course, we give because we owe Him everything, but the reward is an expression of God's generosity, generosity that we are to emulate. (2Corinthians 9:9)

21 And they came, everyone whose heart stirred him, and everyone whose spirit moved him, and brought the LORD's contribution to be used for the tent of meeting, and for all its service, and for the holy garments. 22

So they came, both men and women. All who were of a willing heart ... They brought all the various materials that God had requested to make the tabernacle according to God's design. Notice the expressions, *"everyone whose heart stirred him"* and *"whose spirit moved him"* and "All who were of a willing heart".

Why would our hearts not be stirred and our spirits not be moved? I don't think they had an eternal aspect of the consequences of their giving. They just knew they wanted the benefits of the Lord being among them. But why would someone not be moved? If you have never opened your heart to the wonder of God dwelling in you, it may be that you have believed the old Eden lie, that God is stingy and isn't telling you the whole story. Natural human nature has no desire to sacrifice or submit. It is utterly selfish from birth. (Job 15:14)

The only real cure for selfishness is Jesus. If we see what He endured for us, if we really try to grasp the generosity of His heart towards us, we can't help but want to be generous to others. His life in us is generous. (Matthew 10:8)

25 And every skillful woman spun with her hands, and they all brought what they had spun in blue and purple and scarlet yarns and fine twined linen. 26 All the women whose hearts stirred them to use their skill spun the goats' hair. The offerings included labor. The women spun the materials needed. Notice again it was those whose hearts were stirred. That doesn't mean that all who did not spin wool or yarn or linen were hardhearted. Perhaps some had different skills or possessions to offer. We each have our own gifts. When everyone knows their calling and follows the stirring of their heart within God's guidelines, all that is needed comes together.

There was probably someone out cutting stone that was sure the Lord led them to cut the stone even though the Lord had not asked for stone. And there were surely those who couldn't be bothered with the project, for they were "called" to other things. Even before Pentecost, some of the congregation of Israel in the wilderness were sure that they heard from God that they should take Moses' or Aaron's place. (Numbers 16:13) That is just the nature of humanity. Those who will be blessed are those who let the Holy Spirit stir them to participate in what God is doing. We all have a way to participate whether with material blessings or labor.

29 All the men and women, the people of Israel, whose heart moved them to bring anything for the work that the LORD had commanded by Moses to be done brought it as a freewill offering to the LORD. Whether labor or materials, it was all a freewill offering. The command was through Moses as to the design and substance. In other words, they weren't commanded to bring it, they were just told of the opportunity to participate. We occasionally have the same type of offering. We present a need and ask you to give as your heart stirs you. We took one recently for Mac and Jory and it will help pay a portion of their return flight.

A freewill offering is different from the tithes that the Law will demand shortly after the building of the tabernacle. Today, we are not under the Law. (Romans 6:14) The tithe is a good starting point, but we should be filled with the Spirit and be led by Him as to what to give. Paul took a freewill offering from the churches in Asia for the poor of the church in Jerusalem during a famine. (1Corinthians 16:1-2)

30 Then Moses said to the people of Israel, "See, the LORD has called by name Bezalel the son of Uri, son of Hur, of the tribe of Judah; 31 and he has filled him with the Spirit of God, with skill, with intelligence, with knowledge, and with all craftsmanship, God called people by name to be the overseers of the main craftsman and artisans. They were artists overseeing other artists that crafted beautiful things for Gods glory. That is the work of every believing artist, glorifying God with their gift of artistic ability. From this passage we can see a number of insights into the call of God on our lives. First, not everyone is called to the same ministry. Pastors often speak of the time they were "called". We don't encourage anyone to enter a certain ministry unless they are called and the passage tells us why.

God filled Bezalel with the Spirit of God and all the practical skills and knowledge to do what God had called him to do. When God calls a person, he equips them for the job. The equipping may come through a time of training with another leader just as Joshua was experiencing with Moses. (Exodus 33:11) It may be sudden and supernatural as with Bezalel, but one thing we can be sure, God provides the equipping for those He calls. He doesn't expect you to do it with your natural talent or efforts. He expects you to rely upon Him and His equipping of you for the call He places on your life. (1Corinthians 12:11)

36:1 *"Bezalel and Oholiab and every craftsman in whom the LORD has put skill and intelligence to know how to do any work in the construction of the sanctuary shall work in accordance with all that the LORD has commanded."* He called two particular men to oversee and to do the work, but he also called many others to assist. The Lord gave many people the skill and intelligence to help. The New Testament calls this the gift of helping. (1Corinthians 12:28) This is the most needed gift and so it is the most common gift. Doesn't that make sense? It isn't that the two men that were named were any more special than all the others. They were doing what they were called to do. All the other craftsmen were doing what they were called to do. All are necessary. What is special is faithfulness to carry out your call as the Lord commands. Faithfulness is what the Lord rewards. (Matthew 25:21)

We are blessed with many servants in this church. Our trustees have been a special blessing to me this year. They just quietly go about doing all the work around the church that needs to be done, and there is a lot to do in a building this old. That frees me to do what the Lord has called me to do. When we all do what God has called us to do, we are the most effective for the Kingdom of God.

God didn't call and equip me to counsel people like Pastor Ed does. We can all encourage one another but if you really need some serious counseling, you don't want to come to me. I'm sure that when Ed counsels people he senses that supernatural insight that God has equipped him with, just as I feel it when I prepare or preach the sermon each week. (Ephesians 3:7)

2 And Moses called Bezalel and Oholiab and every craftsman in whose mind the LORD had put skill, everyone whose heart stirred him up to come to do the work. 3 And they received from Moses all the contribution that the people of Israel had brought for doing the work on the sanctuary. They still kept bringing him freewill offerings every morning, Everyone brought the gifts to Moses and he distributed them to the craftsmen. After all, Moses was the only one that had seen the heavenly model and knew what had to go where. Every morning the gifts would come pouring in. God was still stirring hearts!

Have you noticed how many times in our passage today the repetition of the phrase "heart stirred"? When the Bible repeats a phrase that often, it is of great importance. This is all getting done because God is stirring the hearts and the people are responding to that stirring in one accord at God's direction through His appointed leader.

I love to see when the Lord stirs us all in one accord, givers, craftsmen, overseers, helpers and God does something none of us could do on our own. (1Corinthians 12:7) The Tabernacle was a project like that. I'm referring to the Tabernacle Project that the churches here came together on. There was inspiration, skill, divine appointments and a 1000 people heard the gospel. Now it is on its way to Buckeye.

Eventually the craftsmen had to tell Moses that they had more than enough to do the job. That is a sign that God is in something. When God guides, He stirs the hearts and there is no begging and pleading or twisting of arms. His people are excited to participate in what He is doing.

5 and said to Moses, "The people bring much more than enough for doing the work that the LORD has commanded us to do." 6 So Moses gave command, and word was proclaimed throughout the camp, "Let no man or woman do anything more for the contribution for the sanctuary." They brought much more than enough. What a blessing when people cooperate with the stirring of God in their heart! There is more than enough provision, and God's work goes forward. I don't know of any church that ever told the congregation they were giving too much. It seems it is always the other way around. We always have more needs than we can meet or more plans than there are extra funds. I thank the Lord that surplus at Wayside is set aside for future building needs, and for special mission works that can really make a difference. (Philippians 4:17)

So the people were restrained from bringing, *7 for the material they had was sufficient to do all the work, and more.* And I would say that has been true of this church up until July of this year. This particular passage falling on this day is another God incident. I could never have planned it and was amazed again when I saw it land on the day we were to present next year's budget. Every year we have increased in attendance and giving until this year.

So we might ask ourselves, is the vision of Wayside no longer the vision from God so that hearts are no longer stirred to give? Or are we allowing our hearts to be hardened so that we are not giving as we should? Or is it something else? (Joel 1:13)

Let me share with you our vision and you can decide for yourself what the problem might be. Please, I encourage you to look inward, not outward, and simply ask the Lord if you are responding to His stirring. If you are, great! (Luke 6:38) Thank you for being a part of what happens at Wayside. If not, don't miss the blessing! I have no doubt that it is of God.

First and foremost we desire Wayside Bible Chapel to be a safe place to hear the Word taught faithfully and without compromise. It's all about Jesus and He is revealed in the Word. Wayside has taken the vision statement of "Knowing Christ and making Him known." (Colossians 1:9-10) That comes through the study of the Scriptures and walking with Him daily. We want to continue to equip you to do that and improve that this coming year. We make Him known through our life and our witness. We want to continue to help you with life transformations, so others can see Jesus in you.

Wayside has always had a love for missions. While we will cut many areas of the budget, missions will remain over 20% of our total. In America souls trickle in here and there, but revival is taking place in the third world. I'll share with you the struggles of the missions we support in the budget meeting. We don't want give less because they are tightening their belt even more drastically than we are and some are considering closing.

Our desire is to be a body of believers that truly loves one another so that others will know we are Jesus' disciples. (John 13:35) Love is telltale mark of a genuine church. This is the focus of the coming year, increasing in the love of Christ for one another. We have always counted on God and not man to stir hearts and we will continue to do that. You don't hear a yearly tithing sermon; we just go through the Scriptures and let them speak to us.

God stirred Israel to give for a place to dwell among them. Today in a much greater way, we have the opportunity to give so that He might dwell in the hearts of many. What a gracious God who invites us to give back to Him what we have received to advance His goodness in the earth and be blessed in return. (Nehemiah 9:10) I'm excited about the giving opportunities and ministries we'll have in the coming year. If they are of God, He'll stir our hearts.

Questions
1 How did the people know what to give?
2 Why did the people give?
3 What were the offerings called?
4 From where did the craftsmen get their ability?
5 Who directed the work?
6 Who else helped?
7 What problem did the craftsmen encounter? Why?
8 Describe the balance between vision and gifts.
9 What is the vision of Wayside Bible Chapel?

10 Why is today another God-incident?

Heaven Came Down Exodus 40

We've come to the grand finale of Exodus. It is what the story has been pointing to all along. The big picture is that God is fulfilling His promise to Abraham by bringing Israel out of Egypt and to the Promised Land. The even bigger picture is that God is providing a solution to the fall of man that occurred way back in the Garden. Exodus focuses us on a more intimate picture, that of the tabernacle. We should not lose the context, however, that this is all a part of healing the breach caused by sin. It is about God walking among man again as He did in the Garden. (Genesis 3:24) This step of the tabernacle is a necessary intermediate stage of instruction that helps us comprehend the final and complete reality of Jesus.

Most weeks I read the text for the sermon and write it out before referring to commentators. This week, I had in mind what I wanted to share, but I started reading a commentary and got so engrossed in it that I couldn't stop reading it. The writer ended his comments the same way I had planned to end mine, but the buildup was something that I hadn't foreseen. So I owe a debt of gratitude to Philip Ryken's commentary on Exodus. His work helped tweak many of our sermons in Exodus.

In the last chapter of Exodus all the work of the artisans is being assembled and put into place. It is very significant that this is taking place on the anniversary of the exodus from Egypt. God brought them out so that He could dwell among them. In chapter 52 of Isaiah, the prophet sees that God brings His people out from the oppression of the world to be purified from the evil that is so prevalent. (Isaiah 52:11) The Apostle Paul quotes the passage when writing to the Corinthians (2Corinthians 6:17) and the voice of Revelation cites them both. Revelation 18:4 (ESV) *4 Then I heard another voice from heaven saying, "Come out of her, my people, lest you take part in her sins, lest you share in her plagues;"*

The deliverance from Egypt was a picture of our being taken out of the corruption of the world and made the people of God among whom He dwells. (Ezra 6:21) But God did not yet dwell among them. They just had the agreement that He would. They already failed to keep their part, but then the agreement was renewed with the understanding that it would be by grace alone that God dwelt with them. (Exodus 34:9)

There are some who teach that Old Testament folks were saved through the Law. That is not possible! No one could keep it. It was by grace and mercy that God would dwell in their midst. The Law was teaching them that they needed the mercy of God. (Psalm 14:2-3)

The tabernacle construction was completed on the anniversary of their departure. That means it took around nine months to complete the details of all the instructions God had given. Finally, they were ready to assemble all the parts. Finally, God would "come down" and dwell among them. Ryken describes the anticipation they must have felt as they assembled each portion. Those nine months must have seemed to drag on forever. They had seen the cloud that led them, and heard the voice that came from it when it came down Sinai, and the elders had seen a bit of the glory on the mountain. Moses had seen the "back" of the glory which caused his face to shine. (Exodus 34:35) What will happen when God comes down in their midst?

They first erected the tabernacle and the coverings went over it, but the glory did not come down. The Ark of the Covenant where God would dwell was placed inside the Most Holy Place. The Law was placed inside and the Atonement Cover on top. They shielded it with the curtain that divided the tabernacle into two rooms. God's special room, the Holy of Holies, was complete. Still the glory did not come down.

The rest of the furniture in the tabernacle, the table of showbread, the lampstand, and the altar of incense, were all put in place, and the curtain of the outer tabernacle was hung. The tabernacle was complete. Still the glory did not come down.

The furniture of the outer court was set up. The great brazen altar and the brass washing basin were placed, but the glory was still not seen. The outer perimeter curtains were hung from the posts, and the main gate curtain was put in place. Now everything was done. All that God had directed was complete.

Moses and Aaron stood back and two incredible things happened. The cloud came over the tabernacle and the glory of the Lord filled the tabernacle. The curtains and covering must have been radiant with light. Some believe it was a brilliant, pulsating light of the Shekinah. John Currid comments that the form of the Hebrew verb for "filling" reflects a dynamic, ongoing situation. (from John D. Currid, *A Study Commentary on Exodus*, 2 vols. (Auburn, MA: Evangelical Press USA, 2000), 2:369)

The glory that filled the tabernacle was a spectacular display of the radiance of God's being. The God of the exodus—the God of power, who made the heavens and the earth; the God of justice, who plagued the Egyptians; the God of love, who kept his covenant with Israel; the God of providence, who led his people through the wilderness; the God of truth, who gave them his law; the God of mercy, who atoned for their sins; the God of holiness, who set them apart for service—this great God was present in glory. When the people looked at the tabernacle, they could see that God was in the house. (from Philip Ryken - *Preaching the Word – Exodus: Saved for God's Glory*.)

From that point on, wherever the cloud stopped, the tabernacle would be erected and the cloud would then come over the tabernacle. Glory came down and they saw it fill the tabernacle, but the people have only seen the effects.

The irony of the story is that Moses could not enter. This was all about God dwelling with man, and setting up a system of intercession, but Moses and Aaron could not enter the tabernacle. The glory was too brilliant. There is a message here that we have lost in our day. God is awesome in holiness and power. Just as Moses could not see God's face and live

(Exodus 33:20), so he could not just walk into that tent and survive. It is mortally dangerous to stand in God's holy presence! (1Timothy 6:16) Is God a God who is near (immanent) and compassionate or a God who is so great and awesome that we dare not come near Him (transcendent). He is both!

Something else was needed to make it possible for the holy, righteous and perfect God to be in the midst of men. God had already given the instructions as to what was needed at the beginning of the book of the covenant. (Exodus 20:24) Leviticus follows Exodus, without missing a beat, expounding on the details. What was needed was atonement. Leviticus is all about the sacrifices and the requirement of blood. The blood of sacrifice had to be shed so that all would know it was only by grace of another taking their sins that they could ever have God in their midst. The justice of God had to be met. (Exodus 34:7)

Leviticus gives us the details of their obedience to follow the Lord's instructions in regards to the various sacrifices. We have seen how they all point to Jesus. (Luke 24:44) He is our sin offering, our fellowship offering, and the burnt offering. When the sacrifices were completed Moses and Aaron could enter. It was the blood that made it possible. (Leviticus 17:11) The blood pointed to the blood of the Lamb of God, the perfect sacrifice that could take the penalty that we all deserve. (Romans 5:9) That is the only way we can enter into His holy presence. (Hebrews 9:22)

Let's read of the second amazing event from the details we find in Leviticus 9:22-24 (NIV) *22 Then Aaron lifted his hands toward the people and blessed them. And having sacrificed the sin offering, the burnt offering and the fellowship offering, he stepped down. 23 Moses and Aaron then went into the Tent of Meeting. When they came out, they blessed the people; and the glory of the LORD appeared to all the people. 24 Fire came out from the presence of the LORD and consumed the burnt offering and the fat portions on the altar. And when all the people saw it, they shouted for joy and fell facedown.* Now they have seen the consuming fire of the Lord's presence. (Deuteronomy 4:24) They shouted for joy for several reasons. The year of anticipation had reached its climax. The tent of God was complete. God had accepted their labor. But most importantly, God accepted the sacrifice. The evidence was the fire that came out from the Holy Place consuming the sacrifice. Every detail of the picture God was painting was completed as God had instructed. God would live among them and go before them. Could we ask for anything more? Actually, yes, we can. We can ask for the reality of the shadow. We can ask for the substance of which this was just a painting. (Hebrews 10:1)

Let me explain. The people that came out of Egypt were not just Hebrews, but all that accepted the God that proved Himself through the plagues to be the only true God. (Exodus 12:38) They were saved from death by the blood of the Passover lamb on the doorposts, a picture of Jesus' blood on the doorposts of our hearts. (1Corinthians 5:7) They were separated from Egypt which is a picture of worldliness, and passed through the waters of the Red Sea, a picture of baptism. (1Corinthians 10:2) The enemy of our soul can try to pursue us, but he will be destroyed. (Romans 16:20) Jesus is our daily bread, our great provider. (John 6:32-33)

His voice gives us the moral boundaries of life. We enter into a new covenant with God by grace alone. It is based on the blood of a substitute, blood that should be our own, the punishment for our sins. We have the wonderful invitation to have God dwell not just in our midst but in our very heart. (John 14:23) We have the opportunity to be the tabernacle of God. So we give the freewill offering of our very self. (Romans 12:1) This is a one-time act, but it is also a process. We make the decision but then we learn a little more of the cost day by day. Yet, God stirs our hearts and helps us be generous toward Him and others as He is with us.

Exodus began under the cloud of brutal slavery. It ends under a cloud of glory. The people do not need to search for guidance, rather they wait upon the moving of the cloud that guides them. That is the life of the believer in Jesus, waiting on His move. (Psalm 27:14)

In Christ Jesus, we have done all that was commanded of us. We probably erected a golden calf or two on the way to this point in our life, but we repent and realize it can only be by grace that He would live in us. Finally, we accept that He is the sacrifice and His glory fills our heart. There is no room for us. (John 3:30) We face the same irony Moses faced. We now desire to go in and fellowship with God and intercede at the altar of incense, but we can't get in for the glory.

The sin offering has been offered. We have come to the place of the burnt offering. We see He completely gave Himself up for us, and in response as living sacrifices we offer our lives completely to Him. (1John 4:19) Then we can experience the fellowship offering. We find "it is no longer I that live but Christ that lives in me." (Galatians 2:20) Then we can enter in, for it is Christ that enters in. Then we can intercede, for it is Christ in us that intercedes. We can face the fire of His glory, for judgment for our sins was meted out upon Christ, our substitute.

Inside the tabernacle, His light is lamp to our path, directing our steps. We commune at His table eating the bread of His presence, the Word. Our intercession at the altar is sweet smelling incense.

Then, the grace of God lets us see more of His glory. It fills the whole earth! (Isaiah 6:3) The glory is Jesus! We begin to see Him in all the Scriptures. We see Him in the providential details of life. We see Him in joy and in suffering. His fire consumes us as living sacrifices. (Matthew 3:11) We see Him at work through us, and we are humbled.

The reason that some people just can't see what God is doing is because they are still filled with themselves. Everything is still about them instead of being about Jesus. They haven't yet become a living sacrifice. They are still their own lord. They may have accepted Jesus as their sin offering, but they don't want their heart to be broken by Jesus' total dedication to saving us represented in the burnt offering of the cross.

Some people don't like the depiction of Christ on the cross. "He is risen," they say, "Take Him off of there!" True, He is risen, but perhaps we need to take a good, long, painful look at how He had to give it all up because of our sin.

We just celebrated Christmas, and you may be wondering why we are going so soon to the cross. The baby came to live a sinless life and go to the cross for you. He showed us how to become a whole burnt offering! His resurrected life in us is what makes us able, but His example breaks our heart's resistance to His enabling power.

The greatest glory the world has ever seen is the glory manifest in Jesus. Those who won't read the Word will only be able to see His glory when it's manifest in your transformed life. When you are a whole burnt offering, others will see the sacrifice of the cross in you.

One day, the world will see an even greater glory, for Jesus is coming again! Jesus promised He would come again with power and GREAT GLORY! (Matthew 24:30) Every eye will see Him! Every knee will bow, like the Israelites did when they saw the fire come out of the tabernacle. But when we who have believed see Him, we will be changed. We will stand in His presence. (Psalm 1:5) His work in us will be complete! *When Christ who is your life appears, then you will appear with Him in glory.* It's the promise of Colossians 3:4 (NIV).

And here is the grand conclusion: Revelation 21:3 (KJV) It is the same verse we ended the Christmas message with, but notice the fulfillment of the tabernacle type. *3 And I heard a great voice out of heaven saying, Behold, the tabernacle of God is with men, and he will dwell with them, and they shall be his people, and God himself shall be with them, and be their God.* The tabernacle of God is Jesus. (Revelation 21:22) There will no longer be a need for Him to veil His glory. The separation sin caused will be ended. The promises will all be fulfilled. They enemy will be forever vanquished. And Jesus Christ shall reign forever and ever. (Revelation 11:15) To Him be all glory, honor and praise, now and forevermore.

Questions
1 What is the BIG picture of Exodus?
2 Discuss 2Corinthians 6:17.
3 When is the age of grace?
4 Why is the completion date of the tabernacle significant?
5 Discuss the suspense and arrival of glory.
6 What was the irony of the situation?
7 What had to happen before Moses could enter and why?
8 What amazing thing happened next?
9 Review the picture Exodus paints of our life in Christ.
10 What glory do you see?
11 What Great Glory will all see?

Other books by Pastor Paul Wallace:

Through the Bible Daily Devotional
Through the Bible Again volumes 1&2
Jesus Concealed in the Old Testament
John's Rabbi
Divine Messiah?
Preaching Through Genesis
Preaching Through Exodus
Preaching Through Isaiah
Preaching Through Zacheriah
Preaching Through Matthew vol 1&2
Preaching Through John
Preaching Through Acts
Preaching Through Romans
Preaching Through Ephesians
Preaching Through Philippians and Colossians
Coming soon:
Preaching Through Luke
Preaching Spiritual Disciplines
Preaching the Attributes of God

www.ingramcontent.com/pod-product-compliance
Lightning Source LLC
LaVergne TN
LVHW020929090426
835512LV00020B/3278